CRISTOﾠ ﾠL MATTINGLEY is
dmired writers. ﾠ
ﾠmpelling narr
ﾠdinary circuﾠ   ﾠﾠ.ey include radiation in *The*
le Tree, anﾠ   ﾠriences of refugees in *The Angel*
a Mouth   the *Asmir* trilogy. She also edited,
arched   groundbreaking Aboriginal history,
ﾠﾠﾠﾠ   ﾠand – '*Aboriginal*' *experiences in*
ﾠ   ﾠ836; the oral history memoirs of a
ﾠﾠﾠ   *uby of Trowutta*; and the best-selling
ﾠy King, *King of the Wilderness*.

ﾠ author of more than forty books for
ﾠﾠﾠristobel Mattingley's readership spans
ﾠ.   ﾠeration. In 1990 she received an Advance
Auﾠ   or her contribution to literature. In 1995 sﾠ
waﾠ   ﾠtor of the University of South Australia, anﾠ
in 1ﾠ   ﾠer of the Order of Australia, both for serviﾠﾠ
to ﾠ   and to the community through her commitment
to ﾠﾠ   ﾠd cultural issues. In 1999 she received the Pheme
Tanﾠ   ﾠd for her contribution to children's literature, anﾠ
in 2ﾠ   ﾠnaugural South Australian Books Be In It Festivalﾠ
Lifetime Recognition Award.

'This ﾠﾠk is about the quality of courage. There were many
likﾠ ﾠvid but the theme of this book and its importance
is ﾠ ﾠxamination of his attitude, his disregard of self, his
sense ﾠresponsibility and his strong convictions. It is a story
abouﾠ ﾠouth, too. Christﾠbel Mﾠttingley has written this book
with comﾠﾠ   ﾠresentation is gripping anﾠ

David Mattingley on his 21st birthday in New Zealand, 14 June 1943

BATTLE ORDER 204

A bomber pilot's story

Christobel Mattingley

ALLEN&UNWIN

First published in 2007

Copyright © Christobel Mattingley, 2007

The author and publishers wish to thank The Society of Authors as the literary representative of Cecil Roberts for permission to reproduce 'Wings' by Cecil Roberts.

Unless otherwise stated, all photographs are from the private collection of David Mattingley.

The photo of the Lancaster on page 128, and used in the Battle Order segments and on the front cover, is by Paul A Richardson. The publishers have made every effort to locate the copyright holder, without success, and would welcome any contact information.

Allen & Unwin
83 Alexander St
Crows Nest NSW 2065
Australia
Phone: (61 2) 8425 0100
Fax: (61 2) 9906 2218
Email: info@allenandunwin.com
Web: www.allenandunwin.com

Distributed in the UK, Eire and Europe by Frances Lincoln Ltd., London NWS 2RZ

National Library of Australia
Cataloguing-in-Publication entry:

Mattingley, Christobel, 1931– .
Battle order 204.

ISBN 9 78174175 1611.

1. Mattingley, David. 2. Australia. Royal Australian Air Force – Airmen
– Biography. 3. Australia. Royal Australian Air Force – History – World War,
1939–1945. 4. World War, 1939–1945 – Germany – Aerial operations, Australian.
I. Title.

940.53092

Cover and text design by Sandra Nobes
Set in 10.5pt Sabon by Tou-Can Design
Printed in Australia by McPhersons Printing Group

10 9 8 7 6 5 4 3 2 1

Teachers notes available from www.allenandunwin.com

In memory of
Peter Lord
David McNeill
Frank Mattingley
Tas Williams
Joe and Jim Brock
Bramwell Barber
Allen Morgan
Ollie Morshead
Arthur Bruce
Jimmy Wilson
Hugh Brodie
John McGee
and all from Bomber Command who did not return from ops

And for David and his crew
Cyril Bailey
Drew Fisher
Reg Murr
Reg Watson
Noel Ferguson
Allan Avery
and all the others who did return from ops
and have lived with the nightmares

The Bomber Command Memorial Window, Airmen's Chapel,
Lincoln Cathedral (photo courtesy Lincoln Cathedral)

Men find a cause to die for: and the bravery
Of this riper spring, unjust and harmful,
Scalds the wide open eye and sears the tongue.
John Pudney, 'Spring 1942' from *Dispersal Point and other air poems*

Contents

'Wings' by Cecil Roberts 1

BATTLE ORDER 204 (1) Bomb Doors Open! 2

1 A Passion for Planes 5

2 Name, Rank and Number 23

BATTLE ORDER 204 (2) D Dog 42

3 Slow Boat to Britain 45

4 Loving Life 53

BATTLE ORDER 204 (3) Target Dortmund 66

5 Confronting Death 69

6 Airborne Again At Last 81

'High Flight' by John Magee 101

7 Wimpeys and Crewing Up 103

8 Heavies and 'Butch' Harris 117

'An Airman's Prayer' by Hugh Brodie 131

9 625 Squadron 133

BATTLE ORDER 204 (4) Hit! 144

10 Holland, Happy Valley and France 147

BATTLE ORDER 204 (5) Put on Parachutes! 162

11 J Jig 165

12 Erks and Armourers 173

13 Holland, Happy Valley and Operation
Hurricane 179

BATTLE ORDER 204 (6) Take Up Crash Positions! 186

14 'Three of our aircraft are missing' 189

15 'Bold, cautious, true and my loving comrade' 205

16 G George and D Dog 217

BATTLE ORDER 204 (7) A Perfect Landing 230

17 A Fractured Skull and a Headless Crew 233

BATTLE ORDER 204 (8) Outstanding Devotion
to Duty 244

18 'It is so good to be alive!' 247

19 Victory At Last! 261

20 'In hospital again. Nothing serious.
Don't worry.' 273

21 Going Home 283

Epilogue 287

About the Others 293

Writing *Battle Order 204* 300

Acknowledgements 302

About the Poems 306

Glossary 309

Sources 312

Wings

Lord of land and sea and air
Listen to the pilot's prayer.
Send him wind that is steady and strong,
Grant that his engine sings a song
Of flawless tone by which he knows
It shall not fail where'er he goes –
Landing, diving, in curve, half roll,
Grant him Oh Lord! full control –
That he may learn in heights of heaven
The rapture altitude has given –
That he shall know the joy they feel
Who ride the realms on birds of steel.

Cecil Roberts

Battle Order 204 (1)
Bomb Doors Open!

'Bomb doors open!' It was the call that haunted airmen's dreams.

Approaching the target, flying straight and level with its bomb doors open, the mighty Lancaster was at its most vulnerable. Likely to be 'coned' at any second by persistent enemy searchlights. Target for fierce anti-aircraft guns. Prey for deadly fighters.

'Bombs gone!' the bomb aimer reported over the intercom, then 'Bomb doors closed.'

'Bomb doors closed,' the pilot repeated.

But there was no respite from enemy attack.

The plane had to continue straight and level until the camera recording the bombing had stopped running. Then and only then could the pilot turn away and set the Lanc on the first leg of its hazardous homeward course. The crew, with the sick sour taste of fear in their mouths, the smell of cordite in their nostrils and the sight of shells exploding all around and aircraft going down in flames, kept watching, hoping, praying.

· · · · · · · · · · · · · · · · ·

On the morning of 29 November 1944 David and his crew woke to find themselves on Battle Order No. 204. It was a daylight offensive, a Royal Air Force sortie of 294 Bomber Command Lancasters and 17 Mosquitoes heading for the Ruhr, Germany's industrial heartland, the dreaded Happy Valley, as it had been dubbed by the airmen. Today bomb doors would be opening over Dortmund.

David was a Lancaster pilot and this was his twenty-third operation in ten weeks. Only seven more journeys into hell after this one and he would have completed his first tour of duty.

Then, thank God, he would be due for leave.

1 A Passion for Planes

David was only six when his father hired a launch to take the family on an expedition to explore Twenty Day Island in Bass Strait, about twelve miles from the fishing village of Bridport where they always spent the summer. The launch's engine had sputtered into silence near the rocky shore, when David heard the drone of another engine. There was not a boat to be seen in any direction.

Then, above in the sun-bright blue, David glimpsed something extraordinary. An aeroplane! The first he had ever seen! David nearly jumped off the launch into the water in his excitement. He waved and waved. And watched and watched until the little plane disappeared beyond the horizon. He knew then that he wanted to fly too. One day. When he was a man. Bobbing about in a boat over choppy sea was an adventure. But surely it could not compare with rushing through the air, up among the clouds, looking down on the world spread

The vice-free de Havilland Tiger Moth (AWM neg. no. 002157)

out below like a multi-coloured tapestry. The pilot was pioneer aviator Bert Hinkler and David's passion for planes had been kindled.

In 1931, when David was eight, Charles Kingsford Smith came on a barnstorming visit. On 1 March, Tasmania had its first Air Pageant at the recently established Western Junction airfield. Interest was intense and so many people flocked to see the show that the newspapers reported Tasmania's first traffic jam, with cars banked up for a mile or more.

Impatient to reach the display, David hopped out of his father's Essex car and eagerly walked the final stretch. His unmarried aunt, a feisty woman who lived with the family, gladly parted with ten shillings to go up with the famous pilot on a brief circuit beyond the airfield.

'Can I go up too?' David begged.

'No!' said his parents, very firmly.

In those Depression years, times were tough for his father, a dentist whose patients could not always pay their bills. And because David was their youngest son, his mother always worried about him. He had to content himself with inspecting the amazing machine on the ground and questioning his aunt over and over about every detail of the flight.

David cut photos of the historic event out of .the paper. Then over the next months he saved the tuppence his uncle gave him each week for a pie from the tuckshop, until he had enough money to buy a big scrapbook, into which he carefully pasted all the cuttings. Over the years he added other items about aviation as he found them. All the while, watching and waiting for his chance to fly.

*David, Bow in Launceston Church Grammar School
First Four, 1940*

By the time David was thirteen he spent most summer Saturdays on the water. He loved the wide brown Tamar River studded with swans, its tidal waters ebbing and flowing between reedy banks where native hens ran with raucous calls. Training in the mornings, racing in the afternoons, year by year he had progressed from the Junior rowing crew to the Seconds and at last to the Firsts, rowing at Number Three or Bow. He loved the teamwork, the camaraderie, the shrill voice of the young coxswain chanting, 'In. Out. In. Out,' and the deep voice of the coach shouting instructions across the water through his megaphone. He thrilled to the thrust, the glide, the power generated by four sets of shoulders, four pairs of arms pulling on the oars. It seemed like the steady beat of wings making the boat fly across the water.

Winter Saturdays were different. On wild wet days, or when fog seeped up from the river, or dark clouds shrouded the Western Tiers, he stayed home, disappointed but determined, plugging away at the maths he would need if he was ever to become a pilot. But when the clouds were light and playful and the sun danced over Mount Barrow, he would slap together two sandwiches thick with cheese, peanut butter or blackberry jam, wrap them hastily and shove them in a pocket, stuff two apples in the other, and grab his bike, shouting 'I'm off, Mum!'

Whistling, he would pedal uphill out of town. When he reached the flat road that led to the Western Junction airfield, speeding by the clipped hawthorn hedges still speckled with red berries, he laughed as he felt the wind rushing through his hair. He counted down the minutes – fifty, forty-five, forty – until he would catch his first glimpse of a windsock, a hangar, a plane...

The Northern Tasmanian Aero Club had set up its headquarters in a shed at the airfield and members gave joy flights at the weekends. David soon learned to distinguish between the different types of Moth aircraft, boxy little biplanes constructed of wood and fabric. There were Gipsy Moths, Fox Moths, and a Leopard Moth. But his favourite was the Tiger Moth. Each Saturday he promised himself that one day he would learn to fly a Tiger Moth.

He prowled round all the machines, watching pre-flight checks, listening to conversations between pilots and mechanics, thrilled when someone called 'Lend a hand, will you, lad,' or even, 'Want to look at the instrument panel?' The sights, sounds and smells would later fill his dreams.

At school, David persevered with maths, but English and history were his favourite subjects, especially poetry and modern European history. As he scanned the papers for any items about aviation, he could not help noticing news about the growing unrest in Europe. At first, small paragraphs were tucked away in back pages, behind local and Australian news. But as the months went by they moved closer to the front of the paper and had bigger headlines, as the Nazis grabbed more and more power in Germany.

In March 1938, German troops entered Vienna, the once-proud capital of the great Austro-Hungarian Empire, and Austria was declared part of the German Reich. By August, as Germany began to mobilise, the name Hitler had become a household word, evoking anxiety and fears for the stability of the precarious peace established after the Great War.

In September, half a world away, schoolboy David studied cartoons of British Prime Minister Neville Chamberlain caving in to Hitler at the infamous Munich Conference, which established Nazi Germany as the dominant power in Europe, with Fascist Italy under Mussolini in support. As France and Britain followed a policy of appeasement, Nazi troops occupied Czechoslovakia. But in Britain an outcry against Chamberlain arose, and David noted the name of its leader, Winston Churchill, soon to become another household word epitomising resistance to Nazism and Fascism.

If Britain went to war, Australia would follow. It threw a long shadow over the eagerly awaited summer holidays, spent, as usual, at the family beach house. The young people partied around the bonfire on Mattingleys Beach, as they did every New Year's Eve, but lads whose eighteenth birthday would fall in 1939 were quieter than usual.

Staring into the leaping flames, sixteen-year-old David had a heavy feeling he was looking into the fire which seemed about to engulf Europe, its fierce heat scorching and destroying lives around the world.

But despite the foreboding, it was a glorious summer, that last summer of peace. David and his friends swam, sunbaked and walked for miles along the pristine beaches of the great sweep of Andersons Bay. At dusk, they threw their lines into the Brid River for blackfish, though David secretly hoped he wouldn't catch any. On shooting expeditions in the bush with his father and brothers, he deliberately missed the gentle wallabies in the gun's sight, unable to bring himself to kill them.

David had gained the Royal Lifesaving Society's Award of Merit and Instructor's Certificate and now drilled younger swimmers in lifesaving techniques. He had never forgotten the terrible day six years before, when, despite the efforts of his older brothers Max and Brian to save them, two boys, one also named David, had drowned.

When David turned seventeen on 14 June 1939, war in Europe seemed inevitable. Hitler and Mussolini had signed 'The Pact of Steel', a ten-year military and political alliance, and although non-aggression pacts between Germany and other countries were collapsing, a new one with the USSR strengthened Germany's position. Poland's sovereignty was threatened. Britain and France had warned Germany they would stand by Poland. But Germany invaded on 1 September. Two days later Britain and France declared war on Germany.

David, Launceston Church Grammar School prefect, 1939

The heavy black print of the Launceston *Examiner* headline of 4 September seared itself into David's brain. BRITAIN AT WAR WITH GERMANY.

A second headline, TASMANIAN TROOPS CALLED TO THE COLOURS, appeared over a photo. David studied the photo closely. 'How long before I'm in uniform?' he wondered.

By the end of September, when Germany and the USSR had invaded and divided Poland between them, Britain had sent 158 000 men to fight in France and the

Royal Air Force (RAF) had begun its propaganda raids, dropping thousands of leaflets over Germany. David's album bulged with newspaper pictures of warplanes, both British and German.

In December, celebrations marking the end of the school year were subdued. Some boys who had turned eighteen went straight off to enlist. Through Christmas and January, David was aware of faces missing from the beach scene. His older brother Max, home on holidays from teaching in Brisbane, talked of enlisting in the Royal Australian Navy, because the sea had always been his passion. And when term began in February 1940, David found that teachers at his school had left to join the Services.

By Easter, Germany had invaded Norway and Denmark, and a British force sent to help Norway singe Herr Hitler's moustache failed for lack of air power. In May, Germany invaded the Netherlands, Luxembourg and Belgium and pierced French defences. On 29 May the heroic evacuation of British forces began at Dunkirk in France.

Then, on David's eighteenth birthday, the Germans entered Paris. For the free world it was a day of mourning as this great city, symbol of culture and popular revolution, fell once more victim to tyranny.

Every day, David rose early to read the war news in the paper before setting off for school. In the evening he gathered with the family round the wireless to hear the latest broadcast, watching their expressions become more serious as the news worsened. In July, the RAF began night bombing of Germany. Germany had unleashed the force of its *Luftwaffe* on Britain, in an attempt to knock out as many airfields and defences as possible prior to invasion. But the German planes met with valiant opposition. Avidly, David pored over the accounts of the courage and daring of the fighter pilots in their Spitfires and Hurricanes, who with such skill and tenacity harried and attacked the Heinkels, Junkers and Messerschmitts sent by Hitler to blast Britain into submission. The stories of this small band of weary but indomitable airmen in their battle-worn planes, patrolling the English skies, repulsing invaders, inspired him and strengthened his determination to join them in defending the heart of Empire. He was moved by Winston Churchill's tribute, 'Never in the field of human conflict has so much been owed by so many to so few.'

By mid-August, when the Battle of Britain was at its peak, one hundred and eighty German planes had been shot down. But still more came over in wave after relentless wave, pounding London day and night – the beginning of the Blitz.

At sea, German U-boats threatened vital supplies of food and fuel, and troops arriving from Commonwealth countries.

At eighteen David was not old enough to vote. But he could pay taxes and legally drive a car. And he could join the armed forces, which seemed the right thing to do. The only thing. Everyone in the free world had to take responsibility for opposing the evils of Nazi aggression. But war meant mayhem and mass destruction on both sides. Created widows and orphans. Destroyed homes. Robbed parents of children in whom they had invested so many years of care and love and hope. 'How will Mum and Dad feel if I enlist?' he asked himself again and again.

One spring evening David was walking home with his father through City Park, where since he was small he had always loved to watch the monkeys' antics. The question which had kept his heart and mind in turmoil for months spilled out.

'Dad, when I leave school, I want to join the Air Force. That's all right with you, isn't it?'

His father was silent, but a blackbird scratching among the oak leaves scolded loudly. His father's footsteps slowed, then stopped. Two children ran by, laughing as they pelted each other with acorns.

'I've been expecting this,' his father replied at last. 'And so has your mother. Of course we aren't happy about it. But we understand. And you have our blessing.'

David gripped his father's strong square hands. The hands which extracted teeth in the surgery and tended flowers in the garden. The hands which had shown him how to hold a cricket bat, wield an axe, plant a rosebush, prune an apple tree.

'Will you tell Mum or shall I?' he asked.

'Let me break it to her first,' his father said. 'Then you can talk to her.'

When they sat down to tea, David's mother's eyes were red and he knew at once that his father must have spoken to her. But the family talked of other things, focusing on end of year plans and David's brother Brian's return from teaching in Armidale.

After the meal, everyone gathered as usual around the wireless, listening intently to the progress report on the newly opened North Africa campaign, hearing with dismay that the Germans had extended their bombing raids over Britain.

David carried the teacups out to the kitchen where his mother was running water into the sink. 'Dad's told you,' he said. It was more a statement than a question. His mother nodded, not trusting herself to speak. He hugged her and held her close for what seemed a moment, but was actually almost three wordless minutes as he realised, looking up at the trusty old clock on the dresser, which had already ticked through World War I.

'When?' she asked, holding him at arm's length so she could gaze on him.

'As soon as I've left school.'

She nodded again. 'Your father and I expected this. After all, you've always loved planes and this is your chance to learn to fly.' She smiled wanly. 'But you're doing it for the right reason, Viddy,' she added with pride. 'We have to stand up to those bullies. There must always be an England and England shall be free,' she said, referring to a song David had been playing for months on the sitting room piano. 'Now you must get back to your homework. Only six more weeks to your final exams.'

David needed no reminding. He was a conscientious student, and wanted to do well. Before the war had blown up he had set his sights on going to university and becoming a teacher. It was something of a family tradition. His father's parents had been teachers, with their own school at Emerald Hill in Melbourne. Now both his older brothers were teachers. It was a good profession.

In his last week at school, the headmaster called David to his study.

'Has the war affected your plans too?' he enquired. 'Will you be joining up like so many others?'

'Yes, sir.'

'The Air Force, I suppose.' The headmaster knew David's passion for planes.

'I hope so.'

'Well, they'll be getting a good recruit in you. But if you're not called up for a while – lots of fellows have enlisted but had to wait for their call-up – I'd be glad if you'd help us out here. We're losing another couple of teachers to the forces and need replacements. Think about it.'

'I don't know whether I could change from schoolmate into teacher, sir,' David demurred.

The headmaster looked at the tall, fresh-faced young man, whose modesty, quiet humour and sense of responsibility had endeared him to students and staff alike. 'You've been a prefect, wicket-keeper in the Second Eleven, and rowed in the First Four. You're respected and well liked. You won't have any trouble. I'll give you classes in the lower school, where you're looked up to. Share your passion for poetry with them and tell them stories from English history which they'll never forget. Anyway, see how you go at the recruiting office. If they can't take you straightaway, we'll be glad to have you back and pay you for your time and effort.'

His mother was pleased when David told her of the headmaster's offer. It was a good fallback position, if his call-up didn't come straight through. He knuckled down to revision and the approaching exams with some peace of mind, if not confidence.

The final school speech night was emotional. Would David ever again see some of these fellows he had grown up with over the last twelve years? How many would still be around in a year's time? How many names would be up on the school honour board, with a gold asterisk beside them denoting the final sacrifice? Would his? Or would the war be over before he had the chance to make his contribution?

It was a quiet Christmas and New Year. With growing impatience, David awaited his exam results and a response to his application for entry into the Royal Australian Air Force (RAAF). At last one of the letters he was hoping for came. He had passed all his Leaving Certificate (Year Twelve) subjects, with As in English and history, Bs in the rest. Now he must wait for his call-up.

And wait he did, through much of 1941. Processing applications took time, and there were not enough places in the Empire Air Training Scheme for the volunteers who wished to become aircrew. Month after month he waited for the envelope which seemed as if it would never come, while increasingly grim news came from the war zones. These now spanned the Sudan, Eritrea and Abyssinia, (Ethiopia), Greece, Crete, Syria, Iran and the Baltic States. And Germany had launched a new North Africa offensive where the Diggers' heroic resistance led to the insulting Nazi epithet 'Rats of Tobruk' becoming a byword for courage and tenacity.

Air raids on London had been stepped up again. In the industrial city of Coventry, the superb Gothic cathedral was reduced to rubble. Britons had stoically endured the devastation and disruption of their lives caused by the Blitz. But the destruction of such beauty and tradition galvanised a new spirit of determination and resistance. U-boat attacks also intensified. The battle cruiser *Hood*, pride of the Navy, was sunk off Greenland by the

German super battleship *Bismarck*, which was in turn sunk by the Royal Navy. In June, eight days after David's 19th birthday, Hitler broke the non-aggression pact and German forces invaded Russia.

'It's come at last!' David announced to his parents in October, on receiving the letter requesting him to attend an interview for entry to the RAAF.

Wearing his best jacket and tie, shaven, his thick dark hair carefully combed, his shoes polished, David presented himself at the recruiting office. After completing a plethora of forms, answering a myriad of questions, he was called for a short interview. Standing straight and attentive before three uniformed officers, he noted their ranks and focused on the most senior.

'Why do you want to join the Air Force?' the Flight Lieutenant asked.

'To serve my king and country, sir,' David answered without hesitation.

'Do you know anything about flying?' another asked.

'I've been keen on planes, sir, ever since I saw Bert Hinkler, then Charles Kingsford Smith at the Air Pageant.'

The officers smiled for the first time. 'That was a good show!' one exclaimed. After a medical examination David returned by train to Launceston to await results yet again.

On 2 December a letter arrived *On His Majesty's Service,* notifying him that he had been placed on the Royal Australian Air Force Reserve. Call-up was unlikely before April 1942, but he was required to commence a course of ground subjects immediately. Disappointed yet pleased, David began night classes, the first step towards his goal. More maths and some physics, with morse code and aircraft recognition stimulating new interest and promising action in the air eventually.

International events escalated dramatically. Japan, which had invaded China and Manchuria in the 1930s, suddenly revealed further imperial expansionist ambitions. On 7 December, the Japanese Air Force bombed the American naval base Pearl Harbor in Hawaii, and British Malaya. Next day Britain and Australia declared war on Japan. So did the USA, up until then neutral. Three days later the USA declared war on Germany and Italy.

Now the world was at war.

With the fall of Malaya to the Japanese before Christmas, and war raging on Australia's doorstep, David grew increasingly frustrated, chafing to be in uniform. Earlier in the year, the biggest contingent ever to leave Tasmania had embarked on the liner *Queen Mary*, now converted to a troopship. Although the movement was an official secret, it was impossible to disguise the presence of such a large and impressive vessel in Hobart, and people flocked to see the splendid ship and to farewell loved ones.

David caught a special train from Launceston, travelling over four hours, to join the crowds gaping at the great grey giant towering above the fishing boats in the historic deepwater harbour. He took in every detail and would have given anything to change his civvies for uniform, to be striding up the gangplank, kitbag on shoulder. Instead he just had to trudge to the station for the rackety trip home in the cold and dark, with a long walk at the end.

At the New Year's Eve beach party there were now many more girls than boys. David had little heart for celebrating. He just wanted to be up and away. Then, early in January 1942, an unexpected letter arrived. It was a compulsory call-up for Army service. Within days he was in khaki, drilling at the Launceston Showgrounds with more than a hundred other raw young recruits. For four months he marched and trained.

Just before his 20th birthday the long-awaited summons to the Air Force came. David went straight to Hobart for a stringent medical examination, after which he was sworn in.

Australia was a participant in the Empire Air Training Scheme to provide aircrew to supplement Britain's Royal Air Force. Recruits might eventually be sent for flying training to Canada or Rhodesia, but they all did their initial training in Australia. As one of a group of Tasmanians entering No. 1 RAAF Initial Training School at Somers, Victoria, on 19 June, David became a Blue Orchid, as RAAF personnel were dubbed in army slang. Air Force blue was the colour he was to wear for the next four and a half years.

RAAF officer's cap badge, which David hoped eventually to wear

2 Name, Rank and Number

Life at No. 1 Initial Training School at Somers on Westernport Bay was very different from living at home. After David's temporary stint in the army, sleeping in a tent with five others was not a new experience. But being woken by the sound of the bugle playing 'Reveille' was very different from an alarm clock chirring. The new intake quickly learned the refrain *Oh how I hate to get up in the morning,* singing with particular gusto the line threatening revenge on the pup who woke the bugler up! They also relished the old services saying, 'Who called the cook a bastard?', and its reply, 'Who called the bastard a cook?'

The training program provided an introduction to the knowledge and skills needed to become aircrew, as distinct from ground crew. With its regimen and discipline, it also aimed to change 800 free-spirited youthful individuals into three cohesive units who identified themselves as

David, 20, being presented with his Wings,
Passing Out Parade, Point Cook, 1943

23

members of Australia's armed forces, trained to obey orders instantly, without question. Personal identity was submerged under name, rank and number. David became Mattingley, C.D. Aircraftman Class 2, 408458, RAAF.

Each airman was fitted with clothing from the skin outwards – underpants, singlets, shirts, tie, socks, shoes and boots. Only pyjamas were not issued. 'So we're expected to sleep in the raw!' they joked. Full uniform had to be worn at all times, even when on leave. This included the field service cap, with its coveted white flash denoting aircrew trainee status. On the station, long-sleeved overalls, known as goonskins, and jumper and beret, all blue, were to be worn in cold weather; khaki shorts and shirt in summer. Kit included blankets, towels, razor blades, shoe-cleaning gear, clothes brush and cutlery. Each man also received a sewing kit, essential for sewing the badges of rank onto his uniform. David's unit had only to stitch on the *Australia* eagle.

'Ouch! Wish Mum could do this,' they exclaimed, sucking pricked fingers.

Finally, each received a kitbag in which to keep everything, and out of which he would live.

After inspection of tents, kit, uniform, and a full parade, the day began in earnest with a solid timetable of drill and classes. More slogging away at maths and physics, more morse code and aircraft recognition. But now there were new subjects: Air Force law, meteorology, armaments and ship recognition, popularly called shipwreck.

David had always been interested in weather, especially cloud formations which were such an integral part of Tasmanian days, and he became absorbed in the detail and variety of patterns to be learnt and understood if he was to fly safely. Cumulonimbus thunderheads were

David, RAAF Aircraftman Class 2
White flash on cap denotes aircrew trainee status

always to be avoided and cumulus clouds treated with caution, because of the turbulence they caused.

Armaments were another matter. David had to grapple with the thought of being the agent of delivery for loads of bombs. The prospect of using weapons against fellow human beings was not a happy one. But news from the theatres of war did not allow for personal scruples. The German army was advancing steadily across Russia and by late August had reached Stalingrad, while Japan had already become a major threat to Australia itself with the fall of Singapore. So David learned to strip and assemble both Vickers and Browning machine guns and Smith and Wesson revolvers.

The RAF had stepped up attacks on German ports with a 1000 bomber raid on Bremen in June, followed by a raid on Hamburg in July. But British convoys to Malta had suffered heavy losses, not only of merchant shipping but also Royal Navy (RN) escorts. So shipwreck was very important. Ships had to be recognised from above as well as in profile. Not just RAN and RN, but also German, Italian and Japanese – battleships, cruisers, aircraft carriers, destroyers, corvettes. Merchant ships and tankers too. And national markings. David's brain teemed with images.

In aircraft recognition, flash cards, projected images and suspended models were used to familiarise students with silhouettes from every likely angle. RAF and *Luftwaffe* fighters and bombers were shown from above, below, sideways, head on, and turning – Spitfires, Hurricanes, Blenheims and Wellingtons, Messerschmitts, Junkers, Heinkels, Dorniers and almost 150 others, including Japanese planes.

David studied the outlines and distinguishing features. Then he drew the planes and ships over, over, over again until they were indelibly imprinted in his mind and he could pass the weekly tests with scarcely an error.

Drill, marching and physical training before lunch provided a welcome break from concentrated study. The recruits moaned about the weekly cross-country run, but gradually everyone grew fitter and tougher, losing puppy fat or flab.

Daily duties included kitchen work, cleaning latrines and guard duties. Fatigue, punishment for small misdemeanours such as being late on parade, meant extra latrine cleaning or kitchen work.

One day, David and his companion were on guard duty when a carload of girls became bogged in the sandy track nearby. In reward for their gallantry in digging out the car, the girls gave them each an enamel mug full of sherry! The boys were lucky to escape punishment.

At dinner, everyone was also hungry for the mail which was distributed, eager for news from home. The big moment when 'the eagle shat' came once a fortnight at pay parade, and each man received four pounds and four shillings – six shillings per day. Sunday morning church parade was compulsory. If they had Saturday leave, David and other Tasmanians, school friend Peter Lord, summer holiday companion Tas Williams, and Ian Vickers, also from Launceston, would catch bus then train to Melbourne, to see the sights, window-shop or take a tram ride. Often they went to the cinema to see British films with war themes. They were riveted by *Coastal Command*, seeing in action Sunderland and Catalina flying boats and others they had studied so closely in aircraft rec. The bittersweet wartime romance *Mrs Miniver* had many in the audience in tears. But camp life did not provide opportunities for forming attachments, and although David wrote to various friends, he did not have a regular girlfriend. His heart was fully committed to the world of flying.

As the two units ahead completed the course and graduated, David's group counted the weeks until their passing out parade. In the intake after his, David met a staff member from his school who was struggling with some of the subjects and he found himself in the unexpected role of tutor to his former teacher. A natural teacher himself, David also helped other trainees struggling with their studies.

After four months and final examinations, David's unit completed their initial training and graduated with the rank of Leading Aircraftman. They anxiously awaited mustering, as the allocation to specific aircrew roles was known. Their abilities had been carefully assessed and after yet another interview each was assigned to further training either as pilot, navigator, wireless operator or air gunner. It was a tense time because everyone wanted to be selected as a pilot. Many had their hopes dashed as they found themselves scrubbed, their names not on the coveted list. Some of David's friends were sent off to specialised courses in different parts of Australia and he wondered if he would ever see them again. David was elated to find his name on the list for pilot training. He was fulfilling his dream.

On 15 October, those selected to be pilots were posted to their Elementary Flying Training Schools (EFTS). David was thrilled to be sent to No. 7 EFTS at Western Junction. The next three months were to be some of the happiest he had ever known. The morning after they arrived, an instructor said, 'Mattingley, I'm taking you on a familiarisation flight. You'll be learning on the only vice-free plane I know.' Walking out across the grass beside this experienced pilot past the line of training Moths, David, heart alight with excitement, felt as if a thousand moths were fluttering around it. They stopped beside the last Tiger Moth and he watched and listened attentively as the instructor did the pre-flight check, dropped the low

Tiger Moth, used on Elementary Flying Training School courses

door to the cockpit and said, 'Hop in.' David took a deep breath. This was it!

Just one foot after the other on the footholds and he was in, sitting in the rear, strapping himself in under the instructor's watchful eye. David observed over the instructor's shoulder as the instructor checked the controls. The mechanic swung the two-bladed propeller until the engine fired. The instructor checked the engine revs on each magneto.

'All set. Off we go,' he said through the speaking tube.

The little Moth taxied across the grass and turned into wind. As the pilot opened the throttle it moved slowly at first, then gradually increased speed. Almost imperceptibly it lifted and they were airborne. Heading into the blue sky. They cleared the hedge at the end of the airfield as the plane gained height. Up, up and away towards the Western Tiers, which lay like a purple scarf on the horizon. Below, the landscape shone in the spring sunlight. It was David's beloved Tasmania at its loveliest. Green fields pinpointed yellow by clumps of double daffodils, and smudged pearly pink by blossom of ancient apple trees where early settlers' cottages had once stood. Pastures with sheep scattered like grains of rice interspersed with the rich brown corduroy of ploughed paddocks. All linked and overlaid with a network of hawthorn hedges in frothing white spring flower.

The wind whistled in the wires, the engine throbbed sweetly and steadily. At 3000 feet in the open cockpit, David was glad of the goggles, gauntlets and leather helmet he had been issued, and the heavy overalls buttoned at the wrist to keep out the wind.

All too soon the instructor was turning the plane back towards Western Junction. David gazed across at the rolling cumulus clouds topping the chunky forms of Mount Arthur, Mount Barrow and Ben Lomond like clotted cream, and down on the winding course of the South Esk River, glinting through the tender tracery of willows. This was a day he would never forget.

For days after that first take-off and touchdown David felt the exhilaration of his first flight. But although his heart was in the clouds, his head certainly was not. The new course demanded concentration and hard work, with more crucial new subjects to master: airmanship,

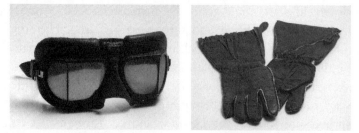

Flying goggles and gauntlets, standard RAF issue

theory of flight, navigation and technical details, aircraft construction – airframes and engines. A pilot was expected to understand everything about the plane he flew. So David learned every part of the Tiger Moth and how it functioned, and studied some of the more sophisticated aircraft he would fly later. Night after night he sat on his bed studying, determined to do well in the final exams.

Flying lessons were the highlight of each day and he awaited his slots eagerly. They were always at different times to allow each trainee to experience varying conditions. After the initial flight as a passenger, for the first week all were with an instructor, practising take-off into wind, powered approach and gliding.

Then, at the beginning of November, David went solo for the first time. It was one of the most momentous days of his life, walking across the dewy grass, knowing that he and he alone was responsible for the safety of the little Tiger Moth which meant so much to him. And for his own life. Heart thumping, he went through the pre-flight safety check with utmost care, climbed aboard and strapped himself in. The mechanic swung the propeller, the engine fired, David signalled 'Chocks away', and under his control the Moth moved forward into the wind and took off.

There was no time to be nervous. He had to perform a set exercise in only fifteen minutes. Tense with concentration, David performed all the actions he had practised with the instructor. He watched the horizon and the instruments. Almost before he knew it, it was time to return. Checking the windsock he took the downwind leg, then the shorter cross-wind and turned into the final approach. Throttling back the engine, he lost height to bring the Moth in to land. There was a rumble as wheels and tailskid touched down. Adrenalin still pumping, he taxied back, uncomfortably aware that a Tiger Moth has no brakes. Finally the Moth came to a stop. He switched off, clambered out and took a deep breath of the bright morning air. David had completed his first solo.

Over the next four weeks he made forty-five flights, totalling sixty hours, half of them solo. He learned to recover from spins, to sideslip and to do climbing turns and steep turns. David loved the cross-country facet of training. He particularly enjoyed navigating visually over pre-determined courses, identifying landmarks – railways, rivers and towns. He practised precautionary and forced landings, and learned to fly at night entirely by instruments.

The altimeter in the Moth did not register small changes in altitude. Soon after take-off one night he was shaken to find that having crossed two hedges and the road between, his wheels were touching the rising ground beyond. He immediately eased back the joystick and opened the throttle fully. To his relief the Moth climbed away instantly. It was a valuable experience, proving that the Tiger Moth was ideal for training because it was so forgiving of beginners' mistakes.

As the young pilots became more proficient, aerobatics, a special thrill, were a regular part of training. They learned to loop and roll and do stall turns, which could be a useful manoeuvre in a tight situation. They learned the truth of the saying, 'There are old pilots and bold pilots. But there are no old *and* bold pilots.' And they were certainly not encouraged to emulate the instructor who flew David between a pair of lofty poplar trees!

David was sorry when the course drew near to its close in December. Western Junction, with permanent hutments and only 50 trainees, had been quite intimate, much more congenial than Somers. With good meals and plenty of Tasmanian beef, potatoes and salad, WJ was almost like a big family, with lots of larks and teasing.

When David found a slug in his lettuce, a mate dared him, 'Bet you can't eat that!' Not to be beaten, he dropped it in his tea and downed it. He was never fond of tea after that. David looked forward to spending weekend leaves at home picking raspberries and strawberries, slug-free, and tucking into his mother's gooseberry pies.

One event stood out during this time. The trainees never forgot their first street march. Rising early, they boarded the train for the long trip to Hobart, laughing and joking like school-children on an outing, enjoying the break from routine. At the station they formed up for the march through the capital. One of the tallest, David was in the front rank. At midday they stepped out to the sound of an army band. It was a chill grey day with a keen wind off Mount Wellington, which stood like a sentinel above the city.

To their amazement, the streets were lined, not just with Christmas shoppers and the idly curious, but with families, school groups, shop assistants and office workers on their lunch break, even hospital patients with their nurses. Country families had left their cows or tractors or apple trees. Even the wharves were empty as fishermen deserted their boats. Everyone was hoping to catch a glimpse of a son or a brother, an old school friend or the boy from across the road. Johnny, Jack or Jim. People from near and far turned out to honour these young men who would soon be going to war in some distant place.

Leading the street march, Hobart, 1942

'Good on ya, Johnny.'

'Good one, Bill. Give it to those Huns.'

'Teach those Japs a lesson.'

There were bursts of clapping, bursts of cheering. Sometimes there was stifled sobbing, sometimes a fluttering hanky or flag. But for the most part the crowd was silent. Awed by the solemnity of the occasion, the sight of fifty of their finest – sons of farmers, fishermen, factory workers, doctors, dentists, bankers, builders – all prepared to lay down their lives.

The men's expressions were serious as they concentrated on keeping in step along the tram lines, while the trams waited by the GPO, whose clock boomed the hour. More conscious than ever of the honour and the responsibility that the dark blue uniform laid on them, binding them together as brothers, in loyalty, discipline and duty. Some of them – no one knew who – would be called to the ultimate sacrifice for king and country. They marched erect, their bearing reflecting this knowledge, this pride.

It was a silent journey back, each man immersed in his own thoughts, wrapped in his own memories, grappling with his own fears. Sunlight shafted across the Midland paddocks, the Western Tiers loomed purple against the sunset which gilded the clouds as the milestone day drew to its close.

Towards the course's conclusion David was assessed as an above-average pilot. Trainees were asked if they would prefer to continue their training in single-engined or multi-engined planes. Like most others, David dreamed of being a fighter pilot in singles, perhaps in Spitfires in Britain, Hurricanes in North Africa or Kittyhawks in New Guinea. But because of the high casualty rate in bombers, RAF Bomber Command needed more pilots. So his next posting was back to Victoria to No. 1 Service Flying Training School at Point Cook to learn to fly multis. After what was to be his last Christmas home for four years, David and his fellow trainee pilots boarded the *Nairana* again for the overnight crossing of Bass Strait.

Point Cook, established in 1914 in Australian flying's infancy, was the Air Force's oldest base. On Port Phillip Bay, in flat terrain between Melbourne and Geelong, its site had been chosen for proximity to both rail and port. After Western Junction's friendly atmosphere, it was a surprise to find other attitudes here, with some condescension shown towards the newcomers. A peacetime station for so long, Point Cook had become focused more on administration than action, and the wartime trainees had quickly coined a phrase passed on to each intake – 'Chairborne versus Airborne'.

The station's permanent brick buildings were not to be used by trainees, who occupied temporary quarters. Nor did the trainees fly at Point Cook. All training flights took place from satellite airfields, just paddocks at Werribee, Lara and Little River. Students were transported by open truck, and the flight office was a large wooden crate. The only amenity was a Furphy cart providing tepid drinking water. It was mid-January. There was no shade or shelter for the young airmen, and the planes, made of wood and plywood, sat out in the sun all day, and were blisteringly hot when on the ground. They were Oxfords, twin-engined monoplanes, more than twice the size of the single-engined biplane Tiger Moths. The landscape, too, was very different. After Tasmania's spring and early summer verdure, rivers and purple mountains, the expanse of sunburnt brown paddocks shimmering in the heat, windswept and treeless, was a shock and the glare was much harder on the eyes.

Unlike the Tiger Moth's tandem seating, the instructor and trainee sat side by side in the Oxford. David concentrated hard as the instructor explained the instrument panel, far more complex than the Moth's, and rehearsed the vital actions before take-off, after take-off, before landing and after landing. There was a lot to learn. Then after the instructor had trimmed elevators and rudders, selected fuel tanks, checked their gauges and cocks, checked flaps and uncaged the gyro which operated the compass, it was the moment for take-off. Each engine was three times as powerful as the Moth's.

David felt the acceleration and found himself looking down on the dry brown plain unrolling ahead, with the

Airspeed Oxford, twin-engined trainer used at Point Cook and in the UK

You Yangs low and mauve-blue to the north and Port Phillip Bay flat and grey-blue to the south. The instructor demonstrated climbing, gliding, stalling and turning, and flying and turning with only one engine, before bringing the Oxford in to land.

Early in the course, the airmen learned a chilling lesson, vital for survival – how to abandon an aircraft.

'Hope we never have to do that,' each man whispered to himself.

There was also the usual full timetable of lectures with new subjects. These included more advanced navigation with some astronomy and knowledge of astro-nav, navigation by the stars. They also had to plot courses on paper as far as Gippsland and the Bass Strait islands. Other subjects included armaments – gunnery, pyrotechnics, bombs and their components (known as bombs and comps) – and Aldis lamp signalling from air to ground.

As they had at Western Junction, the trainees also spent many hours in the Link Trainer, a primitive precursor of the modern flight simulator. Two days after his familiarisation flight, David went on his first solo in an Oxford and by the end of January had tallied 12 hours flying. Then he did his first cross-country lasting two hours. Each was longer than the last, extending into Victoria's Western District.

Night flying was another challenge. The flights lasted up to an hour, and included both instrument flying and some astro-nav. David loved the clear starry nights with the Southern Cross in different positions. But like everyone, he was deeply shocked when a fellow trainee was killed in a crash on a night flying exercise. It was a sobering realisation of the cost of pilot error.

That night boys became men.

In the weeks that followed, the trainees practised precautionary and forced landings on one engine, and low flying was introduced, which David found fun. He enjoyed following the tops of cumulus cloud banks, though on one occasion he was startled to find another Oxford doing the same thing, a bit too close for safety. Formation flying was the next challenge. It required intense concentration and kept the adrenalin flowing.

Stringent revision flights in late March preceded a major test, which examined general proficiency before a pilot was awarded his Wings. An exercise in naval cooperation tested the nerves when David was required to fly his Oxford over Flinders Naval Base as a practice target for ground-based gun crews. He could see the gunners elevating and traversing their anti-aircraft guns, aiming at him, and was thankful they were not firing live ammunition. 'But we will be the target one day,' he told himself.

In Europe, the air war had intensified. The German

air attack on London, renewed in January, had been followed by a heavy RAF raid on Berlin. In March the RAF began systematic bombing of the European railway network. So in April when bombing became the next part of the Point Cook training, every man was in no doubt of its importance and the need to become proficient.

Flying in pairs, each took a turn as pilot, then bomb aimer. It was simulated bombing, with a camera focused on a ground target. It was the pilot's responsibility to bring the plane accurately into position so that the bomb aimer could press the tit (the button which would release the bombs on real operations) when the sights were correctly aligned on target. Results were recorded photographically and assessed later. An inaccurate pilot might result in inefficient bombing.

Even as these young Australian pilots trained, the RAF commenced heavy raids on Germany's industrial heartland, the Ruhr Valley, climaxing in the legendary exploits of the Dam Busters. As the air offensive on Germany became ever more destructive, David's course was coming to a close, culminating in a solid week of formation flying with some air to ground radio telephony.

On 21 May 1943, with a total of 182 flying hours, he was presented with his Wings at a graduation ceremony at Point Cook, which his parents attended. At a celebratory dinner at the Hotel Australia in Melbourne, the menu, drawn up as a flight plan with typical Air Force humour, included a weather forecast: *Very wet night. Depression expected tomorrow morning.* Tomato juice was *90 Octane.* Roast lamb was *cross-country killed*, and the dessert was *Bombe Australia (no dummy runs permitted)*!

David with his parents and brother Brian at home, Launceston, 1943

When David was notified he had a week's pre-embarkation leave, many emotions and thoughts he had pushed to the back of his mind while concentrating on training surged to the fore. He had always wanted to discover the world beyond Tasmania's familiar shores. Opportunities, however, to travel even in Australia, let alone beyond, were rare for most people. He was fortunate and had already visited Melbourne, Adelaide, Sydney and Fiji. But he was hungry for new experiences, new insights into life in places with different histories and cultures. Although a couple of his family's acquaintances had come as migrants to Australia, few of all the other people they knew had travelled overseas. Now, at the age of twenty, he was going abroad. Leaving behind those people and places he had known and loved, perhaps never to see them again. He was about to face challenges and dangers he could hardly begin to imagine.

Now promoted to Sergeant, David returned to Melbourne, sleeping on deck as the *Nairana* was overcrowded with servicemen. At No. 1 Embarkation Depot at Ascot Vale Showgrounds, he was glad to have time for one last visit to the family of Des Hadden, his friend since schooldays, who had made him so welcome on weekend leaves. Then the young airmen travelled overnight by train to No. 4 Embarkation Depot at Scotch College, Adelaide. Four days later David's group embarked on SS *Umgeni*.

Would they head west? North? Or east? Were they bound for the Middle East? Or New Guinea? Or Britain? David was hoping with all his heart that Britain would be their destination.

Battle Order 204 (2)
D Dog

Battle Order 204 was a rushed effort. The
men were disappointed that they were given
an ordinary breakfast instead of the normal
flying meal of bacon and eggs. As was usual
under such conditions, aircrew assisted with the
exacting task of bombing up. As they worked to
hoist their deadly load into place, the men found
wry amusement in the messages the armourers
had painted or chalked on some of the bombs.

Drew, the bomb aimer, chuckled to see *Aggro
for Adolf*.

'*Another addled egg for Adolf.*' crowed Birdy
the rear gunner.

And they all laughed at seeing the supremely
confident *You're history, Hitler*. 'That one's for
you, Skip,' they joked, knowing their skipper's
passion for history.

· · · · · · · · · · · · · · · · ·

David and the crew in D Dog waited tensely on the airfield perimeter for the go signal. At 1230 hours on 29 November, they took off with a bomb load of fourteen 500-pound clusters, two containers of sixty 4-pound incendiaries and one cookie, a massive 4000-pound bomb. Two of the aircraft from 625 Squadron hadn't made the noon deadline, so twenty-seven planes set off from the base at Kelstern that day.

Flying across Lincolnshire, the roar of the Lancaster's four powerful Merlin engines reverberating though them, David and his crew joined their gaggle, as the grouping was known, at the coast. A little further south, they took their place in the stream of aircraft converging from other stations and had their last glimpse of a winter-sombre England. They crossed the sullen grey English Channel churning below, hoping as always they wouldn't have to put their ditching drill to the test in its hungry waters.

On, on, mile after Merlin-driven mile, high above France, towards Germany. Dreading what lay ahead. Feeling the vice grip of terror. Knowing the horrors awaiting every Lancaster bomber and its crew of seven, every Mosquito and its crew of two.

Two thousand and ninety two men going through this ordeal of fire.

For some it was the first time.

For some it would be their last time.

For some it would be their only time.

3 Slow Boat to Britain

SS *Umgeni* was a handsome five-year-old 7000-ton merchant ship with passenger accommodation, much more comfortable than a regular troopship, and David shared a first-class cabin with two others. A good sailor, he was untroubled by typical Bass Strait weather, which laid other men low and sent soup, glasses and cutlery to the floor. Speculation about destination ended. They were heading east. Surely bound for Britain. David was jubilant. But very aware that the rocky Bass Strait islands were the last view of Australia he might ever see. Enemy submarines had been active in the Tasman Sea, so life jackets had to be carried at all times, and every man served on daytime submarine watch and night blackout patrol.

Seven days after leaving Adelaide, *Umgeni* made landfall in New Zealand. For the first time David saw the mighty Avro Lancaster aircraft, the only one in Australasia. Queenie, the Lanc, was visiting from Britain to raise funds with demonstration flights. She was breathtaking. So well

The mighty four-engined Avro Lancaster (AWM neg. no. P00811_003)

proportioned, so much bigger and more powerful with her four engines than any aircraft he had yet seen. She banked and turned so effortlessly on her long elegant wings.

Although David had aspired to be a fighter pilot, he was realistic. With Bomber Command's high casualties, most of the new aircrew would probably be sent to fly heavy bombers. Now he hoped he would be allocated to Lancasters. 'That's the kite I want to fly,' he told himself. 'She's magnificent.'

On his 21st birthday David took eight friends, including Tasmanians Peter Lord, Ian Vickers, Gordon Lawson and Ron Leonard, to dinner at the best hotel in Wellington. They were amazed to find eighteen choices on the menu, in contrast to Australian austerity.

'Tuck in, boys, and make the most of it,' David urged his guests. 'We won't be getting meals like this in Britain.'

They needed no second urging.

When David asked for a bottle of wine the head waiter's surly response was, 'Don't you know there's a war on?' All the young men in Air Force blue, already so far from home, burst into laughter.

Umgeni was delayed for almost four weeks in three ports because waterside workers refused to handle frozen lamb in wet conditions. 'Perhaps we can swing the lead too, and refuse to fly when it's raining!' the airmen joked. But it gave them plenty of opportunities to enjoy renowned Kiwi hospitality and to explore. Eager to experience Maori culture, arriving at Waitara, a traditional village and ancient *pa*, on the occasion of a great gathering, David was moved that the Australians were welcomed as guests of honour, greeted in the languages of the elders.

During their last week in New Zealand, David felt unwell, but he did not report sick for fear of being offloaded. When *Umgeni* finally sailed, the ship's doctor diagnosed jaundice and David was confined to bed on a diet of boiled fish, bread and jam and black coffee for ten days. 'What rotten luck,' his mates sympathised.

When at last he was allowed on deck to watch gunnery practice and take part in lifeboat drill he was glad to enjoy the sunshine and glittering expanse of the azure blue Pacific. Before reaching the Equator, they saw the Southern Cross, now low on the horizon, for the last time. Haunted by the sight of an empty lifeboat drifting on the watery waste, each man wondered if he would ever see the familiar constellation again. They sweltered in stifling heat, thunderstorms and torrential tropical rain before Crossing the Line, which gave the young warriors-in-waiting a chance to let off steam.

Almost eight weeks after leaving Adelaide, *Umgeni* reached Balboa, the Panama Canal's Pacific entrance. During the fifty mile, day-long passage David marvelled at the system of locks and lakes, an amazing feat of engineering which had cost so many lives.

Reaching Colon on the old Spanish Main, they were eager for their first taste of a really foreign port. A night out in the brightly lit old town was different from anything they had known, with its lively Latin atmosphere of night clubs, Spanish dancing and music, its cosmopolitan crowds, horse-drawn cabs, narrow streets lined with Spanish-style houses, and open taverns and shops. Returning to the ship, however, was tricky, cruising from one blacked-out vessel to another searching for the right one. In the morning they discovered that Colon was not so glamorous by day, just sleazy and squalid. Unnerving, too, with large American cars driving on the right-hand side.

Umgeni sailed now as Commodore's flagship in the first row of a ten-ship convoy, which could only travel at the speed of its slowest vessel, a vulnerable 7 knots. U-boat activities had escalated in the Caribbean and only four days earlier a convoy had lost the equivalent of three *Umgeni*s. So everyone was extra vigilant on submarine watch.

As radio communication was forbidden, flags and Aldis lamp signalling were used, and the ship's guns were manned at all times. The tension increased after detectors twice picked up submarines in Torpedo Lane, the narrow passage between Jamaica and Haiti where the Commodore's ship had been sunk on his last two trips.

Three submarines were sighted during one evening, but then black cloud descended, obscuring the moon and reducing the danger of attack. Next morning no convoy vessels had become statistics to add to the grim tally of over 400 lost in Torpedo Lane. The airmen joked about their good Aussie luck. 'The Japs didn't get us in the Pacific, and Jerry hasn't got us here. So we've got to be third time lucky in the Atlantic!' But secretly all were aware that at any moment their number could be up.

The next brief landfall was Guantanamo Bay, Cuba, a US naval base. It was a desolate spot and the men were not sorry there was no shore leave. Joining a bigger fifteen-ship convoy, helping to screen twelve oil tankers from attack, made *Umgeni* even more vulnerable. Only the Caribbean's indigo blue and magnificent sunsets provided relief from tension, unrelenting heat and humidity. Twelve long days and nights after leaving Colon, heat changed into cold wind. Heavy fog enveloped the convoy and ships blew their sirens in morse to indicate position. It was eerie.

But intact and unharmed, the convoy entered New York Harbour. The harbour was dominated by the gigantic figure of the Statue of Liberty and crowded with shipping flying the flags of Britain, USA, France, Netherlands, Norway, Sweden and Panama. From the Little Apple of Launceston to the Big Apple was a stupendous transition. The long watches day and night for weeks at sea had given David plenty of time to reflect on the meaning of life and the question of death. Now, the hurry, bustle and noise of this huge city, with its Manhattan skyscrapers dwarfing the mortals below, seemed overwhelming and superficial. But David and his mates made the most of the long hot days to take in new experiences, using slot machines for food and drink, eating hamburgers and fries, and sightseeing. They were particularly impressed by New York's showpiece, the recently completed Rockefeller Center, with elevators travelling up seventy floors at phenomenal speed to a breathtaking view from its observation deck. David wrote home, *Among its army of maintenance personnel, one man's full-time job was to pick up chewing gum!*

Shopping in well-stocked department stores for items unobtainable in beleaguered Britain, most men bought silk stockings, but David also bought swimming trunks and a silver propelling pencil. And mindful he might find himself shot down over France, a second-hand copy of Alexandre Dumas' novel *The Three Musketeers*, to brush up his French.

A home visit on leafy Long Island provided a welcome break, and a chance to reconnect with the earth and green and growing things. The kindly couple, who provided hospitality to many servicemen, kept in touch for the next thirty years.

After five days in New York, *Umgeni* left on the hazardous Atlantic crossing as part of an even bigger convoy proceeding at 10 knots. On watch early next morning David had the uncanny experience of seeing a notorious Newfoundland fog swallow all thirty-nine ships, including a merchant ship converted to aircraft carrier with fifty-one Thunderbolt fighters lashed to her deck. After another fourteen ships joined, dense fog caused several collisions. Then fog gave way to driving rain and icy winds, and rising seas forced the convoy to slow to an anxious 4 knots, to allow twenty-five ships separated overnight to catch up.

Ten nerve-wracking days out from New York the convoy was split to allow the fastest ships, including *Umgeni*, to proceed at 12 knots. Next day, it was finally disbanded, and each ship headed for its own port. Grateful that none had been lost, even the most hardened atheists secretly murmured 'Thank God!' In the calm Irish Sea, such a relief after the fierce Atlantic, *Umgeni* made 15 knots. On Friday 3 September, the fourth anniversary of the declaration of war, the Allies invaded Italy and *Umgeni* docked at Cardiff. That evening the young airmen staged an impromptu concert, a high-spirited celebration of their arrival in Britain after their three-month voyage.

SS Umgeni

4 Loving Life

The day after docking in Cardiff, the contingent headed for London. The long train journey revealed not only England's rural beauty, but also some of her wartime strategies. New airfields and factories had been sited throughout the countryside to reduce target potential and minimise damage such as London had suffered.

The young airmen arrived late in the blacked-out capital and it was not until morning that they were confronted with the scars of the Blitz. Seeing the skeletons and shells of buildings, and other sites razed to the ground, shocked them.

'Jerry sure has been busy!' they exclaimed.

'And that's what we're going to be doing to Jerryville!' they thought.

Looking eagerly from the bus taking them to their next train, David was agog at the postcard images he recognised as they drove – Nelson on his column flanked by lions in Trafalgar Square, under Admiralty Arch following the

Big Ben, Westminster, in wartime London (AWM neg. no. 002752)

route of royal processions along The Mall, past St James's Palace and Buckingham Palace, where the Royal Standard proudly flew, to arrive at Victoria Station. So different from Australian stations. Not as impressive outside as Melbourne's Flinders Street, but its interior loftier and more extensive, home to multitudinous pigeons which scurried among the feet of the myriads of hurrying passengers.

David had always revelled in English history and literature so he was eager to see for himself the country that inspired England's great poets. As the electric train sped through Surrey and Sussex meadows, woods and downlands, he delighted as more of William Blake's *green and pleasant land* unfolded. They were headed to the famous seaside town of Brighton, 50 miles from London, where the once-crowded shingly beaches, so different from Australian sands, were now mined and laced with barbed wire entanglements. The end of the famous pier was cut off, and even the promenades were partly barricaded. Only the seagulls could go where they chose. Hearing their mournful mewing David exclaimed, 'That's the background sound in British films! Not like our raucous squawking gulls.'

All too soon they heard another new sound. A sound which made the war seem very near indeed. An eerie wailing which made David's spine tingle.

'Gives you goose flesh, doesn't it!' he muttered to his room mate Peter Lord. It was the air-raid alert. A preliminary siren gave the first warning of approaching raiders. If the enemy planes came closer, a series of pips like radio time signals followed. But on that first occasion the German bombers were heading for London, so the welcome steady wail of the All Clear sounded soon afterwards.

Another night the raiders were closer and the men could hear distant gunfire. Then returning from the cinema one night David and Peter watched fighters going up and a German plane taking violent evasive action in the glare of searchlights. When the Bofors gun outside the hotel started firing Peter shouted 'Watch out for your cap!' But the blast blew their caps off. Next morning the Bofors crew claimed the plane as a definite kill.

As the Germans maintained their raids on London, David wrote in his diary, *Jerry has been very persistent lately and the gunfire prevents our sleeping.* Soon they got into the habit of ignoring alerts, not bothering to leave their beds. But when they saw two bombs dropping and bursting only a few hundred yards from the hotel, Peter exclaimed, 'This is it! Down to the basement, boys!' It was the first occasion David had taken shelter, and he wrote afterwards, *I wasted no time!*

The men were based at No. 11 Personnel Despatch and Reception Centre, in one of Brighton's largest and best hotels, the Grand, on the seafront. David was pleased to be still with fellow Tasmanians Peter Lord and Ian Vickers, who had both travelled on *Umgeni* and been at his twenty-first birthday dinner. Ian, tall and lanky, nicknamed Skinny, had an assurance which Peter, quiet and rather shy, envied. But David appreciated the contrast and they made a good team. Their fifth-floor room had the luxury of hot and cold running water, but only standard Air Force iron bedsteads, as hotel furnishings were stored for the duration of the war. Lifts were not in use, so they challenged each other up and down the stairs. 'This'll keep us fit, fellas!' Checking that blackout was observed in every room on all seven floors was another test of stamina.

Lectures had begun the morning after their arrival in Brighton. But if they thought they would soon be ready to go on ops, they were wrong. They still had much to learn and many months of grind, swot and slog ahead.

They also had to hand in their kit, disgusted to be issued second-hand English blankets, very inferior to their good new Australian ones.

'Call these blankets? They're just grey dish cloths!'

Now, instead of life jackets, gas masks had to be carried at all times. Trying them on for the first time, the men exclaimed, 'They make us look like mini jumbos!'

'Mini Dumbos you mean,' others quipped.

'Dumbos if we don't wear them.'

Each respirator came in a small haversack, which, minus mask and filter canister, was ideal for carrying pyjamas and shaving gear when going on leave. To ensure that the men obeyed the regulation, occasional mock attacks using actual tear gas were staged without warning. Sore and weeping eyes were enough to persuade them that carrying the mask was the best practice.

Training also focused on physical fitness, with drill sessions under a Grenadier Guards instructor. 'Slave driver!' David muttered. The first time the airmen were sent to the local rail station to unload steel girders and stores, they were stroppy. The second time they were even stroppier and David wrote tersely, *We didn't come 12 000 miles just to do this!* But compulsory organised sport was popular and he enjoyed swimming in the local baths and playing cricket in surroundings like a village green.

At the conclusion of each day's sessions, the men had leave from 5.00 until 11.59 pm. After exploring the historic town there was little to do. So they often went to the cinema even though most films were revivals or dealt with wartime themes. Occasionally entertainment was put on – a concert by top professional musicians and one by the RAF Band. 'The best drummer I've ever heard,' David exclaimed. Sporting fans were catered for, too, with a boxing tournament and a former champion boxer speaking about his experiences. *And he used me to demonstrate his moves!* David wrote home. After an inter-unit Australian Rules football match David noted in his diary, *The players were rather out of practice, but improved in the second half.*

On other evenings the men sat in their rooms talking or writing letters. In their first mail in over three months, David was jubilant to receive nineteen letters, and he was always diligent in responding. Writing home frequently on Australian Comforts Fund notepaper, he sometimes enclosed a weighing machine ticket to reassure his mother, as she worried that he had lost so much weight during his jaundice bout. A standard six-page airmail letter cost a shilling and threepence and took up to a month to arrive. So he often used airgraphs, which were microfilmed and sent in batches back to Australia. The delivery was speedier, but they were only one page and allowed no enclosures.

David also worked at night on assignments for the Oxford-based correspondence courses in Economics and Modern European History, in which he had enrolled.

Stationed on the rooftops of various hotels, the men watched for enemy aircraft. Gun watch was often cold and wet and was usually uneventful. But one drizzly day at dusk, after anti-aircraft fire had downed a raider, David's team was about to open up on a plane emerging from the mist.

'Hold it! It's one of ours!' David shouted just in time. It was a salutary reminder to concentrate on the vital subject of aircraft recognition.

Out in the English Channel, invasion barges were practising amphibious operations, and aerial activity gave an opportunity to identify Spitfires, Typhoons, Mosquitoes, Mustangs, Marauders and Fortresses. On one occasion they saw over 300 allied aircraft, including American bombers, Mitchells and Bostons, heading for the continent.

'Now the Jerries are getting as good as they gave,' they cheered.

Watching nine Spitfires in a practice dogfight was encouraging. But seeing a German fighter shot down in flames, plummeting into the sea, was a chilling experience. Each man realised more keenly than ever before what was ahead.

'There but for the grace of God,' murmured one.

'Poor devil. He was only doing his job for his country,' David said quietly.

In a new intake of trainees, David found many of his Air Force friends and old acquaintances. One night in the hotel he was particularly pleased to find affable Alan Scott waiting for him. Alan was an old friend from Adelaide, who shared his enthusiasm for rowing, and they spent many evenings catching up. They knew each other's families well. Alan, who had always cared for his

Alan Scott, Navigator and good friend

widowed mother and five sisters, had appreciated holidays
with David's father, mother, and two older brothers.

'I feel so responsible for my sisters,' Alan said. 'They
are pretty independent, but it must be hard on women
when their menfolk go to war.'

David nodded, thinking of his friend Des Hadden,
who also had a widowed mother and three sisters. They

talked optimistically of what they might do with their lives afterwards.

'Engineering's my scene,' Alan said. 'What about you? Do you want to keep flying?'

'If I can,' David replied. 'I love cross-country flying. Maybe I'll buy a second-hand Tiger Moth and stooge around Australia for a while.'

David and Alan spent a blissfully peaceful warm Sunday afternoon walking on the 'blunt, bow-headed, whalebacked Downs' beloved by Rudyard Kipling, lying on the close-cropped turf, overlooking green fields below, gazing up to blue autumn sky latticed with white contrails. Listening to the 'larks at heaven's gate', Shakespeare's sonnet came to life for David, and it was hard to picture the Battle of Britain that had raged above these very Downs three years earlier.

Back in Brighton they were greeted by the joyous sound of a carillon calling people to a thanksgiving service celebrating the capitulation of Italy. It was a day he would always remember.

With four days leave, David, Peter and Ian went to London. 'Let's catch up with other chaps from Somers at the Boomerang Club.' Located in Australia House in The Strand, the Boomerang Club was home away from home for Australian service personnel, a popular place to meet friends, have a meal, nap on one of the big leather sofas, or read Australian news, although the papers were usually at least three months old. All branches of the services were represented in the thousand and more Australians whose shoes sank each day into the thick pink carpet of the marble-walled club. Most were airmen, including some pilots wearing the purple and white ribbon of the

Distinguished Flying Cross or Distinguished Flying Medal. There were ordinary seamen too, spruce in carefully creased bell-bottomed trousers. Officers dashingly smart with gold braid rings on well-tailored jackets, and 'scrambled egg' on their caps (as gold braid was irreverently known); there were even merchant seamen in tweed civvies, whose heroic efforts to bring much-needed supplies were critical to Britain's survival.

Australian women worked cheerfully as volunteers: cooking; cutting sandwiches of grey wartime bread; serving soup, salad and snacks; making tea and coffee; washing up; and, perhaps most important of all, lending a listening ear to the homesick. They looked at family photos and dealt with emergencies like lost luggage; handed out maps, guide books and theatre tickets; assisted with travel information and arranged accommodation, which was always hard to find. A helpful woman booked beds for David, Peter and Ian at a nearby YMCA.

Next morning, David visited Kodak House in Kingsway, now RAAF Overseas Headquarters. All the mail from home was addressed here. Dedicated Australian airmen sorted and redirected the huge volume constantly arriving for all the personnel scattered on bases throughout Britain – no small task as aircrew were frequently moved. The mail was vital to maintain morale. 'Thanks, chaps! Especially for those parcels!'

David, aware that his parents were worried about his affairs, arranged a power of attorney, in addition to the will required on enlisting. Business concluded, he set off on the expedition he had so long looked forward to – exploring London.

Wherever David went, it seemed the Germans had already

been. He passed many skeleton buildings and bombed-out blocks. And obviously Jerry was expected again. Signs to air raid shelters were everywhere. Windows were boarded up or masked with criss-cross tape. Doorways were sandbagged. Porches held lines of red metal buckets containing sand or water, and stirrup pumps for fire extinguishing. Many razed blocks were now occupied by large water tanks, while high above the skyline barrage balloons soared on their cables like giant airborne sausages, to force enemy aircraft higher or ensnare them should they attempt a low-level raid.

But among all the changes war had brought, one well-loved feature remained the same. London Bobbies still patrolled their beats, their presence a source of comfort. Their friendly calm and willingness to give directions lent a welcome touch of normality.

Some of an airman's official documents: Will, Identity Card, Services Clothing Ration Book, lecture notebook, Flying Clothing Card, Responsibilities of a Prisoner of War

David walked down broad Whitehall past the Cenotaph, bleak memorial to lives lost in the Great War, and from Westminster Bridge looked across the River Thames to the Houses of Parliament, even more impressive than he expected, although they had suffered bomb damage. He watched the huge hands of Big Ben, the world's most famous clock, waiting for the chimes he had often heard on wireless and in newsreels, rapt to hear its deep tones. In Westminster Abbey, so steeped in history, he wandered for three memorable hours, pausing longest at the Tomb of the Unknown Warrior.

Next day, David and Peter went to St Paul's Cathedral, masterpiece of renowned architect Christopher Wren, amazed its landmark dome had survived in an area so heavily blitzed. David discovered more of the London he knew from nursery rhymes which his aunt had loved to teach him – 'London Bridge' and 'Oranges and Lemons'. He was glad that London Bridge had not fallen to German bombs, and sad that St Clement Dane's church had been gutted in 1940. *But its splendid 'Oranges and Lemons' steeple still stood proudly tall,* he wrote to his parents. *Let's hope that one day it will be rebuilt in all its glory.*

David and his brothers had often played Monopoly on cosy winter nights by the fire. Now he walked along Monopoly-red Fleet Street and The Strand, to see the offices of the legendary London newspaper *The Times,* and on past now-familiar Australia House. Making his first trip on the underground, he emerged at Piccadilly Circus, disappointed to find the famous statue of Eros boarded up. Wandering along Monopoly-yellow Piccadilly, he visited the Royal Academy's exhibition of paintings and photos of the Allies at war. In royal-blue Park Lane and Mayfair war had also left its mark. Elegant parks and squares had been converted into vegetable gardens, their beautiful iron fencing melted down for reuse. Green Park was a pasture for sheep. Hyde Park bristled with anti-aircraft guns and temporary quarters for AA personnel.

At celebrated Speakers' Corner, David listened to the diversity of orators who mounted their soapboxes to address the crowd. It was a vibrant gathering, orderly and good-natured, speakers jocularly dealing with interjections from persons of different opinions. He admired this society which not only tolerated but even embraced differences. He felt a wave of pride, identifying with the spirit of this great British democracy, rejoicing in this freedom of speech which was part of his heritage. So different from the repressive fascist regime they were fighting, when to voice, even to family or friends, an opinion not held by those in power could lead swiftly to arrest, imprisonment, even torture or death.

David gazed at the people standing around him in their shabby austerity clothing. Men in bowler hats stood shoulder to shoulder with others in cloth caps, their thin pale faces shadowed by lack of sleep from night after night of air raids. He was both humbled and elated to be part of them, come to help them fight the oppressors, to regain freedom for nations struggling under the Nazi jackboot.

From Marble Arch, David walked along Oxford Street, recognising department stores, like Selfridges, whose names were household words. Shortages and stringent rationing meant that most had little to display. But he lingered at a bookshop with the intriguing name of Bumpus and a tempting array of second-hand books. Red and white double-decker buses lumbering by, with equally intriguing destination names like Shepherd's Bush and Elephant and Castle, lent colour to an otherwise drab scene. But on such a fine evening David continued to walk, passing Foyle's and other famous bookshops in Charing Cross Road, until footsore but fulfilled, he finally was back at the Boomerang Club. He was part of London now and London had become part of him.

On another evening, David set out to discover places he knew from Dickens' and Conan Doyle's books. But as the blackout engulfed the city he became hopelessly lost. After three frustrating hours and an unfriendly encounter with a lamp post, he found his way back, only too aware that on future journeys back to base his encounters would be with much more hostile obstacles.

David and Peter then enjoyed a farm stay in Devon, with good-hearted country people pleased to welcome these young men so far from home, and glad of their able-bodied help as labour was so scarce. With fresh farm produce and rich cooking, serene days in meadow-sweet air and quiet starry nights, it was an idyllic interlude. The war seemed very far away – until they watched Liberators from a nearby base being used for searchlight practice, and knew that before long they could be pinned down in similar shafts of light over Germany, like hapless moths on a specimen sheet.

Then it was back to Brighton and the training course.

Battle Order 204 (3)
Target Dortmund

Each crew member kept silent unless addressed over the intercom by the pilot, who was concentrating on the complexity of over 100 switches, gauges, controls and dials in the cockpit. Only the wireless operator was in touch with the outside world, passing on any message to the skipper.

The Master Bomber was code-named *Toby* and the Main Force had the code words, more apt than usual, *Press On*. Their target, Dortmund, with a population of half a million, had already felt the devastating effects of previous raids. One of the most important centres of major German industry, the city was strongly defended, and the light cloud afforded little protection for the raiders.

At 17 000 feet D Dog met severe and concentrated enemy opposition. Anti-aircraft guns, both light and heavy, filled the sky with tracer, which burst on impact, and shells, which exploded at a predetermined height.

'Jerry sure is letting us have it today!' Boz, the mid upper gunner, thought, as from his turret he watched the fierce bursts of flak, smelling and hearing the barrage exploding perilously close on all sides. In some ways it was even more frightening by day than it had been by night. Instead of seeing quickly fading fireworks, David and his crew could see just how close together were the menacing dark puffs of smoke.

The rest of the crew listened intently to the intercom exchanges between bomb aimer and pilot and the tension was almost unbearable as D Dog ran in towards the target.

5 Confronting Death

Chuffed to find three cakes in the mail awaiting him at Brighton, David exclaimed, 'Let's have a party!' and invited some mates to warm their new sixth-floor room in the Metropole Hotel. Then, keenly aware that seamail took three months to reach Australia, he wrote Christmas letters and five dozen cards.

Now the course intensified. The men studied signals, armaments, airmanship encompassing modern combat methods, aerodrome control, navigation and operations, intelligence, leaving a ditched aircraft, and evasion and escape from enemy territory. Operational crews were provided with some ingenious aids to help them escape. A silk scarf, which could be tucked easily into a pocket, was printed with a map. A compass was concealed in a comb or a button, or under the eraser of a pencil. Flying boots concealed a special blade to cut off the tops, leaving footwear like normal shoes. There was a razor for maintaining appearance, and for survival

Metropole Hotel, Brighton, England, home to newly arrived Australian aircrew

a collapsible rubber water bottle and high sustenance Horlicks tablets. A wallet full of money in the currencies of countries in which the airmen might find themselves completed the kit.

A card detailing The Responsibilities of a Prisoner of War, printed NOT TO BE TAKEN INTO THE AIR, was issued to each airman, who was required to memorise the information. It was impressed upon all aircrew that under the 1929 Geneva Convention a prisoner of war is required to give only his name, rank and number. *The Enemy is known to attach the utmost importance to the interrogation and search of prisoners, but he can learn nothing from a silent and resolute prisoner whose pockets are empty.*

The men were urged to remember that *a prisoner who systematically refuses to give information is respected by his captors* and *that a silent and resolute prisoner without articles or papers of any sort is an interrogator's nightmare.*

Point by graphic point instructions were given on behaviour under interrogation: what the Enemy would try to find out; how information would be obtained by the Enemy. Sources included examination of captured aircraft and material, search of prisoners for notebooks, letters, diaries and any other incriminating documents or papers, and interrogation either by direct questioning or by indirect methods. Among many others, both subtle and crude, methods might involve fraternisation, intimidation, bribery, ill treatment, hidden microphones, agents, stool pigeons and propaganda. Do's and dont's and the rights of a prisoner were reiterated, as well as the warning, *A prisoner is always surrounded by his enemies. Trust no one.*

Instructors from three Advanced Flying Units spoke about their courses, and David wondered, 'Where will I be posted?' The men were shown films which dealt with aircraft recognition, camouflage from air observation, protection from gas. They also saw a British film showing the North Africa campaign, plus one about Russian guerrilla warfare and even a German film on the Nazi invasion of Poland. And although they laughed at the poster to be seen everywhere – *Be like Dad, keep Mum* – the film *Next of Kin*, shown twice to drive home the message – careless talk costs lives – was very sobering. No airman wanted his family to receive one of those telegrams KILLED IN ACTION or MISSING, PRESUMED DEAD. David also spent hours in the intelligence library, studying the 'gen' on German aircraft and equipment, location of German units and details of the different war fronts.

There was plenty of practical work too, with more sessions in the Link Trainer, substituting for actual flying. Gunnery practice included clay pigeon shooting – 'Much harder than it looks,' David declared – and firing practice with Brownings from different types of turrets, aircraft cannon, Sten guns, sub-machine guns and pistols.

Nobody enjoyed the afternoon spent in the baths practising how to escape from a ditched aircraft. 'This is no fun,' they spluttered. But the memory of the unforgiving Atlantic motivated everyone to master the skill. Clambering into and out of aircraft dinghies in full flying kit, heavy, sodden and cumbersome, demanded real effort. David, knowledgeable in lifesaving, took it very seriously, encouraging and assisting the others. He was used to small boats and rowing fours, but handling these circular rubber dinghies was quite another matter.

'They've certainly got a will of their own!' he muttered after several attempts to get one right side up. 'Let's hope we never have to use one.' A hope fervently echoed by all the shivering airmen, choking and spitting mouthfuls of water.

'You look like a drowned possum.'

'Well, you look as miserable as a bandicoot.'

The men joked as they stripped off their wet clobber, leaving it to be donned by the next group, but they all knew ditching was no laughing matter.

After the cricket season ended, David continued swimming, and enjoyed trying badminton. He also gave boxing a go, but quickly gave it up, joking to Peter, 'A bloody nose doesn't suit me.'

Now in addition to blackout duty and gun watch there was fire watch, fortunately uneventful, although there were four successive nights of air raid alerts as the German offensive against London increased again. David discovered stargazing and learned to identify the unfamiliar Northern Hemisphere constellations, pleased to be able to recognise the North Star in the Plough. He missed Alan's company when his friend was posted to an Advanced Flying Unit, but an unexpected visit from cousin Phil provided another opportunity to talk about family and home. Phil was in Coastal Command, flying Liberators from Northern Ireland, and David was envious hearing that on recent flights he had been diverted to Iceland and Gibraltar. 'You lucky blighter!'

David and his mates seized every chance to explore more of England's beautiful south coast by double-decker buses, which gave splendid views of country and coastline. David and Ian spent a day's leave at Shoreham Air/Sea Rescue Station, glad to learn how dinghies were dropped to ditched airmen. A Mosquito doing aerobatics with one engine stopped was really impressive.

'I wouldn't want to try that in a Spitfire!' David exclaimed.

'Nor would I,' grinned Ian, appreciating the joke that Spitfires are single-engined.

David and Peter visited Newhaven, base for motor torpedo boats, which they watched on manoeuvres. Travelling west, through woods of yellowing chestnut trees, David was enthralled by the layers of history which every mile revealed – Roman roads, Saxon forts, Norman castles, medieval churches. The most recent layer, imposed by this 20th century war, consisted of well-concealed military encampments in belts of forest, and trip wires at a height of 15 feet above open fields to prevent enemy planes from landing troops.

Quaint place names appealed to his sense of humour and he joked about Henfield, 'Where are the chooks?'; Burpham, 'Who cooked the dinner?'; and Bury, 'How big is the cemetery?' Peter usually responded in kind to David's play on words, but on this day he was quiet. As they wandered into the ancient graveyard of a little Norman church, David could not help quoting from Gray's 'Elegy': 'Each in his narrow cell forever laid, The rude Forefathers of the hamlet sleep'. He roamed among lichened and leaning headstones, reading epitaphs: informative, fulsome, sometimes unintentionally funny, but always revealing in their grappling with mortality.

Peter usually joined David and they would muse and ponder and sometimes chuckle together. But this day Peter sat on an old stone wall, staring at the lengthening shadows, gazing towards the setting sun, 'leaving the world to darkness and to me,' he quoted in return, as David came and sat beside him.

'Do you ever wonder how many more sunsets we will see?' Peter asked.

David nodded. 'Every day.'

In the unit the men did not talk about the likelihood of death which hung over them. Each confronted his own demons in private, secretly. Some considered it bad form to discuss it. Others, more superstitious, feared it might jinx them. Occasionally, someone deeply troubled might talk it over with the padre.

They had survived the perils, day by day and night by night, of the three-month sea voyage. They had seen the devastation of London. They had watched a German pilot plummet to his unmarked grave in the English Channel. They had observed the bombers in purposeful formation heading for Germany. Every man knew his name could be on a casualty list any day – KILLED, or MISSING IN ACTION. Every man knew it could be his next-of-kin, his loved ones, receiving a telegram which would plunge them into mourning and a grief which time would never heal.

So they soldiered on, doing their duty to their nation, upholding the ideals of peace, justice and freedom. They drilled, trained, learned about weapons of destruction, and nurtured the spirit of survival by making fun out of hardships and joking about adversity. Laughter was their most powerful weapon against fear and despair.

'Death is so final, isn't it?' Peter said. 'Or is it?' He turned to David, desperate for the reassurance he knew David could give. They had both been at the same church school, they had attended chapel services together, sung the same hymns, listened to the same talks by the chaplain. David's faith had always seemed so sturdy. He had always seemed so sure, never doubting that this life was a prelude to something even better.

David summoned all his strength for his friend in crisis. With one hand he gripped Peter's cold one. With the other he pointed to a nearby monument, a weather-beaten cross, on which could still be deciphered the inscription, *I know that my Redeemer liveth*.

'Heaven's real,' he said. 'Some of us will make it sooner than others to our Father's house of many rooms. And the place is ready – for you, for me, whenever...'

'I worry about my sister,' Peter blurted out. David knew she had been badly burned as a child and Peter was very protective of her. 'I've left her all I've got, in my will. That's why I might sometimes seem a bit of a Scrooge. I want to make sure there's something for her, if I'm not there to take care of her after Mum and Dad go.'

David nodded in quiet sympathy. He knew intuitively that it would be harder for those left behind than for those who went ahead. He stood up. 'Let's look inside the church before it gets dark, shall we?' They walked past the brooding bulk of yew trees and entered the little church, solid and still under its ancient stone arches. As they were about to kneel in a pew at the back, the vicar came down the chancel steps.

'Hullo, lads,' he greeted them, and noting the flashes on their jackets, he went on, 'You won't find a church like this in your part of the world. People have been praying here for over 900 years. Quite a thought, isn't it? I'm sorry there's not time to show you round. But if you miss the last bus, it's a long way to walk. At least I can say a blessing over you before you go.'

And so the words which had brought peace to the hearts and minds of many generations were said yet again to comfort the young airmen so far from home.

It was a silent ride back. As they climbed the stairs to their room, Peter said, 'Thanks, Dave.' 'Any time,' David replied. That night they had their 12th consecutive air-raid alert. It was Brighton's 876th.

Two days later, David bought a copy of Cassell's *Anthology of English Poetry* bound in maroon leather. At twelve shillings and sixpence it cost almost a day's pay, but was worth every penny. He immersed himself in it in spare moments, finding solace in the words of others who had rejoiced in life and grappled with its deepest questions. Then, on Remembrance Sunday, while all 800 trainees attended a special parade service at 1100 hours, the alert went. David wrote in his diary, *One could not but think what an excellent target we were!* It was a sombre day.

Blustery cold winds had stripped the last crimson leaves from creepers clinging to cottage walls. In the woods, only the oaks still held fast to a remnant veil of their dense summer canopy, dull gold against their massive dark trunks, when David and Ian made another excursion, to Portsmouth. Here sights waited which they would never forget. Britain's chief naval base since Tudor times, Portsmouth had been heavily blitzed. Acre upon acre of the city, especially the old town, had been flattened. Many buildings of great historic importance had been gutted or completely destroyed. Their rubble still lay in great piles along both sides of the streets. Only the occasional building stood intact in the wasteland.

'It's a ghost city!' David exclaimed, more appalled by the utter devastation than he had been so far. 'And this is what we're being trained to do to German cities,' he grieved silently.

They wandered down to the landing where sailors and emigrants in past centuries had embarked for the six-month voyage to Australia. David thought of his great-great-grandmother who had taken a clock inlaid with mother-of-pearl and a fine gilt-framed mirror among her possessions when she set out for Tasmania in 1836. What had been her thoughts, her feelings, as she boarded the sailing ship, leaving behind everyone, everything she knew?

David and Ian walked along the docks to see one of Britain's great national treasures, Nelson's ship *Victory*. The crucial Battle of Trafalgar in 1805 marked triumph over Napoleon, but resulted in Nelson's death. 'What were his last thoughts?' David wondered.

London was still a magnet, with its wealth of places to discover. Thirty-six and forty-eight hour leave passes gave more opportunities for catching up at the Boomerang Club with friends from other units, like Tas Williams from Derby. Tas, sturdy in build and spirit, so typical of the little mining town from which he came, and so worthy of his proud name, Tasman. As he and David laughed at the monkeys in London Zoo, they recalled boyhood days watching other monkeys in Launceston's City Park, and basked in warm memories of Bridport summers they had shared. At Madame Tussaud's Waxworks, wandering among amazingly lifelike figures of the illustrious and the notorious, they laughed again, hearing another visitor mistake one for an attendant and ask for directions.

David visited the Tower of London with Ian, rapt to be shown over it by a Beefeater in traditional livery. On a very different occasion the Agent-General for Tasmania, a family friend, took him to the London Rotary Club weekly lunch, when three lemons auctioned for charity brought £3 each, and a banana, rare indeed in wartime Britain, fetched £3/5/-!

After eleven weeks at Brighton, David was promoted to Flight Sergeant and they all learned of their new postings. According to mustering, classification by specific skills, pilots, bomb aimers, navigators, air gunners and wireless operators were sent on to their relevant units for further training. It was time to say goodbye to many whom David had got to know well since the first days at Somers.

'Be good! Don't do anything I wouldn't do,' they told each other.

'Then that gives me plenty of scope!' came the laughing reply.

But underneath the banter, they were wondering if they would ever meet again.

David was glad Peter and Ian were going with him to No. 3 Advanced Flying Unit at South Cerney near Cirencester in Gloucestershire. After two busy days packing up, obtaining all the necessary clearances and saying farewells, on 23 November they rose before dawn and set out on the next stage of their journey. It would be their third flying course, and they were looking forward to getting back in the air.

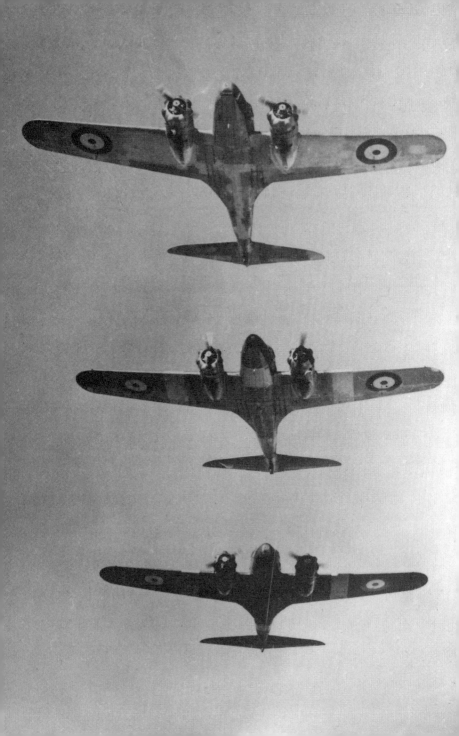

6 Airborne Again At Last

Three trains and six hours after they left Brighton, the young pilots arrived in Cirencester, eager for this new phase of their adventure. South Cerney, like Point Cook, was a peacetime station.

'We'll enjoy it here,' they exclaimed on seeing centrally heated brick barracks with mod cons and huge permanent hangars. But, like Point Cook, it had been expanded to accommodate the wartime influx of aircrew and aircraft.

'Let's make the most of it,' David declared on learning that they would only have twelve days of relative luxury before being dispersed to satellite airfields.

In contrast to Point Cook's flat, dry, sparsely populated expanse, South Cerney was in the heart of the Cotswolds, gentle wooded hills laced with winding valleys, dotted with some of England's most picturesque stone villages and medieval market towns. David could hardly wait to start exploring.

RAAF Avro Ansons in formation

But at first there was no opportunity. The Advanced Flying Unit program consisted of eight-period days, each period filled with lectures on new subjects as well as all the usual. It was a cosmopolitan group of pilots, consisting of French, Belgian, Dutch, Polish and Czechoslovak as well as English, Scots and Australian. The program was designed to cover every facet of the skills and knowledge required for proficient pilots, and also to develop understanding and awareness of the issues of the war in which the men were involved. Experts came to speak on a wide range of topics. This not only increased the pilots' knowledge and expanded their overview, but also encouraged them to think, discuss and debate national and international affairs such as China, Japan and events in the Pacific. David relished these encounters with thinking, informed minds, these perspectives on history in the making. And he himself was asked to give a talk about Australia, which lasted one and a half hours!

More hours in the Link Trainer, and with the bombing teacher, gave further experience of instrument flying conditions that they would encounter on night operations. Climbing into the elevated cockpit, closing the hood which shut out all external light, the trainee pilot saw only the illuminated instrument panel on which he had to rely entirely. The instructor, seated below, gave directions through a voice tube. The pilot at the controls put them into practice and the Link Trainer's simulated flying was automatically recorded on a chart on the instructor's table, to be analysed at the end of the session.

Gunnery practice continued too, and they had their first hands-on experience with grenades, dummies to start with, from which they had to clean the mud after each session. Live ones came later. 'At least we don't have to clean these!'

David enjoyed going out on frosty mornings, crunching over the ice and whitened blades of grass, marching a mile to the firing range. But it was miserable on rainy days and there were plenty of them.

Distances on the station were considerable, so one evening David went looking for a bike, thrilled to know he was walking along an old Roman road, where the legions had marched so many centuries before. In contrast, medieval Cirencester's streets were narrow and winding, but equally intriguing. Because of severe petrol rationing, bikes were in great demand and David considered himself lucky indeed to find the only one for sale. It was old and had obviously been pedalled many miles. 'But I'll have fun tinkering with it,' he told himself, whistling as he rode back to the station.

In early December came the red letter day when David made his first flight in almost seven months. It was his first in England and his first in an Avro Anson. The Anson was similar to the Oxford, but with slightly less powerful engines. David had heard it described as 'one of the most gentlemanly aeroplanes to fly, with no vices'. On this familiarisation flight as a passenger, David was immediately struck by the difference between Australian and British terrain, and noted in his diary *the confusing multiplicity of detail and landmarks*. And after rural Australia's generally clear skies he found visibility much restricted by the haze and smoke from the extensive English industrial areas.

David did not enjoy occasional duties as Orderly Sergeant either, as they precluded him from flying. Inspecting huts for cleanliness and tidiness, David felt like a school prefect again.

However, he was amused to go into the airmen's mess at lunchtime and yell out 'Orderly Sergeant. Any complaints?', muttering under his breath, 'There'd better not be!'

South Cerney's satellite base, Southrop, where David was sent, was only a few months old, a cold raw quagmire of mud and clay. The billets, asbestos huts in a winter-bare wood, were on a rise a mile and a half down dale and up hill from the flights, as aircraft dispersals and flight offices were known. So David congratulated himself on having acquired the bike. Each billet had a coal stove, but as coal was rationed they had to use it sparingly, soon finding it generated scarcely enough heat to take the penetrating chill off the perpetually damp air.

The day after they arrived at Southrop, the weather closed in with heavy mist and drizzle, so, much to the young pilots' frustration, flying was scrubbed until the clamp lifted three days later. Over the next three months the weather would frequently make flying impossible. When winter gales, rain, snow and fog kept the planes grounded, the airmen played soccer in the mud instead. Even when the weather improved, the temporary airfield was still unserviceable, often for days.

Two days before Christmas, David made his first solo flight in England. But while he was up, a fellow pilot was killed when an engine cut out after take-off and his plane hit some trees and caught fire. That night seemed colder than ever before as David thought of the chaps in that other hut with its empty bed, and of the family somewhere for whom Christmas would never be the same again.

By now, many Australians who had survived the hazardous voyage halfway round the world and emerged unscathed from air raids, had developed an 'It won't

Tasmanian pilots at Southrop, 1943, L-R: Peter Lord, Ian Vickers, Gordon Lawson, David Mattingley

happen to me' attitude. But a casualty on their own patch woke them again to the reality of their mortality. So they were determined to extract every ounce of fun out of living while they could. They threw themselves into making the most of every day. They savoured simple pleasures like sitting around the hut stove making toast or feasting when a parcel arrived from home, or enjoying local hospitality.

Once, the local doctor took David and his mates to his house, where he showed them an ancient well and a Roman wall in the garden, regaled them with tales of life as a country GP and gave them two fresh eggs each for tea, a rare treat that was double the monthly ration!

On Christmas Day, the squire made them welcome with sherry and mince pies. He was a Colonel, a contemporary of the Chief of the Imperial General Staff,

Coloured card available for Australian servicemen to buy to send home

and he entertained them with stories of the British army in pre-war India. It seemed almost too good to be true, hearing him say, 'When I was in Poona, old chaps...' and seeing his full dress uniform, complete with tight red tunic, striped trousers and brass hat. 'Imagine if we had to be togged out like that!' the boys exclaimed afterwards. David also had standing invitations from several other families, writing home, *Don't worry, Mum, there are no daughters.*

Over the Christmas break, David and his friends often planned visits to the cinema or live entertainment. But the trips frequently came to nothing when the clapped-out RAF bus broke down; sometimes stranding them to walk 12 miles back to base in the wee small hours, often in rain. No wonder that they were always hungry and food parcels from home were so welcome!

Even though troops were barred from travel over the holiday season, to ease pressure on public transport, and hopes of a white Christmas were not fulfilled, it was a chance to celebrate. Contrary to station regulations, David had double-dinked a mate on his bike, and was pulled up, summoned to the Assistant Adjutant's office.

'Sergeant Mattingley, please explain your action,' the WAAF officer demanded.

'Flight Sergeant, Ma'am,' he cheekily corrected her. 'Just a bit of Christmas spirit.'

Interview ended!

David and the other Noncommissioned Officers (NCOs) waited on the airmen in their Mess, before enjoying their own Christmas dinner. It was a traditional meal with all the trimmings – roast pork, turkey with bread sauce, seasoning and four vegetables, followed by plum pudding with brandy sauce, and mince pies.

'How did they conjure up all this?' they asked in amazement, before putting on party caps and tucking in.

After carols and Christmas music on the wireless, all ranks mixed happily at a social in the Mess before returning to their huts, where partying continued as parcels from home were opened and contents shared. David's thoughts often returned to the sunshine, blue seas and bright sands of Bridport, where his family always spent Christmas, worshipping at the little wooden church while kookaburras chortled in a nearby flowering gum ablaze with red blossom. He wrote to his parents, *It was a vastly different Christmas from those I have spent in the past, but very enjoyable.*

The good cheer continued for a week, as the men opened their Australian Comforts Fund hampers. David, who had just done an assignment on the French Revolution in his modern European history course, quoted Marie Antoinette, quipping, 'Let them eat cake!' But the allusion was lost on the others, who replied through full mouths, 'And there's nothing wrong with that!' It was a bonanza – cakes, puddings, tinned peaches and cream, and chocolate – all luxuries in England where stringent food rationing affected servicemen as well as civilians. Meat, cheese, butter and milk were all rationed, as well as eggs, tea, jam, sugar, chocolate and sweets. Powdered milk, coffee and cocoa were not, honey and golden syrup were sometimes available as sweeteners, and Marmite as a spread. Vegetables were not rationed, though often in short supply. Local apples, pears, and soft fruits could sometimes be found in season, but generally fruit, especially imported, was a rarity. When given two oranges each, the men prolonged the pleasure by placing the peel on their heating stoves, to enjoy its scent before burning it for a final burst of flame and fragrance.

David was overwhelmed by the kindness of the many people who sent him parcels, and he always saved some of the contents to give to the people who showed him hospitality. The Christmas parcel from his parents contained nuts, raisins, tinned jam – apricot was always a favourite on toast at night – chocolate, his mother's incomparable cake and pudding. The parcel also included some newspapers, which the boys eagerly passed round, frequently exclaiming 'Look at this!' and 'What do you know!' as they found hometown news items.

Despite his mother's skill in packing, once a packet of soap flakes burst, impregnating the adjacent chocolate. They devoured it nevertheless, as the ration, only four ounces a week, was rarely available. Another time, vinegar from a jar of onions, pickled specially for him, leaked into the chocolate. David wolfed it down anyway. By the time a parcel posted in mid-August arrived in March, the coconut ice had to be broken with a hammer! But it was a welcome addition to the weekly six-pennyworth allowance of sweets. In another batch of parcels, a cake arrived without even a crack in the icing. Once, when four parcels arrived together, he saved a round tin till last, expecting it to contain a cake. Instead he found several pairs of socks and a scarf!

In contrast to Christmas, New Year's Eve was very low key, and the men were subdued, wondering what 1944 held in store. Only a few more months of training remained before they would be dispersed to start flying operations. Then they would join the war in earnest.

But for David the ecstasy was the flying. The very heart of it. He loved the hours riding the air, looking down on the patchwork English countryside and all its landmarks, or the snow-white tops of fleecy clouds billowing up below. But in January they saw the sun only once in three weeks and the unrelenting grey was dreary indeed. Instead of being skybound, they were earthbound in mud and slush, and they were really browned off. David watched enviously as squadrons of rooks from nearby woods soared and circled in faultless formation against the sombre sky. 'Showing off their superior flying skills!' he exclaimed in admiration.

When fog, worsened by industrial haze, enveloped the whole area the men were given leave. David went to Brighton looking for his recently arrived old school friend, level-headed Des Hadden, whose wry sense of humour matched David's own. It was great to laugh over old times and swap stories of all they had seen and done since they last met seven months earlier in Melbourne. Well worth the ten hours travelling each way, some of it standing in the crowded trains, and the wet five-mile walk to base.

Another 48 hour leave pass was a great boost to morale. David and fellow Tasmanian Gordon Lawson, a likeable larrikin, headed for their customary rendezvous, the Boomerang Club, where David ordered his favourite curried sausages. But he got more than he bargained for when someone accidentally tipped a plateful down his uniform!

'I wish I'd thought of doing that!' Gordon grinned as he helped mop up.

Later, they looked in the visitors' book as usual, and enjoyed catching up with fellows they had known on other courses.

Next day, a notorious London pea soup fog disrupted rail services, then an air raid further delayed their departure. So their train was two and a half hours late. Standing in the guard's van, David made the better acquaintance of Peter's flying instructor, English Sergeant Sam Salter. He was delighted to find they were on the same wavelength, Sam's quirky humour and way with words instantly appealing to him. But at Southrop they were annoyed to find that because the usual fog prevailed, there was still no flying.

'Why the dickens didn't they let us stay on leave?' everyone grumbled.

After four more frustrating days grounded, they were again given leave and headed immediately for London. In retaliation for 2300 tons of bombs dropped on Berlin by the RAF the previous night, German fast raiders came over, dropping bombs a few hundred yards from Victoria Station, where David was staying. Several German planes caught in the searchlight were downed by anti-aircraft guns. Their shrapnel fell like rain. During a second raid at 4 am, David pulled back the blackout curtain to watch the dramatic scene. He knew he was one of the actors waiting in the wings for similar action somewhere over Europe. Soon.

The next day they returned to base, cycling the last five miles in heavy rain, only to find that they had been given another two days leave. Everyone was really cheesed off.

'Bloody hell! We stood all the way on the trains from London for nothing again!'

So it was back to London, arriving at midnight, with the chance to see another national treasure next day, the vessel *Discovery*, of famous Antarctic explorer Captain Scott, one of David's heroes.

Back at Southrop, it was more of the same. At two hours notice, the men were given five days of leave. David was both disappointed and pleased. Disappointed because it was 25 days since he had flown and he longed to be in the air again. Pleased at another opportunity to fulfil his other passion – exploring Britain.

This time David went north. Baby-faced, open-hearted Scots pilot David McNeill, whose wisdom was far beyond his short stature and nineteen years, had become one of David's best friends on the station and had invited him home. The two Davids had to go to London and wait till 4.15 next morning for the train to Edinburgh. David found plenty to interest him on the long journey north. The Yorkshire moors were thick with airfields, and at Newcastle he was thrilled to see one of George Stephenson's early locomotives. Then crossing the wide River Tweed, he had his first sight of bonnie Scotland. From Edinburgh they caught a bus to Tranent, a small mining town, where the McNeills lived in a council house.

David was deeply touched by the warm welcome offered by yet another kindly family, who promptly named him Dights, to avoid confusing two Davids. Mr McNeill, a miner retired after a back injury, was now a school caretaker. Mrs McNeill, a great cook, was devoted to looking after her husband and their four children. Learning of David's interest in education, Mr McNeill showed him over the school where he worked. The headmaster explained the impressive Scottish education system and invited David to speak about Australia to two classes.

David McN took his Australian namesake touring the district, so rich in history. In the village of Prestonpans, scene of the Scots victory over the English in 1745, they

David McNeill, Pilot, with the family dog, Judy,
Tranent, Scotland

had a drink at the Cross Keys pub where Bonnie Prince Charlie had stayed on the eve of the battle. But the battlefield itself was covered in slag heaps and could no longer be seen.

David found Edinburgh most attractive of all the British cities and towns he had seen, with its wide streets, beautiful gardens and gracious stone buildings, all guarded by the great castle on its rocky eminence. Watching a game between crack Scottish soccer teams was another highlight, standing shoulder to tweed-coated shoulder with passionate barrackers shouting themselves hoarse.

After divine service in the wee kirk where Bonnie Prince Charlie had worshipped, Sunday was a relaxing home and family day. The pleasure of walking the dog was followed by a memorable dinner, and visits to relatives and friends who delighted in recounting tales of the past.

On the way south, the Davids congratulated each other on finding seats on the crowded Flying Scotsman. 'Glad we don't have to stand overnight for ten and a half hours back to London.' After several changes of train and the final bike ride, they arrived at Southrop in the early hours.

'We've burned the candle at both ends,' Dights said to Scottish David, 'but it was worth it. The Scots are the most generous and kind-hearted folk I've ever met. And they make the best cakes! And the best porridge of course!'

In February 1944 the British winter was at its worst. January's rain had turned to sleet. Sleet turned to snow. Snow melted to slush. Slush froze into solid chocolate chunks. Gales uprooted trees. And the cloud ceiling came down lower and lower. Flying was out of the question on most days. The trainee pilots, eager to get their flying hours up, sat disconsolate around a huge fire in the mess. Or huddled in their huts, wearing their sheepskin jackets, scarves, mittens and anything else they could put on in an effort to defy the cheek-tingling, finger-numbing, bone-chilling cold.

On one unnerving cross-country flight, David became lost. The strengthening wind had changed direction. Visibility decreased and he found himself badly off course. In sight of the south coast, with dwindling fuel supply, he made for an airfield in the distance. His radio was not on its frequency. But the weather was clamping down, so he landed regardless. Because its aircraft were returning from a mission, landing at much higher speeds, he had to touch down and clear the runway quickly.

It was Dunsfold, an operational station, near Guildford in Surrey, base for one Netherlands and two RAF squadrons. Snow and sleet kept David grounded for the next five days, but he relished the opportunity to absorb the atmosphere and experiences of an operational station, so different from a training station. He also inspected the different kites: Mitchells, flown by the squadrons, and a Beaufighter and a Lancaster which had also landed because of bad conditions. He spent time in the control tower, listening to radio telephone conversations from planes on operations. He heard two distress calls, the chilling 'Mayday, Mayday!' received on Darky, the emergency frequency, and he shared the general elation when both planes were successfully brought home. It was stirring, too, to watch the squadrons set off before dawn on a tactical sortie and return from France after sunrise.

Back at Southrop, where the countryside was quilted in dazzling white, the trainees had bags of fun in the snow, and two Wellingtons and a Spitfire, which landed because of sleet and icing, attracted a lot of attention. When flying was scrubbed David swotted for exams.

Late in February it was time for another move. The men were sent to a specialised course at Lulsgate Bottom in Somerset.

'Ee, lads,' David mimicked the Somerset accent, 'we be goan to Zummerzet where the zoider apples grow!'

BAT Flight instruction, apt acronym for Beam Approach Training, initiated pilots into the system developed to enable planes to land in all weathers. But on the first morning they could not take off because of the weather!

On his first flight, still in the dependable Oxford, David climbed through 5000 feet of cloud and encountered icing for the first time. Thick rime coated the leading edges of the wings. Lumps of ice were flung off the propellers onto the fuselage. The controls became very stiff, and the aircraft became noticeably sluggish. He realised how important and useful it was to experience such an unnerving condition. Real operations were flown at higher altitudes, so David knew he would encounter more icing on bombing runs.

On a dull day, with the aid of the Beam, he climbed through the low cloud ceiling to a wizard new world of warm sun shining brilliantly on the fleecy clouds below. On another flight he landed, again with the aid of the Beam, at Hullavington, the Empire Central Flying School for training instructors, in Air Force slang the home of gen, or genuine information. Here, of course, it was all 'pukka' not 'duff' gen. He saw an amazing array of aircraft, including Magisters, Masters, Bostons, Wellingtons and mighty Stirlings, Halifaxes and Lancasters. And realised yet again how much there was to learn about flying.

David had not seen his brother Brian since leaving Australia ten months earlier. Brian was now an RAAF navigator, and the twenty-three hours David spent in Brighton was hardly long enough to catch up on news of family, friends and acquaintances.

'How are Mum and Dad? I'm afraid they might be depriving themselves of hard-to-get or rationed items, so as to include them in my parcels.'

'Don't worry. Dad is getting a real kick out of finding things for you. I must say those packages look pretty awkward to sew up. But you know how good Mum is with her needle, and it means a lot to her to be doing it for you,' Brian reassured David. 'You've got quite a fan club at home! The Misses Campbell are knitting socks for you. Mr Ingles the grocer has sent you a tin of sugar, even though it's rationed at home too. And the baker has made you a special cake.'

'What about Max?' David wanted to know.

Brian laughed. 'Last time he was home on leave he was mistaken for the Russian Consul at a special service at St John's. Because of his beard!'

David chortled. He could tease his Senior Service brother about that!

'How was your nav course?' he enquired.

'Mt Gambier? Spot on. A good bunch of chaps.'

David hesitated. What he had to say next was awkward. 'I hope you will understand if we happen to be together on the next course and I don't ask you to be my navigator. Too many eggs in one basket.'

Brian nodded soberly. One telegram from the War Office would be bad enough. Two from the same op would be too terrible for their parents. 'Of course. But you should look out for a chap named Reg Murr. We came over on the same ship. He's a bit older than me. Seemed very reliable. Genuine. He could be the nav you want.'

On that trip, David also hoped to see Des Hadden. He envied Des's posting to an Advanced Flying Unit at the King's private airfield, irreverently dubbed Smith's Lawn, in Windsor Great Park. Especially when he heard the airmen were given a tour of Windsor Castle. But for now it was back to Lulsgate Bottom.

At the end of the course, the pilots returned to Southrop for the challenge of night flying. They chafed and grumbled as weather conditions again curtailed or scrubbed their exercises of beacon stooging and circuits and bumps. Fog still obliterated visibility and rain washed out the airfield. But lectures and progress checks continued. One pilot's training came to an abrupt halt when the controls locked during a test flight and his plane pranged on a concrete pillbox. He was lucky to survive but he had two broken legs. 'He almost went for a burton,' they said in the Mess.

Later, another pilot's flying career ended in a particularly grisly manner. As he put on his parachute harness, the propeller struck his arm and severed it. David pitied the men who had to pick up the arm and take it to the Flight Commander's office.

Just when the weather cleared, flying was suspended again – this time for an exercise by units of Transport Command. Troop transport Dakotas and glider tugs flew over, releasing 38 Horsa gliders, designed to be used for invasion, each capable of carrying troops, a jeep, motor bikes or a 75 mm gun. David wrote, *It was wonderful watching a sight which people of occupied countries will see in the near future.* He wondered how near that future was. Weeks? Months?

Whenever the clamp lifted and the weather held good, he noted with satisfaction, *We are getting bags of hours.* But cross-country flying at night was even more challenging, with constant hazards of high tension lines, as well as wooded hilly terrain. When night flying was suspended as unsafe with Dakotas, Stirlings and Horsas stooging over from two newly opened bases nearby, daylight cross-country flights were reintroduced. Eastward flights revealed many operational airfields, with longer sealed runways for heavy bomber use, in contrast to the smaller grass training airfields such as Southrop, mainly in the west. Formation flying also returned to the program.

With spring in the air, romances began to blossom and one lad became engaged to a girl from Brighton. But David still had only one love – flying. He and David McNeill took advantage of double summertime evenings to explore; cycling through the countryside, admiring picturesque villages and bridges, revelling in signs of their first English spring. Tiny buds appeared on bare trees, which gradually turned to shimmering green. Waves of bluebells flooded the woods. And on a Sunday leave in Oxford late in March they delighted in the brilliant swathes of crocuses under the trees in the University Gardens.

On another trip to Oxford, while they were staying in a dormitory, several servicemen stumbled in late, much the worse for wear. In the morning, David's acquaintance Jim got up and shouted, 'Who's been pissing in my shoe?', adding expletives not usually heard from the son of a bishop.

'Well, I hope he's a bomb aimer or a gunner. He was spot on target!' laughed David from his bunk. He observed that thereafter one of Jim's shoes was noticeably duller.

Longer leave allowed the two Davids to return to Scotland for Easter, where Dights was again welcomed warmly into the McNeill family, plied with good home cooking and introduced to a poacher who specialised in salmon. At a woollen mill famous for Border tweeds, David used most of his clothing coupons to buy a length for his mother. Then an unwelcome telegram, unexpected on Good Friday, recalled him to Southrop. It was time to move on yet again.

Easter Monday was occupied by the tedious task of trekking all over the station to obtain clearances, and packing up. *You've no idea how hard it is trying to get all one's accumulated junk plus ordinary gear into a couple of kitbags*, David wrote home. He went into Cirencester with friends, regretting that this would be the last time. He had become very fond of the interesting old town and of the Cotswolds. It was also time to say goodbye to mates who were going on to different destinations. The severing cut more deeply than ever before, as Ian and Gordon were posted to Cairo, and David McNeill, who had become his closest friend, was to be sent to the Middle East. David and Peter were grateful they were going on together.

High Flight

Oh I have slipped the surly bonds of earth,
And danced the skies on laughter-silvered wings;
Sunward I've climbed, and joined the tumbling mirth
Of sun-split clouds – and done a hundred things you
Have not dreamed of – wheeled and soared and swung,
High in the sunlit silence, hov'ring there
I've chased the shouting wind along and flung
My eager craft through footless halls of air,
Up, up the long delirious burning blue,
I've topped the windswept heights with easy grace,
Where never lark, nor even eagle flew –
And, while with silent lifting mind I've trod
The high, untrespassed sanctity of space,
Put out my hand and touched the Face of God.

Written at 30 000 feet in September 1941
by John Gillespie Magee Jr
19-year-old pilot of the Royal Canadian Air Force.
Died 11 December 1941

7 Wimpeys and Crewing Up

The trains taking David and Peter north to their next posting at Lichfield in Staffordshire passed through lush pasturelands and orchards bright with blossom. At No. 27 Operational Training Unit they would be introduced to their first heavy bomber, the Wellington, dubbed Wimpey, or as David described it to beat the censor in his letters home, The Iron Duke.

Lichfield was also a permanent station, the biggest they had been on so far, requiring Service Police to direct traffic at rush periods. For two weeks the pilots enjoyed comfortable quarters while they did an intensive Wellington theory course and inspected the planes on the ground. The lecturers were experienced airmen who had completed a tour of operations and, transferred to other duties, were said to be 'resting'. Most had 'gongs', which impressed David. Lectures started at 8 am and finished at

Vickers Armstrong Wellington, or 'Wimpey', David (centre) with
Noel Ferguson (L), Drew Fisher (R), at Church Broughton, 1944 103

6.30 pm, even on Sundays after church parade. Physical training was held every second evening.

Now, as well as learning about the biggest aircraft they had yet flown, there was an enormous added pressure on the pilots. At Lichfield, men from all musterings were thrown together, and on the fifth day 'crewing up' was to take place. Each pilot had to select the men who would form his crew. At 21, David had to make the most important choices of his life so far. For the first few days the pilots moved around the intake of other musterings, talking to navigators, wireless operators, gunners and bomb aimers; observing; quietly assessing personalities and potential. Each pilot was aware of the long-term implications of his choices – it could be a matter of life or death. It was essential for crew members to be compatible, to be able to work as a team under the most demanding conditions. Two nights before making his selection, David took a long, reflective bike ride, to ponder his choices.

On the morning of Monday 17 April 1944, the aircrew of No. 27 OTU, predominantly Australians, gathered in an empty, echoing hangar. They tended to cluster with others from their own mustering, some stamping their feet on the cold concrete, staring absently into space; others talking desultorily, whistling or humming under their breath. Some were relaxed, some confident, others clearly a little apprehensive.

'It's like a cattle market,' one chap quipped.

'A slave market, you mean,' corrected another.

Meanwhile, the pilots strolled from group to group, speaking with individuals. Everyone wanted to be chosen by a pukka skipper. It was like being back at school, waiting to be picked for a team in a lunchtime game. No one wanted to be left to the last. But this was no game.

A good navigator was crucial for successful operations and David already had his eye on the one he wanted. Reg Murr had travelled to Britain with David's brother Brian, and David approached him first. He was 35, older than most, and married. David thought his maturity would complement youthful impetuosity in others.

'Have you been asked to join a crew yet?' he enquired of the Queenslander, who was pale-faced like all the others after the long sunless winter. Reg, a silent type, shook his head. 'Would you like to fly with me?'

Reg nodded. He too had been observing.

'Think it over,' David suggested, 'and meet me in an hour's time by the hangar door if you're still on.'

Looking at brevets which denoted flying qualifications, David approached a bomb aimer he had already singled out: Drew Fisher, another Queenslander, also married. He introduced himself. 'Would you like to serve with me?'

Drew beamed. 'Sure would,' he replied, and added jokingly, 'I thought you'd never ask!'

David again went for maturity in his choice of wireless operator: 27-year-old Sydneysider Reg Watson. But he chose two gunners for their youthful alertness. Both were short, which meant they would fit more readily into their turrets, so cramped after many hours on a long op. Both were from Newcastle, New South Wales. 19-year-old Noel Ferguson had suggested 18-year-old Allan Avery, with whom he had trained, and David trusted his judgment. The original groups were dispersing and re-forming in small clusters around pilots. It was a momentous day in all their lives.

Reg Murr (Murga), Navigator; Noel Ferguson (Boz), Mid Upper Gunner; Allan Avery (Birdy), Rear Gunner (photo taken 1951)

As David's new crew gathered by the hangar door, Drew was the first to speak, 'I reckon we've got ourselves a gen skipper!'

Reg Watson agreed. 'He won't be flying just by the seat of his pants. Did you notice how he concentrated in those early lectures?'

Reg Murr nodded.

Allan burst out, 'I was hoping he'd pick me.'

'Allan and I wanted to stick together,' Noel added, 'and Skipper took my advice.'

They all looked at one another and the tension of the morning began to melt away. It boded well for a crew when the skipper was prepared to listen to their opinions.

David was pleased to see all the crew he had chosen waiting together for him by the hangar door. 'Let's eat together at lunch,' he suggested, keen to begin their bonding.

That night he wrote in his diary: *I have now decided on our crew*, and listed them by name, state and function.

Some of the gen crew: L-R: David, Reg Murr (Murga), Allan Avery (Birdy), Reg Watson (Pop), Drew Fisher, Church Broughton, 1944

Three have a good deal of experience, while the gunners are young and keen, so we shall make a gen crew when training is finished.

David also made it his business to study all the aircraft on the busy station – Halifaxes, Coastal Command Liberators and Fortresses, as well as Typhoons, Hellcats, Hurricanes, Kittyhawks and Martinets. In the second week, in addition to the usual airmanship, armaments and signals, there were lectures again on intelligence, with gen on escaping from German and enemy-occupied territory. There were also further practical sessions on ditching procedures and dinghy drill appropriate to the Wellington. The men were issued with extra flying kit – wool and rayon underwear for high altitudes and a whistle for blowing in case they were unlucky enough to end up in the drink. With so many possibilities in mind, it was heartening to see a Liberator make a perfect landing on only three engines.

After eleven days of study, three solid days of exams, and a rigorous PT test, David and his crew spent some welcome leave together to continue their bonding. Then it was time to make their seventh move in under eight months.

A beautiful drive through cloth-of-gold countryside shining with buttercups brought them to another satellite airfield, Church Broughton in Derbyshire. Everyone was delighted with the new billets; modern Nissen huts, set among fine old oak and chestnut trees in full spring glory, the ground carpeted with grass and wildflowers. After Southrop's mud it seemed like paradise.

But, best of all, it was back to flying!

The Wellington, designed for operations, was very different from the Oxford, which was mainly a trainer. Bigger, heavier, with considerably more powerful engines, it was almost twice as long, two thirds as high again, with a vastly increased wingspan and area, as well as greater maximum speed and range. David described the Wimpey as 'sturdy and reliable, although very heavy on the controls.'

Familiarisation flights were done with a screened pilot, one who had completed a tour of operations and was resting, although going up with sprogs, as new pilots were known, could not always have been restful. The sprog had to get used to the controls, putting into practice what he had learnt in lectures, going through the actions and manoeuvres already learnt on Tiger Moths and Oxfords. Skill and speed were critical and could mean the difference between escape and being shot down by an enemy fighter. As well as the highly necessary take-offs, circuits and landings routines, popularly called bumps, David learned to put the Wimpey into steep turns and corkscrews for evasive action, and how to handle the plane with only one engine and feather a propeller to control unwanted rotation.

The crew went back to Lichfield for a 'grope', as a synthetic bombing trip was named. It was a five-hour simulated exercise through flak and searchlights, designed as an introduction to the real thing, particularly requiring the navigator and wireless operator to show their skills.

David continued to work in the Link Trainer. Then, flying solo, he took the crew up, stooging around at 4000 feet to give them the opportunity to get used to the aircraft. There were cross-country flights for the navigator, practice on the Gee radar for him, the wireless operator and the bomb aimer, and for the gunners exercises with dummy attacks by Martinets representing enemy fighters. These were carried out with a cine-gun, which filmed the action for later study, identifying errors to be rectified. For the bomb aimer there were runs over bombing ranges, dropping sticks of practice bombs and observing their accuracy.

Everyone was enjoying the milder weather, but the warmth brought its own problems, principally poor visibility on account of the industrial haze. Flying was still sometimes cancelled.

David seized every opportunity to develop the camaraderie so vital for good crew morale. When they had time off they caught local buses or hitchhiked, exploring Derby with its big Rolls Royce plant, now switched from making luxury cars to aircraft engines, Nottingham once renowned for lace, now for Trent Bridge cricket ground, and Burton-on-Trent, famous for its breweries. They were intrigued, too, to pass through the village of Melbourne. *Nothing like the Melbourne we know*, David commented to his parents.

They also enjoyed bike rides in the long summer evenings. They discovered stately homes, ancient churches, Elizabethan manor houses, and quaintly named old pubs, such as The Saltbox, which they nicknamed The Pepperpot. David was pleased to show some of these places to Brian, now posted to Church Broughton too.

One night cycling back, they overtook another pilot who was decidedly under the weather. Weaving his way along the towpath, he overbalanced and toppled into the canal. Water streaming from clothes and hair, he emerged moaning, 'Oh, my profile! Oh, my profile!', much to the crew's amusement. It became their private joke, whenever they were laughing their way through a trying situation, for someone to exclaim, 'Oh, my profile!'

On glorious summer days, their Australian issue shorts and shirts were the envy of British crews, chafing hot in their woollen jackets and trousers. They spent many afternoons by the delightful Dove River, swimming and lying lazily on the grass in the sun, chatting, chiacking, telling their stories and getting to know each other.

Reg M was a man of few words, but when they came they were always worth listening to. Observant and thoughtful, he watched the others with a quiet, almost avuncular smile, and they affectionately named him Murga, short for Murgatroyd.

Reg W, an accountant before the war, who sported a dapper moustache, was as precise in manner and speech

David and Drew outside their Nissen hut, Church Broughton

as he had been with columns of figures. He had a lively side too which made for interesting exchanges and earned him the nickname Pop.

Drew, a primary school teacher, had a quick wit and they all encouraged his quirky repartee.

Nuggety Noel, already known as Boz, had an engaging boyish grin. The shortest in the crew, his arms always seemed to be folded firmly across his chest, as if to say, 'I may be small, but take me on! You just try it!'

Also short, solid and athletic, was Allan, whom they named Birdy. He was a bit of a larrikin, with a mischievous lopsided grin. The youngest in the crew, his old face seemed to indicate more experience than his eighteen years.

David was well pleased. They were a good bunch. Not a clot among them. None was a heavy smoker and all were only light drinkers. It augured well for ops.

In addition to getting to know each man as an individual, it was just as important for David to become fully conversant with the duties of each crew member. He attended the gunners' aircraft recognition lectures, to keep himself up-to-date. He spent a morning in the wireless section with Reg W, and time in an aircraft where Reg showed him how to work all his equipment. He gave Drew instructions on the Link Trainer, to help ensure the critical accuracy needed in bomb aiming.

He also took close note of excellent airmanship and any unusual kites. He watched an Albemarle come in with an engine on fire, and was thrilled to see a new Spitfire Mark XIV land, and later do a remarkable steep climbing turn after take-off. He inspected a Fortress whose internal layout catered better for the crew than the Wellington. 'But,' he declared, 'performances cannot be compared, British aircraft being well in the lead.' He had been observing test pilots on highly secret experiments in jet propulsion and was very impressed with two Wellingtons modified for jets, and two twin jet fighters, known as squirts, whose speed was well in excess of 500 miles per hour. He wrote in his diary with satisfaction, *Squirts should be able to make things somewhat unpleasant for Jerry.*

David's knowledge of Britain's geography and topography was also increasing steadily, as cross-country flights extended to four hours and more. Seeing Wales, the Isle of Man, Scotland and Eire, all on one flight, was memorable. A lecture on German night defence had crews on the edge of their seats, listening intently to information about the elaborate and effective system of controlled interception by night fighters and cooperation with searchlights and flak batteries. David, who already spent many hours in the intelligence library, encouraged his crew to do likewise. A lecture by an RAF official interrogator describing how much gen can be given away by apparently harmless remarks by POWs, quoting German airmen he had questioned, was also very sobering.

At the beginning of June night flying began again. After his first flight David wrote in his diary, *The circuits and bumps certainly make one sweat in a Wimpey.* They were hard work. But night flying also brought the benefit of sleeping in, and much appreciated extra rations. The rigorous mental training plus strenuous physical demands meant the men were always hungry, looking for a feed, calling at farmhouses hoping to buy eggs. Parcels from home, shared among the crew, continued to supplement rather basic meals in the Mess. Everyone contributed what they could for a feast in the hut for the skipper's 22nd birthday, and Drew ribbed David, 'Any tip left under the plate will be gratefully received.'

They made their first night cross-country with a screened pilot, who left them to their own resources, pleased at how well the crew worked as a team. On their second, aware that Reg W had gone to relieve himself, David deliberately put the aircraft into some sharp manoeuvres. He didn't know that the Elsan, the small portable toilet, had not been emptied from the previous flight. Reg copped the lot and was not impressed, though the others enjoyed the prank.

For a change, flying conditions were excellent, with clear starry nights and a young moon. One evening the crew were fascinated by a display of Aurora Borealis, the Northern Lights. On a non-flying night Reg W was tempted to sleep under an oak tree, but found that caterpillars falling on the bed kept him awake. 'First it was crap, now it's caterpillars!' he grumbled.

At the night-flying briefing on 5 June, the men were warned to be careful of large numbers of gliders on an operation, and next morning they woke to the announcement of D-Day, the opening of the Second Front with the landing of Allied troops in Normandy. Reports that the invasion was going well led David to write in his diary, *So let us hope the European war will be over within a year.*

Training flights were temporarily transferred to Lichfield, as Church Broughton was in heavy use by operational aircraft. David was chuffed to see a naval fighter Fairey Firefly, still on the secret list, impressed by its short take-off and very tight manoeuvres.

Fighter affiliation, when friendly fighters took the role of attacking aircraft, was another exercise designed to improve crew responses and give them a taste of what was to come. So was a session in a mobile decompression chamber, from which the air was slowly pumped, allowing crews to experience the effects of oxygen lack at altitude. All wore oxygen masks and headsets, but when one took his off at 25 000 feet he passed out. His speedy recovery when others replaced the mask for him was convincing proof of the purpose and necessity of wearing the gear. Another who wore no mask lasted until 23 000 feet, but his writing became illegible and his calculations inaccurate. It was a telling lesson.

A 'bullseye' exercise involving both night fighters and searchlights on a cross-country was designed to develop crew cooperation. The gunners acquitted themselves well and David was pleased he evaded all searchlights. The final exercise in operational training was a bombing run.

The weather, night flying and gruelling cross-country flights in obsolescent aircraft led to a high accident rate. Almost one thousand Australian aircrew were killed or injured at Operational Training Units. So everyone was chuffed when the course concluded without any casualties.

'Good show, chaps!' the CO declared. 'You're the best lot to go through this OTU.'

In the last week of training, David had three successful interviews for a commission. *Now I'm waiting for the paperwork to come through*, he wrote home. In his diary he wrote *I have enjoyed it. Church Broughton is definitely the best station on which I have been.* But he was tired and had lost 22 pounds in weight over the ten months in England. The strain of flying and the heavy study program had taken their toll. He was glad that after the usual time-consuming task of obtaining clearances, in the rain as always, the men were granted leave – eight whole unprogrammed days for fun and relaxation. David and two friends from another crew headed for the Lake District.

FIG 1

FIG 1

INSTRUMENT PANEL

KEY TO *Fig. 1*

INSTRUMENT PANEL

1. Instrument flying panel.
2. D.F. Indicator.
3. Landing light switches.
4. Undercarriage indicator switch.
5. D.R. compass repeater.
6. D. R. compass deviation card holder.
7. Ignition switches.
8. Boost gauges.
9. R.p.m. indicators.
10. Booster coil switch.
11. Slow-running cut-out switches.
12. I.F.F. detonator buttons.
13. I.F.F. switch.
14. Engine starter switches.
15. Bomb containers jettison button.
16. Bomb jettison control.
17. Vacuum change-over cock.
18. Oxygen regulator.
19. Feathering buttons.
20. Triple pressure gauge.
21. Signalling switchbox (identification lamps).
22. Fire-extinguisher pushbuttons.
23. Suction gauge.
24. Starboard master engine cocks.
25. Supercharger gear change control panel.
26. Flaps position indicator.
27. Flaps position indicator switch.
28. Throttle levers.
29. Propeller speed control levers.
30. Port master engine cocks.
31. Rudder pedal.
32. Boost control cut-out.
33. Signalling switchbox (recognition lights).
34. Identification lights colour selector switches.
35. D.R. compass switches.
36. Auto controls steering lever.
37. P.4. compass deviation card holder.
38. P.4. compass.
39. Undercarriage position indicator.
40. A.S.I. correction card hold.
41. Beam approach indicator.
42. Watch holder.

8 Heavies and 'Butch' Harris

The Lake District is a land somehow apart, reminding one of A Midsummer Night's Dream *or some similar fantasy*, David wrote to his parents. Five idyllic days quickly passed. Walking, climbing, rowing, swimming nude in secluded bays, breathing the soft, clear air, the young airmen were refreshed and reinvigorated in body, mind and spirit by nature and the magnificent scenery. It was too late for the daffodils immortalised by Wordsworth, but David revelled in discovering other associations with both poets Wordsworth and Coleridge, and novelist Hugh Walpole. He had been having difficulty filling a weekly one page airgraph to his parents, as so much about life on an RAF station could not be mentioned. But now he had something to write about, and happily filled eight pages, reporting to his mother that despite all the exercise in those five days he had put on five pounds!

Lancaster main instrument panel

After a pilgrimage to historic York, David caught another train to Doncaster in Yorkshire to meet his crew again and go on to No. 1656 Heavy Conversion Unit, Lindholme. Here, pilots learned to fly Halifaxes, four-engined planes much bigger than the twin-engined Wellingtons, with longer range and increased bomb capacity. The controversial Air Chief Marshal Sir Arthur Harris, Commander in Chief of Bomber Command, widely known as 'Bomber' Harris, was convinced that Germany could be defeated by air power, with strategic bombing to destroy military infrastructure and demoralise civilians. In order to carry out his strategy of mounting 1000 bomber raids over Germany he sometimes used aircraft and crew from these training units. To aircrew who bore the brunt of these operations, he was 'Butcher' or 'Butch' Harris. And David and his crew were aware that, although technically still in training, they might be called any time for an operation. The war was very close now.

The men were issued with more flying kit, including silk gloves and woollen mittens to be worn under leather gauntlets, and began lectures immediately. These covered tactics, enemy anti-aircraft measures, medical aspects of flying and vital survival equipment, parachutes, and Mae West life jackets, with further wet cold dinghy drill. PT featured heavily in the program, and a route march, never appreciated, brought home the point of the nursery rhyme. *The grand old Duke of York, He had ten thousand men, He marched them up to the top of the hill, And he marched them down again.*

David and two others, sent off to do another short course at No. 1 Engine Control Demonstration Unit, had to stand all the way to London, four hours on a packed train in hot muggy weather. The men had been shown a film on the latest Nazi weapon, V1, the dreaded flying bomb, whose speed and unpredictable fall made it very hard to intercept. When David and his companions arrived in London to find a V1 attack in progress they were very glad to catch another train on to their destination. David again came across people he had known on earlier courses, eagerly swapping stories and enquiring for news of others with whom he had lost touch. Four solid days of lectures and practical work on the latest Rolls Royce Merlin engines were relieved by a light-hearted evening on the dodgems at the local fair. After a three-hour exam on the fifth day, it was back to London.

Here the effects of the flying bomb attacks were immediately apparent. Streets were deserted. Many servicemen were now in France and many civilians, especially women and children, had been evacuated to the country, as they were during the Blitz. David was shocked to find that all the glass in Australia House had been blown out, and the noise of the bomb engines and sirens kept him awake most of the night. Standing on another crowded train for nearly five hours they returned to Doncaster.

Then, in the last week of July, the men had to pack up again to transfer from the reception depot to the main camp at Lindholme, a peacetime station with more comfortable quarters. David was very pleased to welcome their flight engineer and introduce him to the rest of the crew. Nineteen-year-old fair-haired Cyril Bailey from Kent was the only Englishman among them.

'An English rose among blue orchids,' they joked.

'Don't you mean colonial thorns?' he retaliated, and the bond was cemented.

Cyril Bailey, Flight Engineer, at home, Birchington, Kent

The course began with a general lecture series that everyone attended before each crew member went to his own specialised section. Sessions on engines, navigation, gunnery and the mechanisms of various gun turrets, evasion and escape tactics filled many hours, both day and evening. They were shown over a Halifax to learn its layout, and spent time in the spotlight trainer, a gun turret sighted on to aircraft projected by film onto a large dome, which David found good practice in sighting and manipulation. They also watched a film about radar, the Y or H2S. This device, which enabled an image of a town, river, lake or coastline to be picked up and shown on a screen in the aircraft, together with bearing and distance, had already proved its value in operations.

On the long summer evenings the crew cycled between fields of golden grain splashed with red poppies. A visit to a village named Spittle-in-Street evoked some joking. 'How unhygienic! Not a desirable address!'

David was annoyed when his bike was stolen, putting an end to jaunting. He wrote to his parents, *News is scarcer than ever, as I have not been out for ten days. Somebody stole, pinched, swiped, thieved, misappropriated, confiscated or otherwise feloniously removed my bike.*

Early in August they had their familiarisation flight in a Halifax. *In good hands the Hali flies well, except that it is heavy on the aileron controls,* David commented. Later, at the controls himself, he found he had to work hard doing circuits and bumps. Twenty feet high, with a 100-foot wingspan and four engines, *The Hali is distinctly different from any other aircraft I have flown,* he declared. When he started to fly solo at night, he was very glad to have Cyril standing beside him, assisting with the four throttles. He wrote in his diary, *The engineer is an invaluable aid – in fact a necessity – for taking off and landing.* Later, on a cross-country in an aircraft with dual control, he took the opportunity to teach Cyril some flying skills.

As ever, training was often interrupted, not only by rain and fog, but because early Mark II Halifaxes were discards from operations because of age or damage. They frequently became unserviceable. 'Hallibags! Clapped out old kites!' the crew grumbled. A bombing exercise was aborted when the sight became u/s. Circuit practice had to be discontinued because of a flat tyre. A cross-country flight had to be abandoned when a broken pipe poured oil onto the hot exhaust. David feathered the propeller and turned back to base, only to find that another aircraft had pranged on the Lindholme runway. They were diverted to nearby Sandtoft, which had earned the unenviable nickname Prangtoft, and landed on three engines. The crew's confidence in their skipper, already considerable, increased further. After another training flight the crew were in the transport on their way back when Pop suddenly exclaimed, 'Where's Boz?'

They returned at once to the aircraft to find Boz asleep in his turret!

'That's a tribute to your landing skills, Skip!' the crew laughed.

But David's awareness of their mortality, already considerable, had also increased. In July, just two months before David was to go on operations, the war had struck deeper than ever into his heart. He learned from his parents that his cousin Frank, a gunner in 463 Squadron RAAF, was missing on a raid over Germany. He and Frank had met only once because Frank lived in Western Australia. But Frank had trained at Western Junction after him. They had been looking forward to meeting and had been exchanging letters in anticipation. Frank had been in Lincolnshire for a week when he wrote in May, *As you can see, I'm just about in the war now. No ops until last night when the skipper went on a second dickey. We should be off next time, I guess.*

They were. And they did not return. Posted MISSING.

But a letter David had written to Frank did return. Unopened. Stamped in purple: RETURN TO SENDER ON AIR BOARD ORDERS.

He cringed as he re-read what he had written when unaware that Frank had gone missing six weeks earlier on his first op. *How are you enjoying life with 463? Apparently they work you fairly hard these days, so you should get through your tour quickly ... If you want a quiet leave, the Lake District is to be recommended.*

Frank would never get through his tour. He had barely begun it. He would never know the delights and serene beauty of the Lake District. What were his last moments? What horrors did he see? What did he know? What were his feelings?

David's last letter to his cousin Frank Mattingley

Frank Mattingley, Gunner, killed aged 21, over Handerath, Germany, 22 May 1944, on his first operation

Frozen with pain, David hid his grief. It was his to bear, not to share. Not even with Brian. Certainly not with his crew. Nothing he did or said must affect their morale. And their lives were dependent on his skills and judgment. This stupid senseless war. This hideous loss of young lives. This sorrow inflicted on parents. On friends. The waste of it all. The wicked waste. But he must not dwell on it. He had a job to do. And he must not let himself think about those other lives that would be lost if he did his job well. About the waste that his skills and judgment would cause. He must not. And he must do his job well. For the sake of peace.

But silently he read and re-read poems by another serving RAF officer, John Pudney, who wrote in 'The Dead', 'These, wishing life, must range the falling sky, Whom an heroic moment calls to die.' And silently he agreed, 'You shall have your revenge who flew and died, Spending your daylight hours before the day began', and made a vow for Frank. Then later, caressed and warmed by his first English summer, he read in 'Men Alive': 'Enough of death! It looms too large in words…Enjoy the sky, Possess the field of air, Cloud be your step, The west wind be your stair.'

David took comfort again in the delights of flying. On a daytime cross-country to the Welsh coast he was exhilarated to fly at 18 000 feet, the highest he had been yet. But a six-hour cross-country two nights later proved very wearying. With no visible horizon and in thick cloud part of the way, he had to fly on instruments the whole time. David, always making light of difficulties, simply wrote in his diary, *We were not sorry to land*. Even under good conditions night flying was a strain. And when they commenced ops, many would be flown at night under horrendous conditions.

One evening a highly concentrated bomber stream passed overhead.

'Just think how the Dutch and French must feel seeing them!' the crew gloated.

Then suddenly it was their turn to gladden the hearts of the French. On 18 August, only 14 days after their familiarisation flight on Halifaxes, David and his crew found themselves listed for a diversionary exercise over the Normandy battlefields, where the fight between the Nazi occupying army and the Allied invasion forces was still raging. This was one of Butch Harris's strategies. Smaller groups of aircraft were often deployed over areas away from the main target to confuse the enemy and divert attention from the Main Force. The casualty rate in Bomber Command was always higher than in Fighter, Coastal or Transport Commands. Although aircraft production had been stepped up, even in 1944 the replacement rate for planes and crews could not keep pace with casualties. During the invasion month of June alone almost 2600 Bomber Command aircrew were lost. To make up the required numbers sprog crews in aircraft that had been retired from active service were pressed into use.

So it was that on the night of 18 August, many young men, not fully trained, set off in defective aircraft to fly as decoys over enemy territory.

'It's one of those sitting duck flights we've heard about,' they quipped as they climbed aboard. 'Let's hope the old girl doesn't conk out tonight.'

*David's notebook with details of corkscrew manoeuvre
for evading enemy aircraft attack*

They flew over the Channel to Caen, where they
could see the mayhem of the battle below, before they
headed for Bayeux and on to the Irish Sea. They were
chased by an enemy fighter, but it sheered off when they
took evasive action. *This was fortunate*, David, master
of understatement, wrote in his diary, *as we had no mid-
upper gun turret*. Thankfully, they flew home through a
strong cold front, to land in rain at base.

'All that corkscrew practice sure paid off, Skipper,' the
crew commented. 'And the old crate made it!'

The rain continued for three days and flying was
washed out. Then, although they had completed only two
out of nine bombing exercises, they had sufficient hours
overall, and were deemed to have completed the course.

David, with a total of 381 flying hours and nine training courses over 22 months, was assessed as a proficient heavy bomber pilot.

Next day he left for London to complete the formalities for his commission, which had come through early in August. Now as Pilot Officer Mattingley he dined in the Officers' Mess. He was sorry to be separated from his crew, but appreciated the opportunity to mix with more experienced men. London was still under flying bomb attack, so Australians were allowed there only on official business. After dealing with his, David went to a tailor in Savile Row to be measured for his officer's uniform. Not only did he now have to pay Mess charges for meals, he was also responsible for providing his uniform. 'Just as well my pay's gone up a bit,' he thought ruefully as he enquired the cost. 'But it'll take more than a few weeks at nineteen shillings and tenpence a day, to cover this lot.'

A flying bomb landed nearby while he was at the tailor's, and on leaving he was stopped by Service Police who checked his pass, then gave him a lift to RAAF Central Stores. Here he bought the rest of his necessary kit, pleased to be at last entitled to a raincoat and a tin trunk. No longer would he have to cram all his possessions into kitbags.

But David still wasn't finished with training. A transport took him and his crew the 20 miles from Lindholme to No. 1 Lancaster Finishing School, Hemswell, and more lectures. On the second day David learned about Lancaster engines and airframes and they all spent time in an aircraft *finding out the whys and wherefores of everything* so that each crew member knew where every item of equipment was located.

Lancaster returning home (Photo by Paul A. Richardson)

'She's longer than a cricket pitch,' Birdy marvelled, 'and I'm on the boundary!'

Everyone forbore to remark that the rear gunner's position, most vulnerable in the plane, was more like silly mid-on.

The Lancaster, almost 70 feet long, stood nearly 20 feet high on massive wheels nearly as tall as a man, with a wingspan of 102 feet. Powered by four Rolls-Royce Merlin engines, it had a cruising speed of 216 miles per hour, bomb load capacity of 14 000 pounds, fuel for up to 2000 miles and could climb to 22 000 feet. It was ideally suited for penetration over Europe. 'What a wizard kite!' they all agreed, appreciating that its black belly made it harder to see from below, and its upper surfaces, painted in camouflage colours and patterns, disguised it from above.

Air-sea rescue and parachute and dinghy drill again featured large. A dummy fuselage fitted with devices registering each crew member's actions made dinghy drill very realistic. As pilot, David would be the last to leave the aircraft and his exit was not easy. The main escape was a hatch on which the bomb aimer lay, forward of the pilot's position in the nose. This would be used by bomb aimer, flight engineer, navigator, w/op and mid-upper gunner, who would all bale out before the pilot. The rear gunner would also leave through the main escape hatch if time permitted, or if necessary direct from his turret.

After a week at Hemswell, and fifteen months since David's first thrilling sight of a Lancaster in New Zealand, they had their first flight. He was ecstatic. *The Lanc is a really beautiful kite, by far the best I have flown. She is remarkably manoeuvrable for her size and is light on the controls.* On this flight they saw a Halifax on fire make a forced landing. Then after a couple of circuits David went solo in a blinding thunderstorm, which tested everyone's nerves.

Lincoln Cathedral, welcome landmark for aircrews returning from ops

David was also ecstatic about a visit to Lincoln. *This is obviously a cathedral city and one can feel the atmosphere.* They climbed the steep hill, and he wrote afterwards, *The famous cathedral almost beggars description.* Nevertheless, he filled more than a page of his diary, extolling its beautifully proportioned towers, west front, wonderful stained glass, superb wrought iron choir screens and the carved angels adorning the choir. But he did not yet know how comforting the sight of the great towers on the horizon were to become to the crew returning from ops.

The following day, 3 September, marked five years since war had been declared. 'How much longer will it go on?' everyone was wondering. 'How many more aircrew will be lost before the carnage ends?' It was also the first anniversary of David's arrival in Britain and he was pleased that Reg Murr had returned from London where he had received his overdue commission. Australian aircrew were often frustrated that despite their intensive training and qualifications, they seemed to be passed over in favour of English crew. Rain interfered with flying, as did an unserviceable aircraft, forcing them to continue until 0300 hours to complete the required number of circuits and bumps. And they had had only one fighter affiliation practice.

At the end of the week, after only three days in Lancs, it was time to pack up again. David's tenth course was over. He and his crew had passed and were ready to join their Lancaster squadron.

An Airman's Prayer

Almighty and all-present Power,
Short is the prayer I make to Thee.
I do not ask in battle hour
For any shield to cover me.
The vast unalterable way
From which the stars do not depart,
May not be turned aside to stay
The bullets flying to my heart.
I ask no help to strike my foe,
I seek no petty victory here.
The enemy I hate, I know,
To Thee is also dear.
But this I pray: Be at my side
When death is drawing through the sky,
Almighty God, Who also died,
Teach me the way that I should die.

Hugh Brodie

Sergeant/Observer Hugh Brodie, old boy and former master of Melbourne High School. Written about 1941, these lines were found in a letter to the boys of the school, among his personal belongings after he had been posted missing during RAAF operations.

Crest of 625 Squadron RAF

9 625 Squadron

David and his crew were posted to 625 Squadron, whose stark motto was *We Avenge*. 625 Squadron was part of No. 1 Group of Bomber Command, based at Kelstern, which had been established only eleven months earlier. Situated on agricultural land four hundred feet up on the Lincolnshire Wolds, exposed and windy, the station was a raw collection of widely scattered Nissen huts. With three concrete runways it was a typical bomber airfield. Under several outstanding wing commanders the squadron had already developed a sturdy and buoyant spirit. David was deeply impressed to learn that he would serve under a 23-year-old Wingco who had been awarded the Distinguished Service Order (DSO) and the Distinguished Flying Cross (DFC) and Bar, and who took part in the squadron's most dangerous ops.

David was going on to active ops just as Bomber Command's part in the war was coming to its peak.

Before joining the squadron, the men had a week's well-earned leave. The ban on Australian troops visiting London had been lifted, but the first V2 rocket had arrived only 24 hours before, and there was still plenty of flying bomb activity. David wrote, *The V1s move fast and low across the skyline and are rather fascinating to watch. But few pass our defences.*

He spent the first morning trying to elicit more information about Frank and wrote to his parents, *There is still no news of Frank, who has been posted as 'Missing'. The majority of his crew were 'Missing, believed killed'.* But he was pleased to be able to tell them that another cousin, Eric Mattingley, flying in the Mediterranean theatre, had been awarded the DFC. At the Boomerang Club, David met numerous friends and acquaintances, and gleaned news of others. Sadly, much of it was bleak. *All too many are now casualties*, was all David allowed himself to write in his diary. He discovered that the fellow who had fallen in the canal near Lichfield was among the missing. So in future David's crew would drop the 'Oh, my profile!' joke.

Back at Kelstern, David longed to go on his first op, but instead was called on for another duty, which gave him a new insight. Told 'You're wanted by the Adjutant,' he walked briskly to the office wondering what it could be.

'You are assigned to stay with Pilot Officer Jackson in sick quarters until he leaves the station,' the Adjutant told him.

'Why?' David wanted to ask. But the Adjutant's manner, tone and expression did not encourage questions.

'Make your way there at once. You will be informed when you are to be relieved.'

'Sir,' David saluted smartly, and headed to the sick quarters at the edge of the station. An orderly showed him to a six-bed ward which had only one occupant. 'Which bed is mine?' David asked.

'That's your choice, sir,' the orderly replied. He nodded towards the airman sitting on a bed in the far corner. 'There'll only be the two of you in here. Your meals will be brought.' The door clicked shut behind him.

As he approached the slouched figure, David's footsteps resounded on the bare floor. But the airman did not even seem to hear. He was in a world of his own. David walked up to the bed. 'Hullo,' he said, holding out his hand. 'Mattingley's the name.'

The young airman stared up at him as if he had not seen or heard. David tried again. 'Pilot Officer Jackson, isn't it? Have you been long on the station?'

Suddenly the eyes focused on David. 'A lifetime,' he said in a flat voice.

'How many ops have you done?

'Too many. Too bloody many,' the other replied. He fumbled in his pocket and withdrew a packet of cigarettes. His hand was shaking as he pulled one out and his lips trembled as he tried to shove it between them and light it.

'How old are you?' David asked. About twenty-two, the same as he was, he judged.

But the other saw it differently. 'The same as Methuselah,' he laughed, and his laugh was hard, hollow.

'Had any leave lately?' David's enquiry was met with the same response and a violent shaking of the head.

'Bloody war,' the young pilot muttered. 'Bloody awful war. Seeing your mates shot to pieces, burned alive. Dropping bombs to burn other people to death.' He lapsed into a silence from which he did not rouse until the orderly entered with their meal. Then he only pushed the food around the plate.

Afterwards, David picked up a pack of cards lying on a locker. 'How about a game?' His charge ignored the question and lit up another cigarette. David dealt himself a hand of patience. He was going to need it, he decided. There was not going to be much conversation here. David chose the bed in the corner diagonal from the other's, who continued to smoke until he fell into troubled sleep. Then David moved quietly across to check that the pilot's last cigarette really was out. Bad enough to be incinerated by enemy fire. Too bad if it was just a careless cigarette.

David was woken by a scream. The young pilot who had seen too much was reliving the night horrors. The horrors David was yet to experience. A strangled groan became choking sobs. 'No. No. NO!'

David shook the writhing shoulders. 'Wake up. It's all right. It's not really happening.' He switched on the nightlight.

The other pilot twisted around and stared up at him. 'Yes it is. It is. Somewhere over there. You'll find out soon enough,' he sobbed. David patted the shaking body and prayed for the soul in torment, until the pilot again subsided into sleep. When the roar of Merlin engines broke the night silence, as Lancasters took off on another op, he moaned, and his occasional babbles of terror brought David to his side throughout the night. David was thankful indeed when the orderly came in with breakfast.

'You're leaving at 0800,' the orderly told the other pilot. He made no response.

'Like a lamb to the slaughter,' David thought as he saw his fellow officer being led away. 'There but for the grace of God go I.' And he resolved to do all in his power to keep up the morale of his crew. Pilot Officer Jackson would never be spoken of on the squadron again. Nothing would ever be heard of him. Nothing would ever be explained.

And he, David, had been chosen as guard because he was new on the station and did not know this victim of stress.

On the OTUs, there had always been rumours swirling around about what happened on squadrons when ops became too much for an airman and he lost his nerve and the will to go on. It seemed these rumours were indeed true. The unfortunate airman was classified as LMF, 'lacking moral fibre', and the consequences were summary, harsh, with no return. Stripped of his rank, all privileges removed, pay frozen, sent to a retraining unit where the regime was severe, then put on ground duties or even sent to work underground in the coal mines. Some were forced to resign with no pension or recourse. Dire indeed.

David remembered the proud day at Point Cook sixteen months before when, watched by his parents, he had graduated as a pilot. With what love and probably secret misgivings his mother had sewn his wings onto his uniform, the wings of her youngest son. Had Jackson's parents watched him graduate too? Had his mother lovingly sewn on his wings, the wings about to be stripped from his uniform? What could her son tell her of his humiliation, the price of this brutal war? David reflected soberly on what he had seen and heard while guarding a casualty of the psychological wounding of war, and promised that that would never happen to one of his crew.

When he rejoined them, they looked at him closely.

'Had a rough night?' Birdy asked.

'You could say so,' David replied.

'Without us? You sly dog,' they teased their skipper.

David managed a smile but said no more.

Finally, on the afternoon of 16 September, David found his name on a battle order for the first time. Battle Order 165. This was it! At last!

Duplicated battle orders were pinned up around the station, which buzzed with a concentrated burst of activity. Telephone lines to the outside were closed to prevent any information being divulged. But the Tannoy public address system crackled with announcements as everyone purposefully went about his or her part in preparing for the operation. The roads were busy with men hurrying on foot, men on bikes, fuel tankers, tenders, tractors hauling bomb trolleys, many driven by WAAFs. In the Messes, beyond the porch where men hung their gas masks, the enticing smell of bacon pervaded the usual smell of wet greatcoats, warm beer and cigarettes, as aircrew queued for their flying meal. 'The condemned man ate a hearty meal,' they always joked. Normally it was the luxury of eggs and bacon with plenty of fat to sustain them while flying. It also ensured that they were well stoked in the event of having to bale out and maybe face German interrogation and POW internment, or hide out in an attempt to escape. There was always a bowl of cod liver oil capsules on the counter too, for those who could tolerate them. The hum of voices and the sound of laughter intensified as the men chatted and bantered to break the tension. And above it all was the growl of engines, as the ground crews worked on the Lancs.

As it was his first op, David would fly as second dickey and flight engineer to a more experienced pilot and crew. The pilot was another Australian, from Melbourne. David was glad that he seemed a quietly confident sort of chap who had good relations with his crew. David spent the rest of the afternoon on a ground test, observing closely all the procedures as the pilot ran up the engines and the crew checked every item of equipment. Then he attended his first operational briefing, impressed at the line-up of senior officers and section heads who outlined the operation and provided the relevant information. The purpose of the raid was to immobilise German airfields in support of a large airborne operation at Arnhem in the Netherlands. Their squadron's target, from 17 000 feet, was the airfield at Rheine on the Dortmund-Ems Canal. Other squadrons were to put nearby radar installations out of action.

David clambered onto the vehicle which took his and two other crews to their dispersal bays, listening to the crews' joking, which covered their feelings.

'Look out, Fritz, here come the Brits!'

'Have a good trip,' they said, as one crew after another was dropped off. David noticed that nobody said, 'See you later.' They knew too much for that.

Then, picked out by the transport's hooded lights, their plane B Baker loomed huge in the gloom. With the familiar pungent smell of oil and petrol filling his nostrils, David was acutely aware, as never before, of all that his senses were telling him. Climbing up the ladder into the aircraft, at each step he felt the metal colder under his grasp. And knew the taste of fear.

Loaded with twenty 500-pound high-explosive bombs, B Baker took off just before midnight, with David, tense yet excited, standing beside the pilot. The sight of his own crew waiting at the edge of the runway to wave him off tightened his throat. 'I'll be back for you, boys. I'll be back,' he promised them silently. As the revs increased, the roar of the mighty Merlin engines filled the aircraft, filled his head, vibrated the fuselage, sent vibrations right through him. Once they were fully airborne, with one hand he unlocked and with the other he raised the undercarriage lever which brought the wheels up with a gentle thump. Then he progressively lifted the flap selector handle. Now the aircraft was trimmed for climbing and David settled on to the folding seat beside the flight engineer's panel on the starboard side.

Ahead, around and behind, navigation lights of the bomber stream glimmered like fairy lanterns. Then, as they crossed the English coast, they were all extinguished. They flew on in darkness, horribly conscious how close other aircraft were, as sickening lurches and bumps indicated they had entered slipstreams. Only too aware that many planes and their crews went down as a result of collisions.

On reaching the Dutch coast they encountered their first flak. The 88 mm shells from heavy Krupps guns exploded at predetermined heights. Others, fitted with special fuses, were set off by the proximity of aircraft. 'Thank God we got through that lot,' the pilot muttered more to himself than David. Then the kindly cover of darkness was ripped by the glare of the flares German fighters dropped from above as they tried to locate victims. Flak could strike anywhere but aircraft on the outer edges of the stream were most vulnerable to attack from enemy fighters.

Shortly before B Baker reached the target, David could see red TIs, target indicators, dropped by specially trained crews, the Pathfinders. The TIs accurately illuminated the intersection of the runways. He felt the aircraft shuddering gently and lifting as the bomb aimer called over the intercom 'Bombs gone!' and twenty high explosives (HEs) left the bomb bay. The doors were closed and B Baker turned away. The target was well pranged, and the airfield was made u/s for some time to come.

But it was not over yet. They still had to get home.

The flak had stopped. But this was only to allow the German fighters more freedom to harry the returning stream. The bombers were even more vulnerable on the homeward flight as the enemy knew their route and enemy fighters often infiltrated the stream and pursued them almost all the way to their base. No aircraft was safe until it had landed. The threat of intruders placed a final burden on the crew. Although exhausted from the operation, they had to remain vigilant from take-off to touchdown. David saw several aircraft illuminated by flares. He watched in shock as two unfortunate crews went down in flames and he thought of their ground crews waiting in vain in the cold and dark for their return.

Almost four hours later B Baker landed safely at Kelstern. David attended his first interrogation, when the crew reported details of their sortie. He wrote in his diary, *It was more or less the ideal op, but of course it did not give me experience in many of the problems I would strike later on in the tour*, concluding with typical understatement, *The flying meal after interrogation was most enjoyable*. All 625's aircraft returned safely. But it was bad news two days later to hear that the Arnhem airborne landing they had supported had failed to outflank the German defence and the paratroops and glider troops had been withdrawn after heavy casualties.

*Map showing Bomber Command operational area, some targets,
and postwar boundaries of Germany*

Battle Order 204 (4)
Hit!

Drew, D Dog's bomb aimer, prone in his position forward of the cockpit, looking out through the perspex nose of the aircraft, gave the order: 'Bomb doors open!'

'Bomb doors open!' the pilot repeated after he lowered the lever.

Drew concentrated on aligning his bombsight on the aiming point, 'Bomb aimer to pilot. Right... Steady... Left Left... Steady... Steady... Steady.'

The crew waited for the aircraft to jump as the weight of the bomb load fell clear, longing to hear Drew report 'Bombs gone!' Then David's 'Bomb doors closed.'

For a few vulnerable moments the Lancaster had to fly straight and level until a photo of the target had been taken. Not until then could they feel the relief of turning away from the appalling blaze below. The blaze it had been their job to help create.

• • • • • • • • • • • • • • • •

But while they were still over the target, only seconds after the bombs were released, bursting flak struck the aircraft.

Dog was hit! A casualty!

Fuselage extensively damaged by shrapnel.

Starboard aileron torn.

No. 3 petrol tank holed.

Almost all the cockpit perspex blown out.

• • • • • • • • • • • • • • • •

And David was also a casualty. Wounded in five places by flying metal. Right knee, thigh and shoulder hit. Tendons and artery in right hand severed. And shrapnel ripped through his thick leather helmet, fracturing his skull.

David lost consciousness.

Dog went into a dive.

10 Holland, Happy Valley and France

Next day, only fourteen hours after returning, David was scheduled for take-off again. He and his crew were down for their first op together, on Battle Order 166, chuffed that the aircraft allotted them was V Victor. 'That's a good omen,' they told each other as they watched V's ground crew working to get it ready. All the same, it was with a certain amount of trepidation that they passed the security guard and entered the briefing room, where the names of all participating crews were chalked up on the blackboard.

Every man had to empty his pockets of anything which could provide intelligence if he fell into enemy hands – notes, coins, letters, photos, dockets, even bus, train, theatre or cinema tickets. Wireless operators were issued with the code of the day, printed on rice paper, so it could be eaten if necessary. David drew the escape

Bomb damage, Cologne, Germany. Factory chimneys often survived the blast better than walls.

aids and wallets of foreign currency for them all. Then he studied the details of the target maps and the large wall chart of Europe with its red tape stretching out along the route, this time into Holland, entering the necessary information on his captain-of-aircraft map.

The atmosphere was tense as they awaited the navs and bomb aimers coming in from their specialised briefings. The tension was partly dispelled when their navigator Murga joined them as they sat at their table, making notes.

'It's a piece of piss,' he told Drew, though to the skipper he said, 'It's a piece of cake.'

The main briefing covered details of the target and the importance of the attack, the route to be followed, which wave the squadron was in, expected opposition and tactics to be used. The method of marking the target varied according to weather conditions and visibility. *Wanganui* was code for sky marking, flares used when the target was not clearly visible. *Parramatta* was code for target indicators like cascading fireworks that were used for ground marking when visibility was good. And as weather conditions were critical to success, briefing always included a forecast by the Meteorological Officer, who described the synoptic situation, and projected a chart. It was a lot of gen to take in, but it was heartening to know how carefully the op had been planned, to cover every detail and foreseeable contingency. The briefing concluded with the CO's send-off. 'Good luck, chaps!'

The airmen, in battle dress and flying boots, walked to collect kit and rations from the crew room and parachutes from the drying room. Then it was 'All aboard' as they climbed with their awkward gear into buses driven by

WAAFs, who ferried them to dispersal bays. 'End of the penny section!' they joked. Their aircraft and ground crew were waiting.

David's pre-flight checks of the aircraft, both internal and external, were even more detailed than usual. He ran up the engines and tested all the systems; brakes, hydraulics, electrical and intercom. Cyril repeated the checks. Then the crew sat on the grass in the shade of the wing, discussing each man's job and the problems it involved, to refresh each crew member's understanding of the others' tasks. David wrote, *I tried to engender confidence in them, suppressing my own feelings, and this certainly eased the tension in the air.*

After the Wingco had driven up on his last-minute round to have a few words with them, David spoke with the ground crew, checking and signing Form 700, that veteran aircraft V Victor was airworthy.

'Time to harness up, boys,' David said, and ensured they had all put on their chute harnesses. The crew climbed up with their cumbersome parachute packs, Mae Wests and gear and groped their way in the dark along the narrow fuselage to their stations.

It was most difficult for Birdy and Boz. They were wearing bulky flying suits, padded and electrically heated to protect them against the paralysing cold they would have to endure. As rear gunner Birdy had the loneliest position in the plane. He had to climb over the spar supporting the tail-plane to get to his turret through small twin doors. It was a snug fit. Once he was shut in, his only contact was the intercom. 'Birdy's in his cage,' he reported. He had earlier checked and installed his four

*Allan Avery (Birdy), Rear Gunner, in electrically heated flying suit
and parachute harness, carrying parachute, flying helmet and
Mae West life jacket, Kelstern, 1944*

.303 Brownings with the armourers. Now he rotated the turret and elevated and depressed the guns to satisfy himself that all were in order. He then cocked them and plugged in his suit. Boz swung himself up into the mid-upper turret and onto his sling seat and went through the same procedure.

The other five had to climb over the main spar supporting the wing, not easy in such a confined space. Murga settled at his table facing the fuselage, changed his cap for his leather helmet, spread out his maps and charts, and arranged his instruments. Pop's table aft of Murga, which housed his radio equipment, faced forward. On a night flight he would draw the blackout curtains, but today the sun was still streaming in through the cockpit's perspex canopy. Drew sat on the step into his compartment in the nose with its commanding view. Cyril perched on his folding seat, looking at his set of dials and cocks.

David, now in his seat to the portside in the cockpit, sitting on his parachute, strapped himself in and put on his flying helmet, with oxygen mask clipped to one side, which he connected to its inlet. After plugging in his microphone, which was located in the oxygen mask, with its earphones in the helmet, he checked with each crew member on the intercom. His procedure began with the rear gunner. 'Rear gunner, everything OK?' Hearing the reply 'All OK', he continued systematically forward, each man hoping that his fear could not be detected in his voice.

Then it was a matter of waiting. Waiting for up to an hour until the signal came to taxi to the end of the runway. Stomachs churning, mouths dry. Shut in this cramped and claustrophobic cocoon of destruction and death, with its all-pervading oily smell, longing for a lungful of life-giving untainted air. Wondering if the op would go ahead. Hoping for a reprieve from hell.

In some ways this waiting was the worst part of an op, David was to find. Once he was up and flying, every atom of his whole being was on the job he had to do, every second demanded his full and undivided attention, his total concentration. But the waiting... After he had gone through every detail of the pre-flight check, ensuring everything, every single thing was in order ... then the fear he had fought so hard to push down would claw its way back into his consciousness. And on his heart and gut heavy as a bomb about to explode lay the dread of all that awaited them...

The danger of collision while orbiting, as all the squadron kites circled to gain height, and as they headed south across England... Then the critical timing needed to move into the main stream of aircraft, and again at the turning points in the blindness of night. Heading out across the Channel or the North Sea into the unknown. Crossing the enemy coast to run the gauntlet of flak, fighters and searchlights. The horror of the sights, the sounds, the smells. The terror, the raw terror, of each moment.

In the late afternoon light of the autumn day, England appeared all the more beautiful, *particularly as the thought was ever there that some of our chaps, maybe some of us, might never see it again*. The target, a V2 rocket storage depot at Eikenhorst in the Netherlands, was in a small wood northeast of The Hague. David had studied the photos closely during briefing, and had a picture of the area imprinted in his mind. Nearing Holland, Drew called, 'Enemy coast ahead', and at 12 000 feet they saw desultory flak, which by day appeared as puffs of black smoke. Drew, using his bombsight, ran up on the target and directed David over the indicators.

What relief they all knew in V Victor as he pressed the bomb release tit! They could feel the bombs falling – twelve 1000 pounders and four 500.

'That's a heap of rockets that won't be coming to Old Blighty,' Pop exulted.

Turning back, skirting The Hague, thankfully they met with little serious opposition, even though the weather was clear. All crews returned safely to Kelstern and David wrote, *It is a pity that the rest of the tour will not be like this. But this easy trip gave us all the more confidence for the future.*

Safely in dispersal three hours later, knots in stomachs loosened, gags in throats gone and the twitters – as the men called the urge to shit – dissipated, they climbed down from the aircraft. And smiled again. Feet firmly on the tarmac which overlaid the precious earth of England, breathing in the free air of the crisp English evening, all except David felt able to admit how scary it had been and their elation at being home. He kept a lid on his feelings, knowing how important it was for crew morale that he always appeared calm and confident.

At post-flight interrogation, they reported their observations and answered the Intelligence Officer's questions. But even as they enjoyed the standard issue biscuit, cocoa and well-earned tot of rum, they could still hear the roar of the engines in their heads and feel vibrations through their bodies.

Next day they saw the photo of their strike up in the nav aids room and the intelligence library. They had achieved the second-best results of the squadron. *After this we got rather cocky*, Drew wrote. But David certainly did not let it go to his head. He wrote, *One cannot relax even for a moment on an op. To do otherwise is to court disaster.*

Because the squadron was acting as army support and could be called at short notice to attack wherever needed, crews were kept on standby, and between concentrated bursts of activity there were lulls. It was frustrating, but David avowed, *The chaps of 625 are the best one could meet, and have the knack of making one feel at home immediately. There is no rank-consciousness and we are all members of one big happy family.* When not out on radar training with the Y, or a bombing exercise, he spent most of his time in the flight office, quietly observing and listening. There was so much to learn from these experienced airmen.

HAPPY VALLEY

On the evening of Saturday 23 September, David and his crew did their first night operation. This time it was into the heart of Germany, 'Happy Valley', as the industrial Ruhr Valley had been ironically dubbed by the airmen who had been pounding it since early in the war. Talking over what was ahead of them, David suggested each crew member try to keep a record of every trip, so that in the event that they did not come back, at least it could be sent to their family. Drew, married and deeply in love, adopted the idea and started a diary for 'My Dearest Thel'.

The target was the railway marshalling yards at the Düsseldorf suburb of Neuss. This was a major traffic centre and one of the enemy's few outlets from the Ruhr to the battle front. Capable of handling 2200 railway wagons every 24 hours, it was of great strategic importance. Navigators and bomb aimers joined the main briefing after their own, and they came in with long faces. Drew muttered, 'I don't mind telling you – it's put the breeze up me.' Nor was David reassured by the intelligence reports of heavy fighter defence and bags of flak, and the Met report of complete cloud cover en route. Obviously this op was not going to be as easy as their first trip.

With a load of twelve 1000-pounders and four 500s they took off just after 1900 hours and were shocked to witness the first casualties even before they left England. At the coastal concentration point where squadrons from different airfields converged to form one stream like a great swarm of bees, two bombers collided. It was a horrifying sight. A vivid flash lit up the sky. Flaming wreckage fell to earth, where it broke up, burning fiercely. 'Two of ours,' Drew groaned, and muttered a prayer. David agonised silently, 'It could be fourteen of our friends "going in".'

All nav lights were supposed to be extinguished at this point. David put out B Baker's, but many pilots, afraid of a repeat episode, continued to burn theirs until they were over France. Here, Murga had to contend with navigation difficulties. First the Gee radar packed up, and then the air position indicator (API) went u/s. They were not permitted to use the Y radar until almost on target, as the enemy was able to pick it up and direct fighters to intercept them. So Murga carried on without aids.

To interfere with enemy radar Drew frantically dropped 'window', long metallic paper strips, through the chute. But in his haste he also threw out the engineer's log, half of his own map and the silver propelling pencil David had bought in New York! Murga's dead reckoning was good and brought B Baker in over the target to drop its load. A dull glow through complete cloud cover, spreading out like red velvet sparkling with sequins, looked unexpectedly beautiful. But for those on the ground it was an inferno. To British aircrew it indicated success by preceding bombers.

The return flight was not easy for B Baker. The flak defence was ferocious. Pop and Boz thought they saw a Messerschmitt flash by, but it sheered off before Pop could stammer out a warning. The wind had changed and without instruments Murga had no means of finding the exact amount of drift. Before the Gee came good they were a fair way north off track and found themselves over the Frisian Islands. The solitary aircraft was an easy target for the many guns which suddenly opened up below and put some small holes in B Baker. *Needless to say*, David wrote later, *we wasted no time in getting out of that area.* He was pleased that they managed to return to base by the briefed time, as did all their squadron aircraft.

Home again after three hours, the crew swapped notes.

'I felt frightened all the way,' Drew admitted.

'Just a little bit shaky,' was Boz's reaction

'More than just a little bit,' Birdy added. 'Had the shits good and proper.'

David saw it as *a good lesson for future ops at night*, because it made Drew, Boz and Birdy search the sky even harder. Their concentration was critical. There might be no second chance.

They had tea, rum and biscuits with an understanding female Interrogation Officer. Drew, who always appreciated a good-looking female, cheerfully handed over the camera magazine to a 'slashing good' WAAF Section Officer. Then at last they could enjoy their bacon and eggs. An open bar in the Mess also helped them to readjust before going off to their billets 'to sleep the sleep of the just,' Drew said.

But David's was haunted by the sight of the two colliding bombers.

Altogether 3500 tons of bombs had been dropped on three major Ruhr targets that night. And twenty-two British planes were missing. One hundred and fifty-four men.

FRANCE

Over the next four days David and his crew made three daylight sorties to France. These were in support of the Allied troops advancing on Calais. One aim was to knock out the enemy's long-range heavy guns trained across the Channel towards Hellfire Corner, as the Dover area was known. Drew lamented, *We were dug out at an unearthly hour for briefing and breakfast.* The first briefing was even more detailed than usual, as the target was very small – railway guns, mounted on rolling stock which could be readily moved. It would require great accuracy on the part of pilot and bomb aimer, flying at a lower level, to pinpoint the target.

It was their first experience of another of Butch Harris's strategies – the Master Bomber. The Master Bomber would broadcast instructions to the main force of Lancasters and Halifaxes, coordinating and concentrating the attack. On this op his code name was *Boxkite 1*. Main Force's was *Samson*. The code word for Abandon Mission, which everybody hoped they would not hear, was *New York*.

Briefed to fly between 8000 and 10 000 feet, at the English coast David was surprised to hear on the radio telephone, '*Boxkite 1* to *Samson*, Basement 5.' Descending to 5000 feet they broke through cloud cover over the Channel at the Straits of Dover. A second command had the force descending to 4000 feet, and it was remarkable to see all the aircraft with their flaps and undercarriages down in order to lose height quickly. Even though the Master Bomber's deputy, *Boxkite 2*, went down to 800 feet, he could not identify the target. So the force was ordered to descend to 2000 feet and orbit while he made another attempt. It was an unnerving experience to have so many bomb-laden planes circling in close proximity.

Then came the unwelcome command, '*Boxkite 1* to *Samson. New York.*' Bombs were in short supply, and it was crucial not to waste them. Drew wrote, *It was enough to make a saint swear. And we aren't saints. So the air was blue around us. We had been orbiting for quite a while and then to have to abandon when we had got that close was lousy.*

Flying so low they could see details of farms, houses and hedgerows, they seemed to whizz along the French coast towards Cap Gris Nez, where they had their first encounter with light anti-aircraft fire. David was intrigued by the patterns woven by the tracers, pretty as a cloud of fireflies, pretty but so deadly. They also met with heavy flak, which burst so close it shook the plane. But even after they crossed the Channel, their troubles were not over. Landing back at base in a cross-wind with a full bomb load was hair-raising. Drew held the seat and glued his eyes to the flight engineer's panel, watching for warning lights. He breathed a silent prayer as *Dave did the ropiest landing he had ever done since we crewed up. It was OK though and nothing happened.* David admitted in his diary, *The landing was not of the best. But it was a consolation to see everyone else doing ropey touchdowns.*

Everyone cheered up when they were told at interrogation that it would be counted as an op. But later in the day, when this decision was countermanded, it raised a storm among the aircrew. Thirty ops had to be flown to complete a tour before an airman had a break from operational duties. To the men who had just gone through almost three and a half gruelling hours, only to have their efforts frustrated by poor visibility, it seemed grossly unfair and was deeply resented.

Next morning they were called early again to repeat the trip to Cap Gris Nez to target another 'Big Bertha' long-range heavy gun emplacement. 'Let's hope the Met does not boob as it did yesterday,' David said tersely.

Again there was a special briefing as this was a very small and sensitive target, with Allied troops within 2000 yards. If necessary, the troops would use yellow ground strips or smoke markers to show their positions. Pathfinder marking and red indicators would show the target and bombing was again to be done on orders from the Master Bomber. His code name was *Toolkit*, Main Force was *Strongman,* and Abandon Mission was *Mincemeat.* David was always intrigued by the code words and would have liked to supply some himself. He and Drew had memorised their target photos thoroughly, and as soon as they had crossed the English coast Drew checked and rechecked his bomb sight settings and fused the bombs. *Pickwick* was the code name for the order to release the bombs and they were glad to hear it, bombing the leading edge of the dense black smoke which was beginning to rise, lit by vivid red flashes.

Flying east toward the target, David had found it rather difficult to see. The bright sunlight reflecting off water and patches of cloud was dazzling. But turning back he was thrilled to see the white cliffs of Dover standing out brilliantly against the green background of England. *I can understand how Englishmen welcome this first sight of their homeland*, he wrote later. But nostalgia for him was the scent of boronia or wattle wafting out when he opened a parcel from Australia.

On the third morning they were called even earlier and briefed again for Calais. *The inhabitants must be thoroughly fed up with our calls*, David observed. *It seems a pity to destroy part of the town when obliterating small targets*. As it was, most of the surrounding country had been flooded by the Germans for defence.

'Poor bloody civilians,' Pop empathised.

It was much easier to do the necessary checks in daylight than by night in the blackout and at 0755 hours B Baker took off with its usual load, following an almost identical route as the previous day's. The MB's call sign was *Nelson*, Main Force *Walpole* and Abandon Mission was *London*. On leaving the English coast they heard '*Nelson 1* to *Walpole* – basement 5', so they had to descend. They watched Baker's bombs straddle the target and could see the blast rings of the 1000 pounders spreading. But they could not turn away until the camera finished running.

Back at the station they were heartened to find that none of 625's aircraft had been lost. Over lunch they

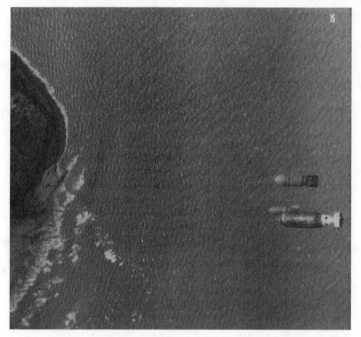

High Explosive bombs going down over Calais, 1944

listened to a BBC report of the heavies' raid, hearing of the damage inflicted by 1000 tons of bombs. And when they saw their own good results in the photos, they were satisfied.

The following day, Canadian troops liberated Calais. All the French Channel ports were now in Allied hands. This was of great strategic importance for getting supplies to the invasion forces, although the facilities required extensive repairs and many sunken vessels had to be cleared. The next major port to be won was Antwerp, still tightly held by German troops. 'Look out, Antwerp!' the crews said to each other. 'We'll be visiting you soon for sure.'

Battle Order 204 (5)
Put on Parachutes!

Coming round seconds later, revived by the rush of cold air, David realised the danger. He struggled desperately with his left hand to pull the aircraft up and get Dog on an even keel.

Then he checked that all his men were unhurt.

'Rear gunner OK?'

'Mid upper gunner OK?'

'Wireless operator OK?'

'Navigator OK?'

'Flight engineer OK?'

'Bomb aimer OK?'

Satisfied that none of his crew was injured, David gave the order they dreaded, 'Put on parachutes and stand by!'

. . . .

From his bomb aimer's compartment in the nose of the plane Drew could see the holes torn by the shrapnel and David's hand dripping blood. 'God, what if we have to bale out here!' he thought in dismay as he put on his parachute.

• • • • • • • • • • • • • • • •

David asked his flight engineer, Cyril, to bandage his hand, which was now bleeding profusely.

Cyril had just done this, when Dog was hit again.

This time Cyril also was hit. In the chest. Luckily for him the shrapnel struck his escape aids, deflecting it and saving him from a more serious wound.

David also copped it again. More in his shoulder. More in his right knee. More in his right thigh.

Resolutely, he refused to have the emergency morphine injection. Although it would ease his pain it would also slow his reflexes. He knew he needed every atom of concentration to bring his badly damaged aircraft and his precious crew to safety.

Because of the damage, David had to drop below the main stream. This made them more vulnerable than ever.

• • • • • • • • • • • • • • • •

As they crossed the Rhine, limping Dog was hit for the third time.

*Crew and ground crew beside J Jig. L-R back: David in Mae West,
Reg Murr in parachute harness, Cyril Bailey, Noel Ferguson.
Front: Curly, Lofty, Drew Fisher, Bill, and Reg Watson in parachute
harness. Note entry door with ladder.*

11 J Jig

A week of frustration followed. All flying was scrubbed because of the weather. No operations were mounted and training exercises had to be abandoned. With the rain the station had become a quagmire and any aircraft which taxied off the perimeter track would have been instantly bogged. So except for a stint of air-to-air firing along the coast, when Boz managed to shoot away an aerial, David continued to spend many hours in the intelligence library, avidly following the course of the invasion across France and the Low Countries, studying reports and photos of air strikes, absorbing as much as he could.

On the fourth day they stood by, tensely waiting for the announcement over the Tannoy public address system, 'Run up aircraft', which usually indicated an op was imminent. It did not come. On the seventh day the call came. But the op did not eventuate, although the aircraft were already bombed up. B Baker had been sent away for engine modification and David and his crew had yet another plane,

J Jig, which they were delighted had been allocated to them as their own. David wrote with satisfaction, *Flying is easier for the crew when they are used to one particular aircraft.*

The next day's call meant business. Serious business. A night operation, which made some of the crew 'feel funny in the tum'. The target was Saarbrücken, a town in Germany that the RAF had rarely attacked, so little was known about its defences. The American Third Army, which was advancing in the area, had requested the raid on the railway marshalling yards in order to block German supply routes. Five hundred and thirty-one Lancs and twenty Mosquitoes were to take part. On hearing this, Drew admitted to 'ring twitter'. When the Met Officer told them that the route was designed to take them under low cloud over France, David felt concerned, as he foresaw the high risk of collisions with a great number of aircraft in restricted airspace.

For the first time their load included a 'cookie' and twelve 500-pound incendiary clusters. The cookie was a massive 4000-pound bomb in a special light casing designed to maximise its blast. The incendiary clusters, dropped after it, should raise a firestorm, as they had done so spectacularly in Hamburg the previous year. At 1000 feet over France all the crew kept an extra sharp watch and David left on the dim resin lights, designed for formation keeping, to minimise the danger of collision. They were relieved to be able to climb to the briefed height of 15 000 feet as soon as they passed the cold front. But when Drew asked for the bomb doors to be opened several minutes too soon, everyone became jittery. With the doors open, the plane was much less manoeuvrable and had to keep a straight and level course, making it more vulnerable. With flak coming up all around, the crew were very jumpy by the time Drew pressed the tit. And at least some said a silent 'Thank you, God,' as David closed the bomb doors and they turned away. It was another useful lesson. He wrote, *The doors certainly will not be opened too early in the future... All these incidents are helping to weld the crew into a fine composite fighting unit.*

Drew was apologetic, 'What a boob! I won't do that again, chaps!'

But another unpleasant experience and test of nerves awaited them on their return journey. Nearing the East Anglian coast, Pop passed on a message he had decoded. The squadron had been diverted to Coltishall, a fighter base near Norwich. There they were 'stacked' up to 4 000 feet, orbiting for one hour and seventeen minutes while other Lancs and Mossies were brought in. With the air full of kites flying in and out of clouds and heavy rain, it was a living nightmare. They were hugely relieved when their call to land came. After a smooth touch down, Jig started jarring and jumping and David thought a tyre must have blown. But it was the steel-mesh landing strip for fighters which was buckling under the weight of the heavy aircraft.

After a brief interrogation they were given a meal of snags and spuds. Drew was irked when he and Pop were taken to sleep in a ground crews' hut, while 'the kids' slept between sheets in officers' beds! David and Murga had to make do with armchairs in the Mess. David wrote afterwards, *It was not too bad.*

They spent the next morning with pilots of an Australian Spitfire squadron, watching with admiration as one made an almost perfect belly landing. They also had their first view of a Tempest, and looked over Mustangs and Mosquitoes.

After Jig had been refuelled by two of the wickedest WAAFs Drew had ever seen, they flew back to Kelstern, where they shared their reactions on the trip.

'Had the shits good and proper over the target area,' Birdy said. 'I kept checking to make sure I could get out of the turret if necessary.'

Cyril admitted, 'I also nearly needed a clean pair of pants.'

'I had a slight attack of ring twitters,' Boz said, 'and at times the aerial insulators gave me mild heart attacks when I thought they were enemy fighters.'

'I was not the happiest little Australian in the world,' Drew confessed.

And they all concurred with Pop's verdict, 'It was a weary journey. Six hours and 50 minutes. And then we didn't even get home.'

All their squadron returned safely, but three Lancasters of the force were lost.

GERMANY AGAIN

Early next morning there was quite a flap when a Tannoy announcement called crews on the Battle Order for briefing at 9.30. They were on it. It was a daylight raid on Emmerich, northwest of the Ruhr, to wipe out a German supply base and communications centre, thus protecting an exposed flank of the Allied army on the Rhine. It was a major operation. Other Rhineland towns were to be attacked simultaneously by other waves.

On the preliminary run-up, Jig was found to have a malfunctioning radiator shutter. Watched by the Wingco, Chief Technical Officer and the Engineering Officer, the erks, as the ground crew were known, worked hard on the replacement, which also proved useless. By then both aircrew and ground crew were in a sweat. Would they get off in time? Finally all was in order and Jig was airborne half a minute before the deadline. By good navigation on Murga's part they caught up with the stream at the concentration point. A group of Halifaxes diverged to another target and David wondered if Peter was among them. The main body of 340 Lancs and ten Mossies carried on across Holland, where widespread flooding caused by the Germans was plainly visible. How much this war had cost the Dutch!

Approaching the target at 11 000 feet was awkward, as both heavy and light flak, the most severe they had yet encountered, were having a deadly effect. Shrapnel was thumping on J Jig, and another Lanc went down in flames only 50 yards away – a gut-wrenching, heart-rending sight.

They dropped their cookie and twelve incendiary clusters, and even at 11 000 feet they could feel the cookies exploding. They were relieved to turn away, only to see two more aircraft ahead in trouble, with smoke pouring from their engines. Their crews baled out successfully and Jig's crew were able to plot the approximate position where those crews would land. In all they saw 24 chutes in the air at once. 'Better to be POWs than incinerated,' they thought. But they knew that the four pilots probably had not got out.

When they were circling over base to land, Drew was irate when 'some whining sod wanted everything cleared out of his way 'cos he had to land on three engines with incendiaries in his wing.' Flying Control wanted him to keep his place in the queue, but David thought it was a valid request and deliberately overshot the runway, as did the pilot behind. So this bod, who happened to be a Squadron Leader, was able to land his aircraft, damaged by incendiaries dropped from a friendly plane flying above it.

The kids ribbed Dave, the perfect gentleman, about it and he lost his temper a bit. 'There, but for the grace of God...,' he reminded them. 'We may need to do the same some time.'

At interrogation, as well as details about the target, David and his crew were able to give information about the men who had baled out. The Groupie seemed favourably impressed. So the men were chuffed. Cyril had found the op 'very exciting'. Birdy was 'too interested to be frightened'. Boz felt 'very confident, like a sightseer'. But for Pop, who 'had nothing to do over the target except watch and pray, the intensity of the AA defences resulted in great twitter'. David, as usual, kept his own counsel.

Next day when the press described it as the biggest assault of the war, with 3000 heavy bombers over the Reich, including 1400 US Fortresses and Liberators, 900 RAF heavies and an escort of 1500 fighters, David went to the nearby town of Louth to church. The beautiful spire of St James', built in the fifteenth century, had been a landmark to comfort him for almost a month now. As had the splendid towers of even older Lincoln Cathedral. And he was deeply thankful for them. He was saddened, too, for the French and Dutch and German churches which had been destroyed by Allied bombing. How much longer would this horrific war, with its hideous destruction of people and beautiful historic buildings, go on? When would it end?

As he sat quietly after the service, gazing up at the centuries-old spacious arches and the lofty vaulted ceiling, David knew he must not let himself dwell on the thought of people maimed and killed, of minds filled with horrendous images and memories, of homes reduced to pitiful rubble and gracious public buildings to smouldering ruins. He must think of them only as targets. Targets which, if not destroyed would allow the Nazi war machine to continue to perpetrate its own devastation, its enslavement of free peoples, its evil values and lust for cruel dominance. As for those crews shot down, missing, lost, dead, whether allied or enemy, they were doing their job, serving their country. 'Let them rest in peace, Lord,' he prayed, 'and let the memory of them stay bright in the minds and hearts of those who loved them, and whom they loved.'

12 Erks and Armourers

There more days of inactivity followed due to duff weather. But that did not stop David going out to J Jig each morning to check the plane and talk with its ground crew, the resourceful and dedicated erks – engine fitters, airframe riggers and others representing the many trades and skills necessary to keep aircraft operational. Each aircraft was allotted its own ground crew, who went into action as soon as the plane returned from any flying, no matter what time of night or day, checking, maintaining, repairing or rectifying any items listed by the crew in the snag book, and searching for other problems only their trained eyes could identify. Regardless of rain, wind and freezing cold, they worked tirelessly to keep 'their kite' in tiptop condition, ready to fly again when the next op was called.

Fitters worked on the engines, which as well as propelling the aircraft, powered all its equipment and accessories. Each of the four operated specific items, such

Sitting on bombs and trailer, L-R: Pop, Boz, Drew, Murga.
The Squadron's code letters were CF.

as gun turrets, bomb sight and doors, and the electrical generators for Gee and Y, to name but a few. Fitters or WAAFs were responsible for the refuelling, an awkward job which usually took three people half an hour. A typical fuel load was 1000 gallons. At a mile a gallon this would take the aircraft to Happy Valley and back, with a little in reserve. If the fuel load was greater, the pilot would know he had a longer haul ahead. Riggers looked for and repaired damage and faults in the fuselage.

Erks would also be there in their oil-stained clothing at the run-up to deal with any defects or malfunctions which might be revealed. They would be there before take-off, hoping the pilot would find nothing to enter on Form 700, which would mean their kite was u/s, resulting in a frenzy of activity to make it airworthy in time. They would chat to their pilot to ease the tension of waiting until it was time to start engines. They would listen to their Merlins throbbing into life, running sweet and true, settling into a steady rhythmic roar. Then when the green signal by Aldis lamp shone from the control caravan at the end of the runway, they exchanged the thumbs-up sign with the pilot. This was the signal they had all waited for, that would set their kite, their crew off. Now it was 'Chocks away'. And they would feel the blast of air from the props and hear the squeal of brakes, as their pilot rolled their kite out of dispersal, taxying along the perimeter track.

They would watch her growing smaller, one in a line of Lancs moving slowly, pregnant with bombs, heavy with fuel, earthbound clumsiness belying her speed and grace in the air. They would suck in their breath as their kite finally reached the end of the runway in use. They

Gunners Boz and Birdy wearing harness and carrying parachute packs

would hear their four Merlins bellow their power as their kite surged forward, gathering speed, lifting off into her rightful element. They would watch her underbelly, black against the grey day, or her nav lights, red and green against the black night, as she gained height, then disappeared from sight.

Heading where? Into what?

'God speed,' they would murmur, knowing they had done everything they could to ensure the safety of their boys.

Then they would load up their tool kits and head back to their quarters to snatch some food and a few hours of desperately needed sleep, before waking in time to return to dispersal to welcome their kite, their boys back home. Or wait, wondering, watching, hoping, praying, for the ones who did not make it. Staring at the empty sky. Staring at the empty dispersal bay. Straining their ears for the sound of their Merlins, their kite. Swallowing hard. Forcing down their grief. Muttering, 'Bloody Huns'. Turning away. Hollow with emptiness. Pierced with pain. 'This bloody war. I could be home snug in bed with the wife now instead of freezing my butt off out here on this wasteland. Bloody war. Bloody Hitler. Blast him to hell.'

Armourers, too, played a critical role in the Lancaster team. Not only did they do the task of bombing up, loading the bombs, they were also responsible for seeing to the armaments, ensuring the guns were all in working order. DIs, as daily inspections were known, were meticulously carried out on all the guns and turrets as well as the bomb gear. Icing at high altitudes affected the guns and could crack the perspex turrets. Guns had to be cleaned after each op or training exercise, ammunition tanks filled and belt alignments corrected to avoid jamming or stoppages. It was life or death stuff for the aircrew and the armourers took their work very seriously. Birdy and Boz usually went out to check the mounting of their guns, which were taken off the aircraft after each sortie.

The first indication that an op was planned was always the call on the Tannoy, 'Armourers report to bomb dump.' Each team usually looked after five planes and had to collect the type and number of bombs specified for that particular raid. It was heavy, exacting work requiring brawn but also brains, manhandling the bombs onto special trolleys to be towed to dispersals. A portable winch put aboard the aircraft was used to lift the bombs into the 33-foot bomb bay in the plane's belly, which extended almost half its length. They had to be stowed according to the order in which they would be used, 1000-pounders before 500s, cookies before incendiaries. It took upwards of 45 minutes to load a cookie and incendiaries. And there was no room for error. Each bomb was clamped for safety in flight and suspended by its own specially designed hook, with an electro-magnetic release for easy dropping over the target. A typical bomb load was 14 000 pounds. In loading over 30 tons of bombs armourers worked under pressure for at least four hours, so were always glad of help from the crew in bombing up if an op was called at short notice.

13 Holland and Operation Hurricane

Despite the erks' vigilance, glitches sometimes still occurred. Called at 0230 for a sortie to Fort Fredrik Hendrik, where long-range German guns protected Antwerp, Drew and Murga made a disquieting discovery while gaining height. The Gee was coded, but the necessary info for decoding had not been supplied, and the Y was u/s. David pinpointed Jig over the airfield so Murga could take a fix, and with some rapid calculation work out their course by dead reckoning. David, as usual, saw the positive side of what could have been a problem and wrote afterwards in his ops diary, *This sort of thing gives us all added confidence in each other – the gen crew.*

When they came out of ten-tenths cloud over the North Sea into clear skies above the target, Drew heaved a sigh of relief. He could plainly see the end of the bridge which was the aiming point, and called, 'Bomb aimer to

Fort Fredrik Hendrik, Netherlands. Smoke on R from Target Indicators. Note bomb craters from earlier raid. October 1944.

pilot. Open bomb doors.' He and Pop watched as twelve 1000 pounders and four 500s went down. But it was scary when one 1000 pounder hung up temporarily, and they were thankful to see it go. All hit very close. The kids rated the trip as quiet and disappointing, but David was satisfied with the good results their photo showed.

HAPPY VALLEY AGAIN — OPERATION HURRICANE

The next two ops were certainly no picnic. As part of Butch Harris's strategy to disable enemy supplies, 625 Squadron Lancs were to join a mighty joint Bomber Command and US Air Force attack on the famous Thyssen steelworks, the largest in Germany, at Duisburg. Harris called for Maximum Effort in Operation Hurricane, to demonstrate to the Nazi chiefs the overwhelming superiority of the Allied Air Forces. The RAF sent off 1013 aircraft, including 519 Lancasters in the first wave, with a second wave of 1005 two hours later including 498 Lancs.

At Kelstern, 32 crews were on Battle Order 178. Woken by orderlies at 0215 on Saturday 14 October, there were groans and rude comments when they heard their daylight destination. 'That bloody Happy Valley again! In daylight, too.'

The Ruhr certainly held no attraction. Drew wrote, *So here we are on 'the effort', though I would just as soon be out of it,* while David wrote with resignation, *Our likes and dislikes have no effect on Butch Harris's policy and strategy.*

As the weather was fairly good, there was to be no Pathfinder flare marking the target. The crews were to rely purely on visual bombing. Extra photographs of the steelworks, as well as the usual topographical and target maps, were provided to assist the bomb aimers. J Jig took off on schedule at 0640 hours loaded with twelve 1000-pounders and four long-delay 500s.

For the Kelstern crews the op got off to a terrible start. As they taxied round the perimeter track, they saw one of the Lancs ahead trying to return to the runway with an engine on fire. But it did not quite reach it. They saw five chutes open as it was losing height. It crashed on a nearby farm. With a horrendous explosion the bombs went up. As the other crews took off, everybody was thinking about their friends who had gone in with their burning kite.

Climbing through high cloud to 18 000 feet, icing became a problem, slowing them down. But Jig arrived just in time over the target and met heavy flak which put holes in the port wing. An aircraft blew up about 50 yards ahead, showering Jig with debris which punctured the metal skin. The computer box was u/s, so bombs had to be dropped using manual settings. Because of the heavy pall of smoke hanging over the steelworks, the buildings could not be identified. Drew decided, 'I'll drop my lot in the centre of the pall.' After watching the long-delays go down, he carried out his check of the bomb bay. No hang-up this time, thank God. He gave the order to close the bomb doors and they could turn away. But a mistake in the course setting took them even further over the target, until David spotted the error and speedily rectified it, much to everyone's relief.

'Sorry, Skipper,' Murga muttered. 'I won't make that error again.'

'Thought we would never get out of it,' Pop said afterwards.

For the first time they saw 'scarecrows', six of them, which they had been told were an enemy device, an aerial flare which simulated exploding aircraft, designed to undermine morale. Drew thought they were aircraft and put on his parachute in readiness for baling out, but David wondered. It seems that the chiefs of Bomber Command hoped that if their crews believed they were only seeing enemy devices, they would not be so stressed by the sight of what were in fact RAF planes going down in flames.

On the homeward flight the cloud base was very low, which necessitated breaking through out to sea, then turning in to Louth at 200 feet.

'Look out for your favourite spire, Skipper!' Boz called from his vantage point.

As Kelstern was 400 feet up on the wolds, they climbed rapidly to come in almost at ground level.

'Glad we haven't got a duff pilot,' the crew agreed.

They had been airborne for four and three-quarter tense hours and they were more than ready for a meal and longing for a kip.

But as they arrived in dispersal they heard an ominous Tannoy message: 'All armourers report to the bomb dump.'

Rumours began to fly immediately.

Bomber Command had just dropped 4500 tons of bombs on Duisburg. It was a record day raid. Thirteen Lancs and two Halis had been lost. Wasn't that enough? No. Not for Butch Harris. Operation Hurricane had not blown itself out yet. He had already ordered a second raid to follow that night. The pre-flight meal was scheduled for 1730 and the briefing for 1815. 'What does he think we are?' men grumbled. 'Robots?'

After lunch, many, including Jig's crew, went to snatch

Lancaster dropping bombs, a cookie and incendiaries
(AWM neg. no. 12293)

some sleep. But David spent the time checking the work on Jig. Noticing a large fuel load, he knew they were in for another long trip.

At the briefing they were told that their target was again Duisburg, a city of 450 000, the world's largest inland river port. The aim was to remove it from the map. 'No wonder Butcher has earned his nickname,' some of the men were heard to mutter.

Five aircraft of 625 Squadron were to go in as part of a separate smaller attack two hours after the first major wave. On hearing that Jig was one of these, Drew said, 'I felt like howling.'

It was the last straw when all take-offs were delayed

by one and a half hours. So the hunt was on to find a place to catch a bit of shut-eye. They finally took off thirty minutes after midnight with their deadly load, twelve 1000-pounders and four 500s.

Over 150 miles from the target the glow was visible, and it spread even further as they approached. Numerous fires were merging into one huge conflagration. The whole city was like a writhing mass of bloody entrails, a seething mass of flames. Despite this, flak was intense and searchlights swept the sky relentlessly. After dropping its load, Jig was almost 'coned' by them – a sitting duck. But David put the nose down to pick up speed and headed for home. Drew reported that the clock registered more than 210 miles per hour, *But it wasn't anywhere near fast enough for me. 310 would have been better.* Alone and vulnerable, they had to run the gauntlet along a lane of fighter flares from three JU88s and had to take evasive action from one. When the Junkers saw Jig prepared for its attack, it sheered off in search of easier prey, to the relief of everyone on board Jig. They were glad to rejoin the stream over the French coast. After four hours and thirty-five minutes flying, the weary crew landed thankfully at Kelstern at 0505. David wrote, *I have never appreciated bed more, having been out of it for twenty-nine and a half hours. Two trips in one day make one excessively tired.*

Cyril's memory of the raid was a complete blank. Birdy said, 'I was too tired to be scared, but was worried about my night vision from searchlights.' Boz said, 'I was weary and not at all happy when the fighter made a pass at us.'

Pop's comment summed it up: 'The outstanding

feature was the terrific red glow from previous attacks.'

All 625 Squadron's aircraft returned, but five Lancs and two Halis were lost from the main force. Over 10 000 tons of bombs had been dropped in the two raids.

David wrote, *I feel I have now avenged Frank, who was killed over this target in May.*

But there had been another death, though David did not know of it. Peter was a Hali pilot.

Peter Lord as trainee

Battle Order 204 (6)
Take Up Crash Positions!

'Third time unlucky!' each crew member muttered under his breath, frigid with fear as he prayed.

'But if anyone can get out of this, it's our Dave,' Drew thought, taking comfort in his skipper's skill and determination.

'Pilot to wireless operator. Fire a Very light for assistance.'

'Wireless operator to pilot. Very light going up.'

After Reg sent up the red Very light for an escort, a couple of RAF fighters checked them out. But as Dog's engines were still functioning, the fighters left them to it.

Putting on speed, David headed for the emergency airfield at Juvincourt in France. But then, even though he was weak from loss of blood, he decided to try to carry on to Woodbridge, an emergency airfield in England.

Dog's instrument panel was badly damaged,

and all the radar sets were out of commission, so Charles navigated by dead reckoning while Drew map-read. 'Thank God it's daylight,' Drew thought.

Boz and Birdy in their gun turrets scanned the sky in every direction for more enemy fighters harassing the returning bomber stream. Always on the lookout for an easy kill, the deadly swift Messerschmitts and Junkers 88s would find the disabled Lancaster a ready target to down.

• • • • • • • • • • • • • • • • •

But the skies remained clear and Dog limped across the Channel.

'Over England at last!' they all breathed.

But the crew's relief was short-lived. Despite the holed petrol tank, Cyril judged there was still enough fuel for one more leg. Summoning every atom of his rapidly dwindling strength, David set course for Lincolnshire and their home base, Kelstern. Fearing that he might not be able to land the damaged kite safely, he asked each crew member in turn if he wanted to bale out. Everyone opted to stay. So David gave the order no one wanted to hear.

'Take up crash positions!'

They braced themselves and crouched through the last fateful moments as Dog descended.

• • • • • • • • • • • • • • • • •

Would they make it? Was this the ending each man had always known might be his – burned to death as his plane crashed down?

4,500 tons –and they strike again

Express Air Reporter

WAVE on wave of R.A.F. heavies again began going out over the East Coast just before dusk last night.

Achtung radio soon reported bomber spearheads over Western Germany, "with more coming in," and later said that raiders were approaching the Hanover-Brunswick area.

The R.A.F. were swiftly following up their Monday night blow at the Krupps city, Essen, which was blasted by 4,500 tons.

This arsenal, now more important than ever, has lost one of its main defences—the radar network stretched along the French and Belgian coast which gave warning long in advance of the R.A.F.'s approach.

Though every available gun round Essen was put into action, R.A.F. losses were only eight out of 1,000 planes.

In the last 1,000-bomber raid on Essen on April 26, losses were 29.

4,500 TONS ON ESSEN BY 1,000 BOMBERS

THROUGH SNOWSTORMS AND INTENSE FLAK

More than 1,000 R.A.F. bombers flew through severe snowstorms and an intense barrage on Monday night to make a very heavy attack on the great armament and ... centre of Essen, the home of ...

...rms lasted from soon after the Con... reached to within 50 miles of the ... over Essen itself the cloud was so ... the Pathfinders had constantly to ... the area. The sky markers were ... by the crews of the main striking ... on after the first bombs had gone ... began to glow with the reflection ... es started below. Towards the ... attack the defences were ... trong forces of fighters, whose ... een along the route leading ...get.

...tons of high-explosive and ... were dropped on Essen ... mand has now dropped ... s on the Ruhr during ... icked the four largest ...rg, Dortmund, and ...

...has lost much of his ... it along the coasts ... he no longer has ... approach of our ... t the enemy had ... and guns and mass ... city. Crews reported ... ble gun was brought into

Newspaper reports of Bomber Command raids on Essen in Happy Valley

14 'Three of our aircraft are missing'

Four welcome days of stand-down followed the Duisburg raids and Jig was given a thorough cleaning and overhaul. David commented, 'It is remarkable what a mess rain can make.' Equipment became wet and the damp affected engines, made radar sets and intercoms u/s, and electrical equipment, with over 400 valves, could be damaged. He was glad Jig was in good trim when the next battle order was posted. It was to be their deepest penetration yet into Germany, to Stuttgart. On the fourth night after Duisburg they took off, again part of the second wave in a total force of 565 Lancasters and eighteen Mosquitoes.

At briefing they had been warned to expect fighter resistance and heavy searchlight concentrations on the devious route across southern Germany, especially in the vicinity of major cities like Frankfurt, Mainz, Karlsruhe and Mannheim. But

Year 1944 Month | Date	Aircraft Type	No.	Pilot, or 1st Pilot	2nd Pilot, Pupil or Passenger	Duty (Including Results and Remarks)
—	—	—	—	—	— Totals Brought Forward
OCTOBER	2 LANCASTER 1	C	SELF	CREW	AIR-AIR FIRING, BOMBING EXERCISE
"	5 LANCASTER III	J	SELF	CREW	OPERATIONS — MARSHALLING YARDS
					SAAR BRUCKEN
					1 X 4000 12 X 500 INC. CLUSTERS HT. 15,000
					DIVERTED TO COLTISHALL
"	6 "	J	SELF	CREW	COLTISHALL - BASE
"	7 "	J	SELF	CREW	OPERATIONS — TOWN, DOCKS
					EMMERICH
					1 X 4000 12 X 500 INC. CLUSTERS
					... X 4 INC. HT. 11,000
"	10 "	J	SELF	CREW	FIGHTER AFFILIATION
"	12 "	J	SELF	CREW	OPERATIONS — GUN EMPLACEMENTS
					FORT FREDRIK HENDRIK (SCHELDT EST)
					13 X 1000 4 X 500 HT. 9,500
"	14 "	J	SELF	CREW	OPERATIONS — STEEL WORKS
					DUISBURG
					12 X 1000 4 X 500 HT. 18,000
"	14 "	J	SELF	CREW	OPERATIONS — CITY AREA
					DUISBURG
					12 X 1000 4 X 500 HT. 20,000
	19 "	J	SELF	CREW	OPERATIONS — MAGNETO, SPARK PLUG
					FACTORY STUTTGART
					12 X 1000 4 X 500 HT. 17,000
			GRAND TOTAL [Cols. (1) to (10)] 458 Hrs 00 Mins.		Totals Carried Forward

An opening from David's flying logbook

not long after take-off they had a more immediate problem. While they were climbing through cloud, snow leaked into the front turret, dripping into the intercom plug, rendering the system practically u/s for the remainder of the trip, so most of the time they had to fall back on using signal lights. But the intercom still emitted shrieks and squeals which added to the stress. To make matters worse, icing caused the air-speed indicator to cease functioning and David had to judge speed by other instruments, the artificial horizon and engine revs. It was exhausting.

SINGLE-ENGINE AIRCRAFT				MULTI-ENGINE AIRCRAFT						Passenger	INSTR/CLOUD FLYING [incl. in cols. (1) to (10)]		LINK TRAINER
DAY		NIGHT		DAY			NIGHT						
Dual	Pilot	Dual	Pilot	Dual	1st Pilot	2nd Pilot	Dual	1st Pilot	2nd Pilot		Dual	Pilot	
(1)	(2)	(3)	(4)	(5)	(6)	(7)	(8)	(9)	(10)	(11)	(12)	(13)	
29.35	27.10	2.55	1.05	98.25	139.55	20.05	26.20	73.55	3.45	10.15	38.55	5.50	65.55
					2.30								
								6.50				2.25	
					.45								
					3.30								35
					1.20								
					3.05							.25	
					4.45								
								5.05				1.36	
								7.00				2.20	
29.35	27.10	2.55	1.05	98.25	155.50	20.05	26.20	92.50	3.45	10.15	38.55	12.35	66.30
(1)	(2)	(3)	(4)	(5)	(6)	(7)	(8)	(9)	(10)	(11)	(12)	(13)	

Nevertheless, they arrived over the target on schedule to see a good healthy glow through the heavy cloud cover and they carried out their part in yet another of Butch Harris's strategic raids, dropping their twelve 1000-pounders and four 500-pounders on the Bosch factory, whose spark plugs were a vital component in every engine. It was a long, cold, tiring trip back. As it was a seven-hour flight, they had taken 'wakey-wakey' pills for the first time, to keep them alert. It was the last time too. 'Never again!' they all declared on return. The bitter caffeine left a most unpleasant taste, and had made Birdy sick and Cyril and Boz sleepy!

The next op was back to Happy Valley, in yet another massive attack on the industrial city of Essen by 1055 aircraft of Bomber Command. Jig was one of the nineteen from Kelstern among the 561 Lancasters in the heaviest raid on Essen so far. David wrote, *Many a good crew has 'gone' here and losses have been heavy*. He had just learned that Peter had gone missing in that area on his first op six weeks earlier and he was desolate. *One more friend to avenge*.

Now promoted to Flying Officer, David was acting Flight Commander at the battle conference prior to the briefing. The target was the Krupps armament works, and they were taking one 4000-pounder, five 1000s and eight 500s. It proved to be an exceptionally gruelling trip. The Met briefing that there would be a high front to negotiate both going and coming proved only too accurate. They struck it on reaching France, flying into cloud at 19 000 feet, keenly aware of the danger in cumulonimbus formations with their deadly anvil tops. If caught in one of these the aircraft could be flung out of control or even disintegrate. Small wonder Butch Harris conceded that Bomber Command was fighting the weather as well as the enemy. David pushed Jig hard and they topped the frontal cloud at 23 000 feet. Quite an achievement with a full bomb load for an aircraft whose ceiling was nominally 22 000 feet. Outside, the temperature was below minus 50 degrees Celsius. Inside the nose it was minus 22 degrees Celsius. David was relieved that although it was so cold the aircraft suffered minimal icing.

Because of the weather, no fighters were about when they reached Essen. But the flak was accurate and they were glad to see the cookie and high explosives go without hang-ups, and to turn away, leaving the smoke to rise to 10 000 feet. Homeward bound, they had to fly high again to avoid the front. This time, bombs gone, they reached 24 000 feet without so much effort, but not without incident. Drew left his compartment to go to the nav table, but did not take his portable oxygen bottle, thinking he could make the short distance without it. But he did not. He sprawled over on top of Murga. Cyril grabbed the oxygen tube and plugged him in to the main supply. It was ten minutes before he came round and then he was horribly drowsy for the rest of the trip. *Lucky it happened on the way back. It would have been bad if the b/a was u/s over the target*, David wrote. It was a salutary experience for them all. In an unpressurised aircraft oxygen *was* vital.

While they were still at a considerable height they were fascinated to see St Elmo's fire for the first time. A form of static electricity, it played around the prop tips and on the metal framework of the cockpit canopy. When David reached out his hand the blue light jumped from the metal to his fingers. 'We always knew we had a wizard skipper,' Pop quipped.

Back at Kelstern, they learned that three of the squadron's aircraft had failed to return. They were shocked. They had always expected that one or more might go missing, but this was the first op on which it had happened since David had joined the squadron.

In his hut with Murga, David looked at the six empty beds. 'They're all pukka pilots,' he declared. 'They could still make it back on a wing and a prayer.'

They fell thankfully into their beds, but although he was desperately weary, David stayed awake. His body still jangling with vibrations. His head still throbbing from the rumble of engines. Hoping, listening for the sound of returning aircraft. But there was only silence. At last he fell into the heavy sleep of exhaustion.

When he woke in the morning he was thrilled to see the beds occupied. But only for a moment. Six strangers lay there. Aircraft from another squadron had been forced to land at Kelstern during the night. Quietly David left the hut, devastated.

After breakfast he was stopped outside the Mess by a pilot from another station.

'I'm looking for Flying Officer Morshead. Can you tell me where I'm likely to find him?'

'Ollie?' David exclaimed. 'He went missing last night.'

The pilot struggled to keep his composure. 'He's my brother,' he explained himself.

David wished he had thought more before he had spoken. Blurting out his own pain like that. Too late now to take the words back. 'I'm so sorry,' he mumbled. 'He was a good bloke. He joined the squadron five days after me. We shared the same hut. I'll show you to the Adjutant's office. It's a rotten war.'

Two aircraft had gone missing days before David had arrived at Kelstern. And that had brought keenly home to him what he had been observing and mulling over for months. It seemed as if some chaps formed romantic attachments, determined to experience while they could all there was to life. Others, he suspected, found in the arms of a girl a way of forgetting the horrors they saw and relief from the fear they felt on ops. But for him that was not the way to go. Because of the work he had to do, he had already brought about pain and suffering for more than enough women on the other side. For them he was faceless, nameless, just *ein verdammter Englander* (a damned Englishman), to be feared and hated.

But here on the station it was different. The WAAF who smiled at him as she handed him his mail from home. The WAAF who prayed for him as she folded his parachute or checked his name on the pre-flight meal list. The WAAF who issued his escape aids or drove the tender to dispersals before take off, farewelling them with a heartfelt 'Godspeed!' The WAAF who did not go to bed on op nights, who stood waving at the end of the runway at take-off, then waited for all the hours it took, straining her eyes in the darkness for the returning Lancasters, biting her lips as names were checked off the blackboard. He had seen the disappointment when an airman who had become special was posted to another station. He had observed the drawn face, the dark-ringed eyes, the forced smile when someone to whom a WAAF had given her heart did not return. The scarcely concealed anguish when he was posted MISSING. The grief when he was listed KILLED IN ACTION. He must not inflict that on anyone. Drew, who always commented on a good-looking WAAF, teased him about being impervious to their charms. 'You old woman hater, Dave!' But to do his job he had to stay focused on it. He had to concentrate on his crew, and his crew only. Give them all his energy and his care. England and flying must remain his only loves. Afterwards perhaps... if there was to be an afterwards...

Life on the station was going on as normal. It had to. Sixteen crews had just been posted out to form the nucleus of a new squadron. Replacement crews had come in. And another op was scheduled. David wondered how the rest of his crew was coping, how they were handling the wiping out of twenty-one good blokes. He always made it his business to be available to listen to their gripes, their problems, their worries.

Murga and Drew both tended to get edgy when the long-awaited letters from their wives still did not arrive. 'Don't worry,' David would try to reassure each of them. 'She's probably writing to you every day. You know what the mails are like. You'll get five or six letters in a batch soon.'

Pop fretted about his mother, a heavy chain-smoker. 'I'm worried she'll fall asleep with a fag in her hand one night, and the place will burn down around her,' he confided in David.

Boz had just become engaged to Ann, a feisty ATS girl, in charge of an anti-aircraft gun crew on the East Anglian coast. Separated from his fiancée, he had the mood swings of someone in love. And he worried about her, knowing the danger she faced on the battery, target for enemy raiders.

Birdy was still a high-spirited youth, liable to break out with pranks which could have undesirable consequences, such as the time at Coltishall when he wanted to nab the camera from a fighter.

It was important, too, to ensure that Cyril, the last to join and the only non-Australian, felt included in the team.

Although trying not to show it, they were hard hit, as David was, by the tragedy which had befallen their mates. But everyone focused now on the next op. Briefing and run-up completed, they were sitting in Jig awaiting the green

Aldis signal to move out of dispersal. A red Very light showed from the control tower, the air was blue. 'We're not a bunch of happy chappies!' The op was off. What a let-down when they had screwed themselves up to it!

To defuse the tension, David suggested they all went off the station for a break, meeting in Louth for dinner. 'See you at the King's Head at six,' he told them. He himself felt sorely in need of time out to deal with his own feelings and there was nowhere on the station he could find privacy and a quiet space. So he put the last letter from Peter and the one from his parents which had come yesterday in his greatcoat pocket and caught the bus to Louth. In St James' church he would be alone.

The first snow of the season had blanketed the wolds in glistening white. It seemed like another world, so pure and unmarred by ugly human intrusion. He rested his tired eyes on it as the bus rattled slowly down to the plain. In St James' it was cold, icy cold. David tugged his scarf, knitted by loving hands half a world away, high up round his neck and wriggled his fingers gratefully in the warm lined gloves his aunt had sent to replace those he had lost, and he gave thanks for all the love which had surrounded him all his life. He gave thanks too for the healing silence and stillness which enfolded him in his pain, this piercing pain for Peter, and for the shaft of late sunlight striking the west window, sending a rainbow down into the encroaching darkness.

Settling where he had sat on his last visit, he pulled out the letters which had first plunged him into this grief, this aching void. He was glad that he hadn't answered Peter's last one. If he had it would have been destroyed by now. There just wasn't room in his trunk to keep all the letters he had received. Addressed in Peter's neat sharp hand, so different from his own open rounded writing, it had been posted in York six weeks earlier. *Dear Dave,* Peter had written, *Just at the moment I am feeling pretty cheesed with life.* His bomb aimer had been sick for three weeks and was not likely to be fit for duty for another two, so Peter and his crew were still waiting to go to their squadron.

But you *were* alive, Peter. You were *alive.* And now you are missing. Although they haven't put the rider to it yet. *Killed in Action.* The terrible certainty that destroys all hope, every last vestige to which family and friends cling through the terrible uncertainty. Perhaps you *are* still alive, hiding out in a wood somewhere, or in a barn, or in the attic of a friendly farmhouse. Or in a POW camp. Perhaps you got out of your burning kite. Perhaps you made a good landing in a field. Or even if it was in a tree, you are still *alive.* Perhaps you hid your chute, like they told us, and cut the tops off your flying boots with that knife. Hope your station issued your bacon and eggs as a pre-flight, not a post-flight, meal. Hope you're not injured. *Alive.* Hope you're not incinerated in the wreckage of your kite. Hope they find you soon. Hope they don't have to rely on an identity disc among bits of a charred and blackened airframe.

Remember those days back at school, Peter? It seems like another life now, doesn't it? Those early mornings on the river, the mist still rising. You were a better rower than me. It wasn't fair that you got appendicitis just before the Head of the River and that I took your place. It wasn't fair. But lots of things in life aren't fair, are they? This war, this hideous war isn't fair. Why should innocent people lose their lives? So violently. So horribly.

But then, although we were always mates, we probably wouldn't have become such good friends if it hadn't been for the war. Funny that. You would have gone your way and I would have gone mine. But the war brought us together again at Somers. Do you remember that sergeant, and the voice on him? 'Sounds like a saw,' you said. Just as well he didn't hear you! And it was great to meet up with you at the pre-embarkation depot at Ascot Vale in Melbourne, and that train trip to Adelaide. Remember? 'Sardines,' I said, and you replied, 'Where's the oil?' And that route march they made us do up the hills. You said, 'Whoever ordered this march must be the bastard son of the Grand Old Duke of York.'

We had some fun on the *Umgeni*, didn't we? You were good at the deck games. And those snow fights in New Zealand. And crossing the line. The music in Colon and the dancers, and the view from the top of the Empire State Building in New York. The Caribbean and the Atlantic were pretty breezy though, weren't they? Wouldn't care to do that again, would you? Brighton was all right. Our first taste of Olde England. Remember that little church we found, and that old priest who gave us a blessing? I'm glad he did that. And if you are in one of those rooms now in Our Father's mansions, I know that your place *has* been prepared for you and that He *is* looking after you. Always will.

David looked towards the altar where the brass cross gleamed in the growing gloom, and the anthem he and Peter used to sing at school sounded in his mind. '*I know that my Redeemer liveth.*' He got down on his knees and committed Peter, who had signed himself *Your old friend Peter*, into His gracious keeping. Peter, twenty years old. Peter who would always be twenty years young now.

Sliding back onto the seat, he unfolded the airletter from his parents, the first half in his mother's deliberate square hand, the second in his father's strong pointed script, both smaller than usual, to fit as much as possible into the limited space. Even so, even in this fading light, he could read the words on the dingy yellow page. They had seared themselves into his brain on first reading. *Darling Viddy*, his mother had begun. *You may not yet have heard about Peter, so we thought we should tell you how we learned the sad news that he is missing.* David knew that his mother and Peter's mother had developed the habit of phoning each other, when either had a letter from her son and reading between the lines, he could hear them now. His mother had been in the middle of sewing up a parcel for him – *This is number 47*, she wrote – when the telephone rang.

It was Peter's mother.

'How is David, Mrs Mattingley?' she asked first.

'He was well, thank you, the last we heard a week ago,' David's mother replied, asking in turn, 'And how is Peter, Mrs Lord?'

There seemed to be a slight pause, very slight, before Peter's mother answered, 'He's well. He's very well. And how are Max and Brian?'

'They're well, too,' his mother replied.

'I'm glad for you. I'm very glad,' Mrs Lord said.

'I'm just sewing up a parcel for David now,' Mrs Mattingley said. 'It's quite a task, isn't it? But the boys do appreciate some home comforts, don't they?'

'Yes. I sent the last one off to Peter a week ago,' Mrs

Lord responded, 'and I'd just started collecting things for the next one.'

'That takes some doing, doesn't it?' David's mother said.

'Yes,' Peter's mother agreed, 'and I mustn't keep you from it.'

She hung up.

David's father took over the account. His mother was still stitching at the calico – it *was* an awkward job – when the phone rang again. 'I'll go,' he called and his footsteps sounded down the long passage. David could hear his voice as he answered. His footsteps seemed slower, heavier, as they came back to the cosy little sitting room where his mother sat at the table. David could see the room now, big cedar book-case along one wall, glass-fronted cabinet with family treasures beside the fireplace, framed photos of Max and Brian and himself as boys on the wall.

'Who was it?' his mother asked, not pausing in her task. 'What did they want?'

His father came and stood beside her. His face was grave and his voice was serious. 'It was Peter's father. His mother couldn't bring herself to say it to you. Peter is missing. They got the telegram late yesterday.'

The sharp curved needle slipped in his mother's grasp, pricking her finger. She did not notice. 'Peter?' she murmured. 'Not Peter. He is their only son. Missing? Then there may still be hope for him.'

'Yes,' his father concurred. 'There may be. We can only hope and pray. I'd drive you to Devonport to see his mother,' he went on. 'But we don't have enough coupons for the petrol. This war...' he groaned almost to himself.

David's mother put down her needle and pushed aside her work. 'Then I must write,' she said, 'to her and to Viddy.' She picked up paper and her pen and started at once.

David could see a tiny fleck of blood on the airletter by Peter's name. He thought back to Peter's letter. He had mentioned one of their school friends, Jim Brock, who had at that time just gone missing, flying a Beaufighter in Coastal Command. *It is jolly bad luck and makes things very hard for his mother*, he had written. Now it was *his* mother for whom life would never be the same. Hoping, praying for the news that her son was still alive somewhere. Waiting, always waiting, looking for the letter that would not come to gladden her heart again.

Would his parents get a telegram too? Or two telegrams? Or even three? He could see a telegraph boy walking up the slope to the house. He could hear the sound of the doorbell echoing across the tiled hall down the long passage. See his mother coming to the door. No, not his mother, please. Let it be his father. He stopped himself. These thoughts were no good.

And somehow he must switch off the words of Rupert Brooke's poem which had been running through his mind ever since he heard about Peter. He had won a prize at school for his recitation of it, and he could still see Peter, smiling encouragement at him from the audience as he walked out onto the stage, glad of his long trousers to hide his shaking knees. *If I should die, think only this of me: That there's some corner of a foreign field That is forever England* ... And Australia, Peter. *A dust whom* Australia *bore, shaped, made aware* ... I'll never forget you, Peter, he promised.

But now he must be with people again. And his boys were waiting for him. He got up from the hard cold pew and walked slowly into the blacked-out street.

In the cosy fug of the King's Head his boys were gathered by the bar. 'You all right, Skip?' they asked. 'You look as if you've seen a ghost.'

'Never better,' David lied to them. 'And the only ghosts around here are the smell of the long departed soles.'

His crew laughed in relief. This was their Skip, who could never resist a pun.

David looked at them, reading the concern in their faces, hearing it in their voices. His boys, his team, his crew. 'The first round's on me,' he said, putting a pound note on the bar and downing his first half pint of warm ale in one go. 'Your shout, Murga.' But before Pop's turn he said, 'No good drinking on an empty stomach. Let's eat.'

Always hungry, they agreed and were soon tucking into a typical English wartime meal – spuds, cabbage and sausages almost 100 per cent grey austerity bread.

'Now it's your shout, Pop,' David said. Better a sore head in the morning than a sore heart tonight. But the sore heart would be with him for a long time.

15 'Bold, cautious, true, and my loving comrade'

Life on the squadron had to be lived from hour to hour, minute to minute, as the weather and its vagaries played such a crucial part in determining operations. The morning after their evening at the King's Head, the crew heard that the op which had been cancelled at the last minute was now on as a daylight raid. 'Let's hope it is. Let's get it over,' they said. No one liked going to Happy Valley. And this was a return visit to Essen, with a Master Bomber, to pound what was left of the Krupps armament works.

They were not pleased either to find that their Jig had been allocated to another crew with a Canadian pilot, but consoled themselves that she would be in good hands, when David assured them 'Arthur's a gen pilot.'

Cologne Cathedral standing amidst ruins of buildings, and the Hohenzollern railway bridge across the Rhine

'They're all decent chaps,' Drew added.

Although they were really sorry not to be flying in Jig, they were chuffed that they had been given a new aircraft, R Roger, to take on its first op. But over France they were shocked to notice a smell of burning and to see blue smoke starting to fill the cabin. The Gee had fused. So Cyril disconnected it. Nearing Essen they noticed the wavering almost vertical trail of a V2 rocket, far above their own cruising height of 20 000 feet. 'Let's hope it gets iced up too.'

Over the target, heavy and accurate flak shook the aircraft badly several times. When Boz reported a two-foot hole in the port elevator, David took even more care than usual with the elevator controls. Although the outside of the windscreen had been sprayed with glycol anti-freeze, he had trouble with damp air freezing on the interior. Icing had reduced vision uncomfortably, and as Gee was u/s, he was pleased with Drew's and Pop's teamwork on radar, using Y to bring them home.

Fog was the final hazard, but before it closed in totally they managed to land at Kelstern. On investigating the damage to Roger, they found that the main elevator spar and hinge had been almost completely severed, only held in place by half an inch of metal. 'Another in the Lucky Stars series! Half an inch between life and death!' David joked, secretly shocked to see how near to fatality they had been. R Roger had had its baptism of fire. Ground crew went into action at once to repair the damage.

COLOGNE

The following day they flew another new aircraft, ferrying it from Binbrook to Kelstern. But again fog was so thick they were not able to land at Kelstern. Returning to Binbrook, they made several attempts before they put down. Then, for the second time in four days, an op was cancelled after briefing just as they were boarding transports out to dispersals, much to the crews' frustration.

Also of great strategic importance, it was rescheduled, too, as a daylight raid. The target was Cologne with its railway marshalling yards, power stations and harbour installations on the Rhine.

David, who had resolutely buried his grief deep in order to concentrate on the work he had to do, wrote, *The inhabitants must be a little fed up with the raids by now*, and exulted, *We feel we are settling old scores for London and other British towns. It is also one in the eye for Goering who said that not one British bomb would fall on German soil.*

Ironically they were flying L Love.

As they neared the target in the first wave, flak was accurate and Cyril windowed furiously to try to jam enemy radar. Brown smoke was billowing out in huge clouds from a large explosion, indicating something vital had been hit.

'That's blasted the shit out of them,' Drew said with satisfaction.

But Pop murmured, 'Poor bloody civilians.'

After they turned away Cyril dropped 'nickels', the British propaganda leaflets designed to warn German citizens of ultimate Allied victory, in the hope of undermining their faith in their leaders and encouraging a grassroots movement towards surrender.

Home again almost five hours later, David was relieved to see that two of his English friends, jovial Jack Ball, who had taken over R Roger, and Clem Koder, whose impeccable English gave no hint of his Czech parents, had returned safely. As for David himself, this had been his fifteenth op. He was half way to completing his tour. Another fifteen ops to go. He must focus on each sortie as it came up, each one another nail in Hitler's coffin, each one a day nearer to victory and peace, in Europe at least. So he worked hard to maintain his crew's morale.

When he received news that another good mate, Tas Williams, with whom he had trained and who was on the same squadron as Peter, had been killed only nine days after Peter, it was almost too much to bear. Tas had already had one close call over Germany. This time it was final.

Quiet, gentle Tas. Only 21. 'They shall not grow old, as we that are left grow old: Age shall not weary them, nor the years condemn. At the going down of the sun and in the morning We will remember them.'

'I won't forget you, Tas,' David promised. He re-read Tas's last letter. Tas mentioned another lad from Hobart who had gone for a burton and that his own brother was now a POW in Japanese hands. Two more Tasmanian homes plunged into mourning and anguish. How much longer until this madness was over? The war in the Pacific, where David's brother Max was serving as captain of a patrol boat, was not so close to its end.

HOLLAND YET AGAIN

David's crew was now rated as an A category bombing team and chosen as one of six from the squadron to take part in the next tactical op the following day. In yet another aircraft, D2 Dog Two, they flew in a force of 358 aircraft, 194 of them Lancasters, led by a Master Bomber. A pinpoint target, demanding great accuracy, it was the last battery of the long-range German guns on Walcheren Island. Commanding the Scheldt estuary, the guns were impeding full and effective use of port facilities at Antwerp to supply the Allied forces now advancing on Germany. When the target indicator fell in the water, the instruction was given to overshoot it by three seconds. Bombing had just commenced when they saw a Lanc going down with smoke pouring from it.

'The Master Bomber's got the chop,' they groaned.

His deputy, in another aircraft, took over and kept the force orbiting. But drifting clouds obscured the target and they groaned again as they heard him repeat, *Sugarplum, Sugarplum*,' the code word for Abandon Mission.

Dodging through clouds and rainstorms they flew back at 200 feet across East Anglian airfields, where ground crews stopped work and people rushed out of their houses to stare up at 25 heavy bombers at such a low altitude.

Landing with a full bomb load in driving rain and poor visibility was no picnic.

'I had butterflies in the tum,' Boz admitted.

'Emperor gum moths more like it,' Birdy corrected him.

David simply wrote, *After interrogation we were glad to reach the cheerful fire in the mess and sit listening to the rain.*

Everyone was relieved when the decision was announced it would be counted as an op. Only fourteen more to go now, David told himself.

COLOGNE AGAIN

On 30 October David and his crew found their names on the Battle Order for the third day in a row. Battle Order 187. This time it was to Cologne again, for another massive raid on the railway marshalling yards. Back in

Jig, their load a cookie, seven 1000-pounders and four 500s, they were airborne just as darkness was seeping over the ground. Flying between two layers of cloud, they experienced considerable icing on the leading surfaces and edges, and were glad to run in over the target and lay their eggs. When the upper layer thinned out they could see numbers of suspicious contrails circling above and all kept a close watch for fighters. A JU88 cut across their bows, but was gone before Drew could fire a shot. Then in his panic he mistook a friendly aircraft for an enemy fighter, his false alarm causing bags of flap.

When Birdy sighted two 'jetties' heading for them on either quarter, David smartly increased revs and put the nose down into the shelter of a nearby cloud bank. The full moon was illuminating everything too well for comfort. He wrote: *We felt distinctly naked either silhouetted against it or lit up by searchlights against the cloud.*

A warning of intruders over England heightened the tension and David wrote: *We did not feel fully safe until our feet were on the ground again.*

The whole operation had been completed without the loss of a single one of the 905 aircraft, and after these knock-out raids little remained standing in Cologne except its cathedral.

It was 4 am before they got to bed, peeved because they were due to go on leave that morning. Leave was due only after six weeks of ops, and they resented missing even half a day. By sleeping in they were late arriving in London and had difficulty finding accommodation. *C'est la guerre*, David wrote in resignation.

He spent next morning at RAAF HQ, seeking more information about cousin Frank and Peter, devastated to learn that Peter, like Frank, had been on his first op. In a Halifax on a raid to Sterkrade in Germany he had been second dickey to an experienced pilot on his 29th, so he could not have been in better hands. It just went to show the hazards they had to contend with and the diabolical effect of flak. As for Frank, the casualty section could tell him nothing more and did not hold out much hope for him.

Lunch at the Boomerang Club was more cheerful and he heard that Ian was still enjoying the warmth of the Middle East, where Gordon was finding interest in identifying Biblical sites.

David had not seen Alan Scott for a year, since Brighton, and, keen to catch up with his old friend, made the journey to the station in Essex where Alan was a navigator flying in Stirlings, dropping troops and supplies at Arnhem.

After a day together, Alan sent him on to friends, Dr and Mrs Noble, who had been for some time in Sydney, and now lived in Cambridge. David could not have had a better guide to show him the beautiful old university city than Mrs Noble, and she enjoyed showing its sights to this thoughtful young Australian, so interested in history and appreciative of architecture. David was delighted when they drove out to Grantchester, the home of Rupert Brooke and subject of one of his best-loved poems. The highlight of the visit was evensong by candlelight in King's College chapel, where the voices of the boy choristers sounded quite ethereal floating up to the glorious fan-vaulted ceiling. But afterwards parts of a Bach organ concert were almost drowned by the sound of bombers outward bound.

HAPPY VALLEY AGAIN

Back at Kelstern, David was dismayed when the Medical Officer pronounced that Murga, who had been moved to sick quarters with a bad cold and chest problems, would not be able to fly again in winter in England. He had been a first-rate navigator, reliable, painstaking and accurate, and the thought of losing him saddened all the crew. They had grown so close and had developed loyalty and bonds which went very deep.

'It won't be the same without old Murga the unflappable,' they agreed.

They were sad, too, that while they were on leave, J Jig went missing with a sprog crew. Sad for the crew and sad to lose the kite to which they had become so attached. Now they would have to use whatever spare aircraft was available, which was not nearly as good as having their own.

The very next morning on 9 November they were awakened at 0430 to prepare for an op in B Baker, with a spare navigator from a crew which was not flying. It was another Happy Valley destination, the oil refineries at Wanne-Eickel, so vital to the enemy. At dispersal it was bitterly cold and the cold intensified as they climbed to 19 000 feet through a snowstorm, which covered the front turret with snow and obscured the clear vision panel. In a temperature of minus 46 degrees Celsius all the aircraft suffered severe icing problems and the sortie became known as the one on which the fighter pilots' eyelashes froze. B Baker was an old aircraft, and icing made it even slower. When they broke out above the cloud they found they were no longer part of the gaggle, the grouping to assist fighters to protect them. Because of a navigation error they were well behind time. And alone. 'Like a country shithouse!' Drew groaned.

They heard the code word *Applesauce* for the bomb drop and pressed on as fast as possible amid the flak. While Drew windowed with his usual frenzy, David took evasive action, weaving the rest of the way, to arrive on target 14 minutes late. It was terrifying. *All on our own over Happy Valley. Never again*, David later wrote.

After dropping their load they lost no time in getting away and were congratulating themselves on having got out of a nasty fix, when Drew caused another flap, calling, 'Fighters on the port bow! They look like jetties!' David's long hours of swotting aircraft recognition again paid off as he was able to reassure the crew they were US Thunderbolts.

'Phew! Thank Gawd for that,' Drew muttered, abashed.

Heavy cloud produced more icing on the return journey, again obscuring the front of the nose, and they had to descend to 800 feet before they were below it, flying through torrential rain almost all the way home.

Talking it over afterwards, only Birdy played it cool, dismissing it as most uninteresting.

'I was more frightened than I had ever been before, with the icing and being alone,' Drew said.

And Cyril agreed, 'It was not very nice playing the Lone Wolf.'

Boz admitted to offering a few silent prayers, while Pop summed it up for them all, 'A hazardous journey.'

Walking into the briefing room for interrogation was always a tense moment. Looking round the room of familiar faces. Were any missing? 'They went with songs to the battle, they were young, Straight of limb, true of eye, steady and aglow, They were staunch to the end against odds uncounted'...Laurence Binyon's words, written in the last war, were true for their generation too. Looking across to the ops blackboard, eyes travelling down the list of aircraft, their crews and their take-off times. Scanning for return slots that were still empty. Listening for the sound of returning aircraft. Even the sound of three engines better than silence. Looking, listening, hoping, praying.

Tonight, late as they were in old B Baker, there were still other crews who were not checked off on the blackboard. The adrenalin which had flowed ever since hearing they were on an op suddenly ebbing away. The exhaustion rolling in. The longing to put the head down. The overwhelming longing for the merciful oblivion of sleep. Blotting out glow of fires, fighter flares, tracery of light flak, flash of heavy flak, glare of searchlight beams, sight of planes going down. And laughing faces never to be seen again?

But before that, interrogation and a meal.

Despite the hazards only two aircraft from the whole Bomber Command force of 256 Lancasters were missing. But they were both from David's squadron and *my particular friends*, he wrote briefly and bleakly.

Next morning he was called to the Wingco's office.

'You're one of our most senior pilots now, Mattingley. In future you'll be taking some sprog crews.'

One of the most senior? He hadn't been on ops for two months yet. Although it did feel like a lifetime. Jimmy and his crew had been on for nine weeks, Arthur and his for eight. Surviving eighteen ops made him senior?

Shortly afterwards, the Adjutant detailed him for one of the tasks everyone hoped they would never have to do.

David's chest was tight as he carefully sorted and listed the possessions of his former comrades, packing them into the standard cardboard storage boxes used in this poignant procedure. Letters. Photos. Such intimate personal things. Shaving gear. Underwear. The best uniform. One with a Canada shoulder flash. A clock still ticking. A man's life in one metal trunk by an empty bed in a metal hut.

'Brave, cautious, true, and my loving comrade.' Walt Whitman's words from an even earlier war running through his mind. And outside the snow on the wind-swept wold. White cold. The pitiless snow that might have helped to bring them down. Remembering Robert Bridges' words. 'I shall never love the snow again Since Maurice died: With corniced drift it blocked the lane And sheeted in a desolate plain The country side.'

Pray God that Arthur and Jimmy and their crews are still alive somewhere.

He snapped down the lids of the two empty black trunks and wrote the names and numbers of his Canadian friend and his English friend on the brown cardboard boxes. He must not let himself get so close to anyone again. Never again. It hurt too much.

16 G George and D Dog

There days of snow and gales. Ops and training scrubbed. Getting out of bed, slipping on the ice on the hut floor. *No wonder the Romans did not enjoy building Ermine Stree*t, David wrote in his diary. 'Any more than I enjoy going to Happy Valley,' he thought. Aircraft run-up, briefing done, sitting in the aircraft, engines running, about to take off, red Very light. Infuriated crew. Briefing and scrubbing becoming monotonous. Foul foul weather. Too foul even for Bomber Command. *Obviously the European winter leaves much to be desired*, he wrote. Oh for the sun and warm sands of home. Two more days of snow and every wind that blows. All hands to shovels to try to keep the runways clear.

Then on 16 November they were up and away again at last and in daylight on Battle Order 196. It was another tactical raid, with the grim purpose of obliterating the town of Düren, a major supply base for the German army, and cutting communications behind German lines

Smoke clouds from bombing raid on Düren, 16 November 1944. Smoke often rose to 10 000 feet or more.

at Julich and Heinburg. A special message from Bomber Command was read at briefing, informing them that the trip was in support of the biggest operation since D-day – the American Army advance on the Rhine. 'So we need a good prang, boys,' the Wingco said.

Flying in G George, they were joined for the first time by their new navigator, Flight Lieutenant Charles Gardiner DFC, who was on his second tour of operations. The crew were a little apprehensive at having a screened bod of such experience. Drew was especially nervous as Gardiner was also 'the Y King', the station's radar instructor, and he felt sticky in case his own technique was not approved. But David was pleased. G George was to be one of the three lead planes in a gaggle, which required accurate navigation and flying. Charles was an efficient navigator and fitted in well.

They had their first scare of the op before they even took off. While still in dispersal a gunner from another aircraft accidentally fired some rounds which passed over their heads. 'A close shave,' they all agreed.

The Lancasters seemed to fill the sky like a flock of giant black crows as the stream flew over England. Over France it divided into three groups, each heading for its specific target with Pathfinder Master Bombers leading the way. They had another scare when one aircraft did not follow the instruction to bomb at 10 000 feet and dropped its load from above them. 'What bastards!' they yelled, as David had to jink, manoeuvring violently to avoid the bombs.

Turning away from the burning and blackened ruin of what had been known as the Queen City of the Rhine, with the sickening smell of cordite and the sound of exploding flak so loud it could be heard above the engines, David joined the stream heading for England.

Flying in the fading light over Lincolnshire, featureless under snowdrifts, he was grateful, as always, to see the splendid shape of Lincoln Cathedral on the skyline. They were nearly home. Wonderful how the faith and vision of men so many centuries ago, and their magnificent handiwork, still proclaimed hope and salvation. Now, other men, in circumstances so different, also needed the message.

Breathing easily again in air unpolluted by funeral pyres, they made their way to interrogation. One of 625's aircraft was missing.

'That was no scarecrow we saw. Could have been our mates' kite going down in flames,' Drew said sombrely.

The lost crew had only been on the squadron for four weeks.

The reconnaissance photos showed a concentration of bomb craters without parallel in any previous attack by the RAF. Virtually one hundred per cent accuracy had been achieved. It was the good prang Butch Harris had hoped for.

Two days later it was back to the oil refineries at Wanne-Eickel. This time David flew with a sprog crew. All his crew went out to George in the morning for the run-up, and to show the new crew their daily inspection routine and their particular jobs. Then, after briefing and their flying meal, they took off at 1540, with second dickey pilot, wireless operator, bomb aimer, flight engineer and rear gunner. Of the regular crew, David had only his own navigator, Charles, and Birdy who took the place of mid upper gunner.

A/C LTR	A/C NO.	PILOT	E/ENGINEER	A/BOMBER

No. 625 Squadron, R.A.F.   22nd November, 1944.   BATTLE ORDER:

	A/C LTR	A/C NO.	PILOT	E/ENGINEER	A/BOMBER
1.	Y(y)	NG.267+	F/O WARD	SGT HARRIS	F/S RUDD
2.	L(y)	LM.747	F/O MATTINGLEY	SGT BAILEY	F/S FISHER
3.	Z(y)	PD.388+	F/O HAZELL	SGT PULFORD	F/O SHENTON
4.	A2(y)	PB.574	S/L HAMMOND	SGT STEVENS	F/S RONEY
5.	P(y)	PD.204+	F/O MALONEY	SGT PEARCE	F/O DART
6.	T(y)	NF.995+	F/O CROOKS	SGT INWOOD	SGT SIMPSON
7.	G(y)	FB.136+	F/O KIDER	SGT BULMAN	SGT DONOHUE
8.	F(y)	PB.536	F/O PARKER	SGT BUTTERFIELD	F/O CROWTHER
9.	W(y)	PB.404	F/O DALLEY	SGT WILLIAMS	F/O LUSH
10.	F2(y)	NG.240+	F/O SUTTON	SGT PENN	F/S MACNEILLAR
11.	M(y)	NR.294+	F/O JAMIESON	SGT CUTHILL	SGT AICKEN
12.	A(y)	ME.700+	F/L COONOR	SGT FULLER	F/O RUSSELL.D.T.
13.	S(y)	NE.237+	F/L FRY	SGT SYKES	F/O DAVIES
14.	K2(y)	PA.175+	F/O MOFFITT	SGT JENKINS	SGT MILLER
15.	J2(y)	NF.996+	F/O MONDAY	SGT GEORGE	F/S COONEY
16.	D2(y)	LM.679	F/O BATTIN	SGT STEEL	SGT DINGLE
17.	O2(y)	PD.376+	F/O CHAPLIN	SGT LYONS	F/O ARKWRIGHT
Spare:B(y)		ED.200+	F/L JARDINE	SGT MILES	F/O COTTRILL

DUTY CREW: F/O BULMAN AND CREW.
RATIONS: F/S BROWN AND F/S JOTHAM.   )To report to N.C.O i/c
RATIONS "G" FLIGHT: SGT.DAVIES.R. AND SGT.DAVIES.V.)Sgts.Mess at the time
                                                   of briefing.
RATIONS AT 1/- = 126.
RATIONS AT 6d = NIL.   TIMES TO BE NOTIFIED LATER.

A typical Battle Order of 625 Squadron, No 200, for 22 November 1944

Pop, Cyril, Boz and Drew went out to see them safely aboard, then cycled to the take-off end of the runway.

Drew said, 'I felt like a lost soul. For the first time it was brought abruptly home to me just how attached to one another we have become.'

They hated to think of their skipper, their Dave, going off without his team, the crew he knew he could rely on. He had a tough enough job as it was, without worrying

	Serial No. 200.	O.C.,Flying	: W/C.BARKER.
		Despatching Officer	: F/O Travis.
		"C" Flt. Despatching Officer: F/L.ORR.	

NAVIGATOR	WOP/AIR	M/U/GUNNER	R/GUNNER
F/O THOMSON	F/S ROWELL	F/S SYKES	SGT MURCOTT.
F/O GARDINER.DFC	F/S WATSON	F/S FERGUSON	F/S AVERY.
SGT SELLARS	SGT HUGHES	SGT HALL	SGT HARRISON(807)
F/S VINEY	F/S FARRELL	SGT ROSE	SGT WAKELING
F/O SHEPPARD	F/S DICKSON	F/S THOMPSON	F/S HARDING
F/O FLETCHER	F/S PORSCUTT	SGT POULTER	F/S BRADY
F/O ZLOTNIK	SGT STEWART	F/S SHEEHAN	F/S SHARMAN
SGT COLES	SGT CASEY	SGT HORSFORD	SGT LOUGHRAN
SGT GEMMELL	F/S JAMIESON	F/S ROUT	SGT LINDSAY
F/S CAPPS	F/S WALKER	F/S SMALLWOOD	F/S MILLINGTON
F/O O'REILLY	SGT SMITH(998)	SGT ELLIOTT	SGT WILSON
F/O RUSSELL.S.T.	SGT MELLOR	SGT WILKINSON	SGT WAGGOTT
SGT CORRIGAN	F/S SOULE	F/O HARPER	F/S MACCANDLISH
SGT BANHAM	F/S BOON	SGT EDWARDS	SGT COX
SGT BROWN	F/S MARTIN	SGT COLLINS	SGT COOK
F/O CARTER	SGT MULLIGAN	SGT WILKES	SGT BARRETT
SGT LEE	SGT CROOSMAN	SGT REID	SGT WALKER
F/O ERLING	SGT THALE	SGT THOMPSON	SGT SMITH(262)

Wing Commander, Commanding,
No. 625 Squadron, R.A.F.

about men who might not cope when things got hot. They joined the Wingco, padre, airfield controller and other officers, together with another crew whose pilot had a second dickey too.

'I damn near howled before George even came along,' Drew said.

They gave G George the thumbs-up sign as it came abreast with their Dave at the controls. 'Godspeed and a safe return.'

David returned the thumbs up and Birdy went one better, swinging his gun turret onto his mates and pretending to fire a burst at them.

The engines roared into life, the tailplane, fins and rudders shuddered with the blast. Moving slowly at first, George gradually gathered speed down the runway and still more speed until it took off. Drew watched until it disappeared into the mist, afraid to look at the others in case they saw the tears in his eyes. Empty and lost, they returned to the Mess, their ears reverberating with the roar of the kites circling to gain height. Five hours to wait until the first ones would return.

Aloft in George, David was not happy either, wishing he had his own crew at their posts, fearful that these sprogs might inadvertently do the wrong thing under pressure and make a fatal mistake. He told the flight engineer to do exactly as he was ordered and nothing else. He ensured that the bomb aimer did not have the doors open too early, that the w/op checked that the photoflash had gone, and that all crew members were properly on the job.

It was a clear night. The target indicators were easily visible, so the attack was concentrated. Particularly active searchlights coned several kites. But with good cooperation from Birdy, David evaded them all and wrote afterwards, *This part of the attack should have proved most instructive to the new crew.*

On the return flight, the w/op picked up a message near the English coast, diverting them to Knettishall, where George landed first in blinding rain. It was a US base for Flying Fortresses and the Intelligence Officer who questioned them was amazed at the bomb load they carried, compared with that of the Fortress.

They enjoyed American hospitality, delighted at the excellent meals in such stark contrast to what British services and civilians were used to. 'Grapefruit juice, peaches and cream, *and* bacon and eggs! And this is just an ordinary breakfast, not a flying meal!'

At Kelstern, the others had waited up to see them home until advised of the diversion. On seeing them safely back after more than 24 hours, they disguised their relief with banter. 'You bludgers! Living off American fat while we didn't even leave the station, not even for a night out in Grimsby!' Grimsby, as they all knew, was singularly devoid of attractions.

Dense fog rolling in from the North Sea brought everything to a standstill on the station. Visibility was nil. But there were two unwelcome personnel movements. Everyone was disappointed to hear of the Wingco's posting to another station. For two months he had been a good leader and they would miss him.

The crew were sad, too, to learn that Murga had now been moved to Rauceby Hospital, and was likely to be repatriated. Another fracture, another loss.

For his part, David was keeping a close tally of his own movements. He had now completed two-thirds of his tour. His next op would be his twenty-first.

BACK TO GERMANY

David and his crew were on the Battle Order again three days later. Going into the Mess for the pre-flight meal with his friend Jack Ball, they had, as usual, to be checked off a list of crews, ensuring they were entitled to the coveted bacon and eggs.

'Mattingley's,' he said, and the WAAF ticked off his name.

'Ball's,' Jack said.

The WAAF looked up from her clipboard. 'Balls to you too,' she retorted.

The queue broke into laughter.

Jack explained, 'Ball's my name'.

She blushed furiously. 'Sorry, sir.'

'No hard feelings,' he assured her.

Jack, David and his other English friends Clem and Sandy chuckled as they polished off their bacon and eggs. It made a good start to the op and a good story to share with the rest of the crew.

David was very glad to be flying with his own crew again, especially as it was to be their longest trip yet, to southern Germany, almost seven hours in the air. This time they were in L Love again, with a cookie and sixteen 500s. Because they were penetrating so far, it gave the enemy more time to organise defences. At briefing they were told to expect heavy opposition from fighters, so the normal strategy was to be followed. They were to change route several times to confuse the enemy and to try to lure the fighters away from the intended target. This was the railway marshalling yards at Aschaffenburg, another major supply depot, and the attack was in support of the advancing French army.

The outward flight was uneventful. Drew recorded that the only happening of note was *Dave having a leak out the port window while Cyril held the plane steady.*

David always flew hands on. He never used the automatic pilot, as it required precious seconds to disengage, which could be crucial in an emergency. So he could not use the Elsan like the rest of the crew. Some pilots carried a bottle or tin, but he did not. Nor did he use the flare chute, as others did, because this would also mean leaving his position at the controls.

When the bombers ran into ten/tenths cloud as they approached the target, an elaborate tactic with Pathfinder markings and Master Bomber had to be abandoned. But to everyone's consternation sky-markers which had been dropped instead were bursting above the planes. Drew and Charles worked well together and Drew gave the Y king full credit for perfect timing as he let the bombs go over the red glow already visible below.

On the return, Pop picked up enemy aircraft on the Fishpond warning radar screen, and soon afterwards fighter flares began falling. It was a stomach-churning moment when one fell within a hundred yards and David wrote, *We felt singularly naked expecting attack*. Drew admitted he felt scared sick and everyone kept an extra good search going. Seven other Lancs were illuminated and they saw a number of attacks over the next half hour. All 625 Squadron's Lancs returned, but two from the force were lost.

Over the next five days the weather was impossible for flying. Snow was falling almost daily, culminating in a mini blizzard which created drifts several feet deep in places. It was frustrating. The leave to which they had been looking forward was postponed by a week because they were needed on the squadron, and yet they were unable to fly.

As usual, when not in the flight office or out at dispersal, David put the time to good use in the intelligence library.

Sawing up wood for the Mess fire helped keep them warm. The coloured lights of half-a-dozen Very cartridges tossed into the fire made for a brighter and more lively evening. Especially as the Groupie was standing with his back to the fireplace!

There were not many options for entertainment, but as always they enjoyed simple pleasures. *Making toast on the hut stove and eating anything we could scrounge was a good deal of fun.*

On the Saturday they took some of the ground crew to dinner at the King's Head in Louth. *As they always serviced our aircraft so well and were most willing and helpful, it was the least we could do for them.*

Then, at last, they were given their own aircraft again, D Dog. David was delighted. *It is much easier having one of our own, as we can take good care of it and have everything to suit us.* On their first flight in D Dog they again took a second dickey crew, mainly Canadians. The sprog w/op and gunner were sick, so David was thankful to be able to take Pop and Boz, though Drew was again left lamenting, as was Birdy this time and Cyril too. At the morning run-up they took the new crew through the routine checks and all they needed to do, and at the briefing David showed them the procedure for emptying their pockets into named paper bags.

But they could carry a talisman. And many did. Teddy bears and other soft toys were popular. Or it might be a so-called lucky rabbit's paw, a trusty pocket-knife, or perhaps a cigarette lighter with sentimental attachment. Perhaps a cherished lock of hair from a wife or child. Or a St Christopher medallion. Sandy always took his officer's cap. On one op it was ripped by shrapnel. Much to his annoyance, while he was home on leave an uncle who was a tailor mended it very skilfully. David carried the small black Bible he had bought at St Paul's Cathedral in Melbourne during his training at Somers. It fitted snugly in the left-hand pocket of his battledress, just over his heart, and it had been on every flight with him since his first at Western Junction.

After obtaining escape aids, maps and currency, David ensured that the sprogs noted all the necessary gen from the blackboard, including the method and time of target marking and the wave in which their aircraft would fly. After the talks on tactics and weather, they collected flying kit and rations from the crew room before boarding the transport out to dispersal. David was concerned that the engineer seemed uncertain about parts of his duties, so he took him through many details himself. Nor was the new crew disciplined or trained well. David found their habit of leaving their mikes switched on very annoying, as the static interfered with his concentration.

It was another long flight into southern Germany, almost seven hours overall. This time the target was Freiburg, a minor railway centre, held by German troops who would impede the advance of American and French troops from the west. In bright moonlight they were horribly exposed, so with an inexperienced crew David was extra thankful that opposition was not too heavy.

On the homeward route skirting neutral Switzerland, the sight of the twinkling lights of Basle was amazing after blacked-out cities, and the snowy grandeur of the moonlit Alps was awe-inspiring.

Descending through cloud they again experienced the uncanny effects of St Elmo's fire playing along the wings, props and guns, turning the perspex windscreen bright blue and sending flames leaping from its framework to David's hands. He was glad to break through the cloud at sea – a much safer alternative to coming out over land – and came in low towards Louth with its familiar radio beacon call sign.

As the weather was rapidly closing in, he was thankful to see the Kelstern searchlights making their distinctive V pattern to guide them. David ensured that the men put their names on the returned list, and took each one through his specialist interrogation, reporting any snags, then went through the general intelligence interrogation with them all. By 4 am he was more than ready for bed, glad to be finished with his duties and relieved of his responsibility for the sprog crew.

David woke at midday and went out to D Dog to check it was ready for the next trip. But during the afternoon another crew used it for a training flight and on take-off had flown into a flock of plovers, damaging perspex and two radiators. Quick to make the best of a bad situation, David collected some of the birds and while the erks worked into the night to get D Dog in flying order again, he and the MO enjoyed cooked plover for dinner.

Next morning. he was glad to have had the meal,

when they were served an ordinary breakfast instead of a flying meal before being sent off on a rushed op.

It was 29 November. Dortmund was their destination, in the deadly, heavily defended Happy Valley.

And they were flying on Battle Order 204.

Battle Order 204 (7)
A Perfect Landing

David called up control and asked for a priority landing, with fire engine and ambulance. And got them all.

In calling for the ambulance he had not mentioned himself, simply saying there was a wounded man on board.

Because the skipper's arm was useless, Cyril operated the throttles and trims under his direction, as well as performing his own duties, monitoring engine and fuel gauges and lowering the undercarriage.

· · · · · · · · · · · · · · · · ·

Four hours and forty-five minutes after take-off Dog made a perfect landing. David had returned from his 23rd journey to hell.

· · · · · · · · · · · · · · · · ·

'Cyril did a very good job throughout, as did all the crew. I was proud of them,' David later said.

And they were proud of their Dave too. None of them knew how seriously their skipper had also been wounded. When they saw the blood congealed around his helmet and on his ripped trousers and jacket they were shocked.

Right arm dangling helplessly, David climbed with difficulty out of the cockpit, over the main spar, along the fuselage, to be assisted down the ladder by the Medical Officer. He and Cyril were taken to sick quarters where their wounds were dressed. It was an emotional crew who came to see them after interrogation.

'Thanks, Skipper. You're a damn good pilot. You did a bang-on job.'

'There's bags of sympathy,' Drew offered.

'The kite's a sieve,' Pop reported.

'Like me,' their skip replied. 'Dog's back in its Kelstern kennel and there's life in the two young Dogs yet.'

They grinned. No damage to their Dave's sense of humour.

'It was a good prang,' they assured him. 'And Jerry can't claim us,' they boasted.

David felt their love and faith in him like a shot of adrenalin, better than any painkiller. He would pull through this and come back to fly with them, he told himself with resolve. Their faces smiling encouragement were the last he saw as he was loaded into the ambulance again. And they stayed with him for the agonising 54-mile trip to Rauceby RAF Hospital. After X-rays, he was taken immediately into theatre, where surgeons removed all except one of the pieces of metal.

• • • • • • • • • • • • • • • • •

By 1 am, the 10 hours since Dortmund seemed like a lifetime.

T.G.428.

This Telegram has been received subject to the Post and Telegraph Act and Regulations. The time received at this office is shown at the end of the message.

Sch. C. 4163
7/1943.

COMMONWEALTH OF AUSTRALIA.
POSTMASTER-GENERAL'S DEPARTMENT.

TELEGRAM

The date stamp indicates the date of reception and lodgment also, unless an earlier date is shown after the time of lodgment.

Office Date

Office of Origin.   No. of Words.   Time of Lodgment.   No.

EW 420 MELBOURNE 133/1 4 P

TELEGRAPHIC ACKNOWLEDGMENT DELIVERY PERSONAL   MR P F C MATTINGLEY
138 ELPHIN RD LAUNCESTON TAS

408458 ACTING FLYING OFFICER C D MATTINGLEY SERIOUSLY INJURED
STOP REGRET TO INFORM YOU THAT YOUR SON ACTING FLYING
OFFICER CECIL DAVID MATTINGLEY WAS SERIOUSLY INJURED AND
ADMITTED TO HOSPITAL IN RAUCEBY ENGLAND ON 29 TH NOVEMBER

T.G.428.

This Telegram has been received subject to the Post and Telegraph Act and Regulations. The time received at this office is shown at the end of the message.

Sch. C. 4163
7/1943.

COMMONWEALTH OF AUSTRALIA.
POSTMASTER-GENERAL'S DEPARTMENT.

TELEGRAM

The date stamp indicates the date of reception and lodgment also, unless an earlier date is shown after the time of lodgment.

Office Date

T.
C.
B.

Office of Origin.   No. of Words.   Time of Lodgment.   No.

1944 SUFFERING COMPOUND FRACTURE SKULL RIGHT UPPER TEMPORAL REGION
PUNCTURE WOUND RIGHT HAND WITH ARTERIAL BLEEDING AND
PUNCTURE WOUND RIGHT ARM AND THIGH RECEIVED AS RESULT
AIR OPERATION STOP KNOWN DETAILS ARE HE RECEIVED HIS INJURIES
WHILST MEMBER OF CREW LANCASTER AIRCRAFT WHICH WAS HIT BY
HEAVY FLAK WHILST ATTACKING TARGET AT DORTMUND GERMANY STOP
DESIRE TO EXPRESS SYMPATHY IN YOUR ANXIETY STOP WHEN ANY
FURTHER INFORMATION IS RECEIVED IT WILL BE CONVEYED TO YOU
IMMEDIATELY ... AIR FORCE 391 LITTLE COLLINS ST MELBOURNE
(138 408458 29 1944 391)

17 A Fractured Skull and a Headless Crew

It was a shock for Murga to learn that his skipper was now in hospital too. He made his way at once to the surgical ward and was even more shocked to see David lying comatose, heavily drugged for his injuries. Head in a skullcap, and swathed in bandages. Right hand heavily bandaged. And a frame under the bedclothes to protect his right leg from their weight.

Overcome with grief, Murga looked down on the still, young face, pale and etched with pain, the observant eyes now closed. His Skipper. Their Skipper.

The ward sister came by. 'Someone you know?' she asked.

'He was my skipper,' he replied huskily. 'One of the best. How is he?'

'He has multiple gunshot wounds. Pretty nasty. Fractured skull. Tendons and artery severed in his right

Official Air Force Telegram to David's father,
advising of David's wounding

hand. Damage to his right leg and shoulder. And he's lost a lot of blood. But he'll make it,' she reassured him.

What had happened yesterday? Murga could hardly wait for the rest of the crew to come, so that he could find out.

When they arrived later in the day, they all stood around the bed, numb with the trauma.

'You've got to pull through, Davy Boy,' Drew murmured. 'You can't leave us.'

'You're a bang-on pilot, old chap,' Pop muttered. 'We won't get another one like you.'

'Just wish we could hear one of your isms now,' Boz said wistfully, and the others nodded in agreement.

Birdy spoke last. 'It's not fair, Dave. You shouldn't be here. Everyone knows that the bloke in the back end is the bunny who usually cops it. It shouldn't have been you,' he blurted.

Murga put his hand on the young gunner's shoulder. 'I haven't heard anything yet about how it happened. Come and let's find a cuppa and you can tell me all about it.'

They stood silently looking down on their Skip for another moment. 'Keep saying your prayers, boys,' Drew urged as they turned away.

Down in the canteen they sat bunched close round the table, clasping their mugs of tea tightly, as if warming their hands might somehow help to warm their hearts again.

'We were going to the infernal Happy Valley. Again,' Drew hissed.

'In Dog,' Boz put in.

'Dortmund in daylight,' Pop groaned. 'In a wave of just over 300, mostly Lancs with a few Mossies,' he added.

'The flak was ferocious,' Boz said.

'Worst I've ever seen,' Birdy declared.

'It was the devil's shooting gallery. Nightmare stuff,' Pop muttered.

'We'd laid our eggs and the bomb doors had just closed,' Drew went on. 'Then WHAM! Dog lurched and shuddered and we knew we'd been hit.'

'We went into a dive. We all thought our number was up,' Boz exclaimed.

'But then she was on the level again and the unflappable old Dave's voice comes over the intercom. Can't you just hear him, all cool, calm and collected?' Pop asked.

The others nodded.

'Pilot to rear gunner. Are you OK?' Birdy quoted.

'We felt better then,' Boz declared. 'Until he gives the order, "Put on parachutes and stand by!"'

'This is it, I thought,' Birdy admitted, 'and felt sick. It's a long scramble to the escape hatch from my perch.'

'Then more hot stuff from hell,' Drew continued. 'The action wasn't over yet. We were hit a second time. It threw us about and Dave had to drop below the stream.'

'Talk about a sitting duck!' Birdy's face was tense with the memory.

'Over the Rhine we cop it for the third time,' Pop shuddered.

'But it was third time unlucky for Jerry,' Boz exulted.

'Skip told me to fire a Very light with the colours of the day,' Pop went on. 'A couple of our fighters checked us out, but stooged off when they saw we still had four engines. Even though one of the petrol tanks was holed.' He laughed ironically.

'It wasn't for nothing that Main Force's code word was *Press On*,' Drew said. 'It was tailor made for our

Dave. He puts on speed and heads for Juvincourt. But then, trust him, he thinks he can do better.'

'And there we are, crossing the Channel!' Boz announced. 'And I'm remembering all that ditching practice we'd done.'

'But we're heading for Woodbridge. Then Dave and Cyril thought we had enough juice to get home,' Pop added.

'But he did ask us if we wanted to bale out,' Birdy said. '"Pilot to rear gunner. Do you want to bale out or stay with the aircraft?" Jeez, I hoped I'd never hear him say that.'

The others nodded sombrely. Murga munched his lip and swallowed hard. If only he had been there doing his bit to help.

'Of course none of us wants to leave him to it,' Drew said. 'So there he is again on the intercom. "Take up crash positions!" I tell you, Murga, we were all saying our prayers.'

'It was a pukka landing,' Pop said proudly.

'And then the blood wagon comes racing up,' Boz chipped in.

'We thought they'd come to the wrong kite,' Birdy said. 'But it was for our Skip, and he hadn't told us,' he concluded, his voice breaking.

'I'd seen blood dripping from his hand,' Drew said. 'But Skip never let on he'd been wounded. And Cyril copped some too in the second burst.'

'We miss you, old chap, but you were well out of this lot.' Pop shook Murga's hand as they prepared to leave.

'Look after him for us, won't you, and let us know if he needs anything,' Drew said, gruff with emotion.

Murga nodded. This would be his bit now.

Jolting back in the bus to Kelstern, everyone was silent until Birdy suddenly burst out, 'You know how after every op Skip would always ask each one of us, "What was it like for you?"' They nodded in agreement.

'It was a sort of ritual almost, wasn't it?' Boz said.

'It was his way of showing he cared,' Pop reflected.

'And he did care,' Drew affirmed. 'He gave us the chance to tell how we felt, before we went to interrogation to tell what we had seen. He understood that feelings are important, just as much as facts.'

'Though he never let on about his own,' Boz observed.

'Somehow he was there today, giving us the chance we didn't have last night.' Birdy was struggling to express what he meant. But the others knew. They fell silent again for the rest of the journey, each immersed in his own memories of yesterday.

Back at the hospital, Murga sat by David's bed, imagining all that had happened in D Dog on its fateful sortie to Dortmund.

Next day David, drifting in and out of consciousness, was comforted to find Murga at his side.

'You've had a lot of visitors while you were out to it,' his old navigator told him, 'and a lot of messages. I reckon we ought to start a logbook. Your brother came. So did the crew. Not Cyril. He's still in Louth hospital. And Charles had business on the station. But Drew and Pop and the kids were here. It was a real mothers' meeting for a time.'

He was pleased to see his remark raise a grin on

David's face. 'I thought you might like me to write some letters for you. Brian said he'd write to your parents, but they'll be keen to hear from you too.'

'Thanks,' said David. He knew how anxious his parents would be. 'Let's send a cable first. IN HOSPITAL. NOTHING SERIOUS. PLEASE DON'T WORRY. CHEERIO. DAVID. Can you see to that, Murga?'

Murga nodded. 'Now what about a bit more detail in the letter?' He produced a pen and an airgraph form and with the meticulous precision which had made him such a good navigator, he wrote to David's dictation:

3.12.44

Dear Dad and Mum,
This should wish you and the family all the best for Xmas.
I am sorry I can't write myself as I have hurt my hand
– nothing serious. I am dictating this letter to Reg Murr,
who is writing it for me, and who hopes to be home early
in the new year himself. I have had several visitors so am
quite fortunate. Brian came to see me the other day so he
has probably given you all the latest news.
The weather here is definitely chilly now – I would
not mind being on the beach at Bridport this year again.
Best wishes to all, and don't worry.
David.

David was glad of Murga's company and grateful for his assistance. But as soon as he could sit up, he started trying to write with his left hand. It was not easy. He persevered, however, determined to be independent. All the shrapnel had been removed from his wounds except for one piece in his right hand. The doctors had expressed doubt as to

P.F.C. MATTINGLEY, Esq,
138 ELPHIN ROAD,
LAUNCESTON,
TASMANIA,
AUSTRALIA.

956069

CHRISTMAS GREETINGS 1944

SENDER'S NAME AND ADDRESS: C/O C.D. MATTINGLEY, AUSt. CoNPa

Dear Dad + Mum,   DECEMBER 9, 1944.

Thank you for your letters, which have been arriving regularly, and for an EFM and a GLT call. Everybody is very kind, and I have had a number of visitors — Brian has been able to come over here twice. I have had a good parcel from the Australian Red Cross and am quite happy. My chief annoyance is that I have lost my crew, who cannot wait for me. One could never have better friends.

Please do not worry about me at all as there is nothing seriously wrong. You will have to excuse my left-hand writing, but it will continue for some time, as some of my right tendons are damaged.   Best Wishes
                                        — David.

NEW YEAR GREETINGS 1945

Airgraph written left-handed by David from Rauceby Hospital 10 days after his wounding

whether he would regain full use of it. David was worried. If his right hand was not fully functional, it could put an end to his flying. And that was unthinkable.

He was concerned about his crew, too. Without a pilot they were likely to be split up, especially as he was obviously not going to be fit to return to active service in the near future. After receiving a letter from Drew confirming his fears, David summoned all his strength and wrote shakily with his left hand to his Wingco, asking that his crew be kept together. Charles, with his senior status, also campaigned with the various section leaders on the squadron to try to circumvent the move to separate them.

But it was all to no avail. Only days after the Dortmund raid they learned that Birdy was to stay at Kelstern as a spare bod, although he was not required to fly with any crew who had done fewer ops than he had. Cyril would also return to 625 Squadron when discharged from Louth Infirmary. Charles was 'looking miserable and still wondering what would happen to him'. But Drew, Pop and Boz were to be posted to another squadron.

Drew was furious. *Unfolding a tale of woe into your little pink ear*, he wrote to David. *It is with the deepest regret that we say farewell to Kelstern-in-the-Mud, and to one of the best skippers we have known or are likely to know.* Reporting that he and Pop and Boz had been posted to 576 Squadron as members of a Squadron Leader's crew, he wrote with disgust, *He has some double-barrelled name and I bet a pinch of shit to a gum leaf he speaks with an Oxford accent. I nearly had a howl when I got your letter. I can't find your things. They have been stored away in a neat pile and though I searched through it I can't find them to send to you.'*

He closed, saying, *We are pleased to hear you are improving and would most earnestly like to thank you for what you did and express our sincere admiration of you. Dave, old boy, you are the hero of the place. Rightly so too, say I.*

David was cheered up by his steady trickle of visitors, including his Wingco, the padre, the Adjutant and others from the station. Several Air Vice Marshals and an Air Chief Marshal also visited the hospital and David enjoyed a long chat with Air Vice Marshal Wrigley, Commander of the RAAF overseas.

On his second visit, Brian brought a bunch of grapes, an almost unheard-of luxury in winter in wartime England. David and Murga speculated afterwards on how much each grape had cost.

Des Hadden and Alan Scott made the long journey from their bases to see their friend. Since Rauceby had formerly been a mental hospital, few of David's visitors could refrain from teasing him about his confinement in a lunatic asylum, especially as he occupied a padded cell! He took it all in good part, and joked himself about being certified. He was grateful for the modicum of privacy and quiet which his cell afforded, being off the main ward.

Drew, Pop and Boz described their new station, Fiskerton, in a joint letter. It was written not on the usual flimsy buff Comforts Fund paper, but as an indication of their special regard for their first skipper, on some beautiful heavy cream prewar sheets which Drew had managed somehow to procure. He lamented, *It's not the same, Dave, and we aren't our old selves.* Pop was more explicit. *Not that I have anything against his lordship. But I steadfastly refuse to call his nibs Skipper.* He was irked at the slack intercom procedure, so different from what David had expected of his crew. Cyril complained about it too. He had joined a Canadian crew and was disgusted that they addressed each other over the intercom by first name instead of by function. After more chiacking Pop concluded in a serious vein, *Let me say that your true worth as a pilot and a man has been brought home to us even more forcibly since we have been separated from you, and I am in deadly earnest.*

For his part, David, wrote to his parents making light of his situation, *My chief annoyance is that I have lost my crew, who cannot wait for me. One could never have better friends. Please do not worry about me at all as there is nothing seriously wrong. You will have to excuse my left-hand writing, but it will continue for some time, as some of my right tendons are damaged.*

Homesick and in pain, David felt the loss of his crew deeply. Lying in his hospital bed, he pondered the torment of others who had occupied this cell before him, and the anguish he was now suffering. Remembering the pain of the past 21 months since Point Cook. Fellow trainees dying in accidents. Friends blown to smithereens. Burnt to ashes. Drowned in the killer sea. Or missing. Hideously. Anonymously. Missing presumed dead. Now it was his own crew he was losing. Alive, alert, aware, loyal as blood brothers, bonded forever through the experiences they had shared. Going on without him. Leaving him alone. And desolate.

Once more he resolved he would never let himself become so attached again. It hurt too much. His heart was also a casualty of war.

COMMONWEALTH OF AUSTRALIA

ROYAL AUSTRALIAN AIR FORCE,
OVERSEAS HEADQUARTERS,
KODAK HOUSE,
63, KINGSWAY,
LONDON.

TCENT, LONDON."

ATIONS TO
ANDING."

TO FILE NO. 1401/8984/P4.

16th December, 1944.

Flying Officer C.D.Mattingley, D.F.C.,
Aus.408458,
No.625 Squadron,
R.A.F. Station,
Kelstern,
Louth,Lincs.

Dear *Mattingley*,

  I have just received the good news from
Air Ministry that you have been awarded the Distinguished
Flying Cross.

  2. Please accept my heartiest congratulations on
this award.

  3. With this note I am forwarding a small piece of
D.F.C. ribbon in case you are unable to obtain this
locally.

  Kindest personal regards,

      Yours sincerely,

      Air Vice Marshal,
      Air Officer Commanding.

Encl.

*Air Vice Marshal Wrigley's letter of congratulation to David on the
immediate award of the Distinguished Flying Cross*

Battle Order 204 (8)
Outstanding Devotion to Duty

The Wingco, deeply impressed with David's courage and superb airmanship in bringing home his crew and his aircraft, recommended David for an Immediate Award of the Distinguished Flying Cross. Writing to David to send the squadron's love and congratulations, he said, 'Never was there one more gallantly earned.'

• • • • • • • • • • • • • • • • •

The official citation reads:

> As pilot and captain of an aircraft, Flying Officer MATTINGLEY took part in an attack against DORTMUND in November, 1944.
>
> Whilst over the target, the aircraft was badly hit and Flying Officer MATTINGLEY was wounded about the head, arm and thigh. In

spite of the hits he carried on and afterwards flew the damaged aircraft back to the United Kingdom.

His indomitable spirit, superb captaincy and outstanding devotion to duty set an example of high order.

18 'It is so good to be alive!'

It was a great day for David when, a week before Christmas, he was allowed out of bed and took his first steps with the aid of a crutch on his left side. All this left-hand business took some getting used to. First the basics of eating, drinking and washing. Then shaving. What a challenge! He felt tempted to grow a beard. Writing too. Now learning to use a crutch was another. But he was determined to master it as quickly as possible so that he could escape from his cell and fraternise with the chaps in the main ward. It was good to swap stories, reminisce and exchange information about home.

They came from all over – London, Leeds, Birmingham and Derby, Wales and Scotland, as well as some local Lincolnshire, Lancashire and Yorkshire lads. There were a couple of Canadians, a Pole and even a chap from Turkey. And he was pleased to discover four other Australians,

David by Spitfire, Loughborough Medical Rehabilitation Unit.
Airmen from overseas who had no civvies were issued with
trousers and white jumper.

one from Tasmania, two from South Australia, and a West Australian, 'Ted' Bear from his own squadron, who had also been wounded on the Dortmund raid. 'We're quite a little League of Nations here,' they told him, pleased to greet their released cell mate. Suddenly the boundaries of his world expanded again.

David was sobered to see how severely some had been wounded – aircrew members who had lost an arm or a leg or an eye, and in the padded cell next to him an erk who had fallen on a circular saw with shocking consequences. But most of them were stoically making the best of their situation. He was thankful that burns patients were in a separate ward. Some of those poor fellows were hideously scarred. It was anguish to see them and think of what they had been through and would always have to endure.

When Alan Scott came to visit, caring as always, he took David on his first outing. 'Have to get you out of this place for a while, old chap, before they certify you!' They went to Sleaford, the nearest town, where Alan was keen to acquire the purple and white diagonally striped ribbon which would denote David's award. David was too embarrassed to ask for it, but Alan certainly was not. Walking into the haberdashery, he enquired, 'Do you have the ribbon for the DFC? It's not for me. It's for my friend here.' Afterwards he wrote to David's parents, *He turned all sorts of colours! He is most modest about it. Because he wouldn't, I had to ask one of the nurses to sew it on his uniform.* It was his walking-out uniform. They had had to cut his battledress off him when he was brought in. But David refused to wear the two narrow gold stripes which denoted wounds received in two attacks.

*Another coloured Christmas card available for servicemen
to buy to send home*

A large bough cut from a pine tree in the garden was brought to the ward for the men to decorate before Christmas. 'We've got all the snow and tinsel we need,' they said, raiding the store for cotton wool and cadging bales of Window from mates on nearby stations. It was completely different from all the Christmases David had ever known, but he wrote to his parents, *I was surprised how cheerful a hospital could be at a time like this.* On Christmas Eve he joined the group of staff and up patients going round the wards singing carols, and afterwards laboriously made his way out to the little chapel in the hospital grounds to attend a midnight communion service.

It was the coldest Christmas for over fifty years and the white one they had hoped for. On Christmas morning he limped again to the chapel for the service of lessons and carols, delighting in the fur of snow like ermine over the shrubs along the path and the tinsel of icicles glittering on the trees after a hard frost, while floating fog billowing around the old buildings softened their stark institutional outlines. Everyone enjoyed the luxury of a traditional Christmas dinner with all the trimmings and received presents from the Red Cross. And in the evening David shared a splendid cake from his mother.

But as ward lights were dimmed and men settled down for the night, the same thoughts were in each mind. Would he see another Christmas? Would the war be over by next Christmas? When would they be able to go home to their families? And everyone thought of families they knew where there would never again be a son or brother or father or uncle in the circle around the Christmas table.

Brian, now at Binbrook, the RAAF 460 Squadron station near Kelstern, visited on Boxing Day and together the brothers went to fog-shrouded Lincoln. They struggled along the slippery cobbled streets, glimpsing medieval buildings ghostly in the drifting mist, and slowly toiled up Steep Hill. Then suddenly as they reached the top they emerged from the fog to see the cathedral in all its ancient splendour bathed in sunshine. David caught his breath. It

David's medals; L-R: Distinguished Flying Cross, 1939-45 Star,
France and Germany Star, Defence Medal, British War Medal,
Australian War Medal

seemed an epiphany, an allegory of the triumph of light
over darkness. Entering through the great west door they
paused to take in the sweep of the lofty arches with the
light streaming through the windows above and his soul
sang with the glory of the great church, hallowed by
worship for almost a thousand years. As they sat quietly
in the nave the sound of the mighty organ rolled forth,
reverberating through them like a score of musical Merlin
engines. Then from the exquisitely carved Angel Choir
voices soared in the powerful anthems of Handel's *Messiah*.
David felt washed, bathed, soaked, steeped in its healing
affirmation. He truly knew that his Redeemer lived and
whatever might happen, held him in His almighty love.

Early in January David was thrilled to be given three
weeks leave, the most he had ever had. Thankful to escape
for a while from the sounds of pain and haunted dreams,
he was determined to enjoy it. His head bandages and
skullcap had been removed several weeks earlier, and he

had had a second round of X-rays, much less painful than the first, which had revealed satisfactory healing. The hospital barber had cut his hair, a difficult job as it was still matted with blood, and it had now had time to grow a little and begin to cover the wound. He had discarded his crutch but still had to wear a sling on his right arm, and when he returned he would have to undergo a second operation on his right hand. But for now the horizons of his world had increased.

His first port of call was Kelstern where he was deeply touched by the warmth of the welcome he was given. Everyone was so glad to see him and he was delighted to see Birdy and Charles again and his ground crew, but not surprised to find that D Dog was still out of service. 'The poor old Dog took a hiding and she's still licking her wounds,' an erk told him.

Then he went to Brighton to see Reg Murr, who was awaiting repatriation. 'No more waiting for letters from Mary,' he smiled at his old navigator. 'Won't she be pleased to have you home!' Reg brightened. 'Think of us shivering our socks off here when you're basking in the warmth of sunny Queensland stuffing yourself with bananas,' David said, half enviously.

Murga smiled. 'I will,' promised the man of few words. Then, suddenly serious, he said, 'Thanks, Dave. It was an honour to be in your crew.'

David looked at the thin figure with the greying face which betrayed the stress and sickness Murga had suffered. 'I'm glad you were part of it. You are a gen navigator. We certainly had some moments, didn't we? But we've done our bit for peace and freedom.'

Murga nodded.

They shook hands, looking long into each other's faces. Then David squared his shoulders and turned away. No looking back, he told himself. He could not bear to see Murga's face crumpling. And he knew he could not hide his own feelings. These partings…At least this time he had been given the chance to say goodbye.

From Brighton, he made his way to Kent, where Cyril was home on sick leave. It was good to meet his parents and sisters and to be so warmly made part of a family again. Next stop was Birmingham where, in driving snow, he met up with Pop and Drew to attend Boz's wedding. Looking at Boz's face, so young and happy, and Ann's bright with love, David felt a lump rising in his throat for the pair in their uniforms. 'Let neither Hun nor gun put these two asunder,' he prayed. He felt a pang, too, at parting again from Pop and Drew, but at least he was on his way to another reunion. David McNeill was being invalided home from the Middle East and Dights had been invited to stay with the usual warm welcome.

Arriving before his friend, Dights watched the family reunion, wondering when it would be his turn, moved by the emotion of it all, as the sturdy little Scots mother embraced her oldest laddie and wept, while his father struggled to restrain his tears. When Dights was introduced to Scottish dancing he exclaimed, 'It certainly warms you up. Now I know why Scotsmen wear kilts.'

The highlight of the week was a Burns Supper. He was fascinated to see the fierce pride with which his Scots hosts and friends celebrated their *ain* poet. Robbie Burns knew about farewells and death, the pain of parting and loss. 'When day is gone, and night is come And a' folk bound to sleep, I think on him that's far awa' The lee-lang night, and weep.' He knew the value of friendship. 'It's coming yet, for a' that, That man to man the world o'er Shall brothers be for a' that.' Dights found himself listening with new ears, identifying with the meaning of the poems in a deeper way than ever before. When it was time for 'Auld Lang Syne', he was moved by its poignancy, 'Should auld acquaintance be forgot And never brought to min'? Should auld acquaintance be forgot, And days of auld lang syne?'

'I'll never forget you, David lad,' he said as they climbed the stairs to bed. 'You're the best friend I've made since I came to Britain. And your family has certainly given me 'a cup of kindness', full and overflowing.'

Back at Rauceby, a bumper mail awaited him – letters, airgraphs and parcels. So he set to at once to answer at least some, before the second operation on his hand. The surgeon, who was a King's Honorary Surgeon, was still in doubt what it would achieve. Fortunately it went well. The last piece of metal was removed and the tendons rejoined. And after a few days he was allowed up and about. But it was still uncertain whether he might require further surgery.

He was writing left-handed again, as his right hand was in a splint once more. After receiving 23 more letters and five parcels in one batch, he wrote to his parents, asking them to thank the donors. *Parcels are always acceptable in hospital, and I have been distributing largesse like a philanthropist or public benefactor.* Alan Scott also wrote to David's parents. He had received a letter after the second operation, *but as usual David gave no personal information whatever*, so Alan planned to visit and check up.

The hospital atmosphere in the grim old buildings with their barred windows was depressing. And David wondered yet again if and when he would get back to active service. He himself unwittingly caused a delay in his discharge. Italian POWs awaiting repatriation were working on local farms and one day just after the splint had been removed, a group saluted him. Without thinking he returned it, ripping stitches out of his right hand. So, more had to be inserted.

Men were moving in and out of the hospital every week. New casualties from missions were being brought in. Others were moving out, which was encouraging or unsettling, depending on whether they left by the front door on their own feet or were carried out through the back in a box. Even with those who walked out, David knew it was unlikely that their paths would cross again.

Then suddenly at the end of February, the future seemed brighter. It was decided that he would not need a third operation. After three months in hospital he was to be transferred to a convalescent and rehabilitation unit at Loughborough in Leicestershire. Run more as a club than as an Air Force station, uniform was not worn, rank was ignored and patients, who ranged from an Air Vice Marshal to Pilot Officers, mingled freely, with a fine sense of camaraderie, understanding and respect for what others had gone through. There were amputees who had lost a foot, or a leg, some below, some above the knee, others still right up to the thigh. Some had lost a hand or an arm. David counted himself lucky indeed and was inspired by their fortitude, encouraged by their positive attitudes, philosophy and humour.

The program began at 9 am and finished at 4 pm, and the men worked hard with exercises, basketball, badminton, archery and swimming. David's first treatment for his hand was rather painful, as it was bathed in almost boiling hot wax, followed by massage and exercises to strengthen the tendons and regain mobility in his fingers. Treatment was holistic, much attention also being given to social interaction, relaxation, and mental stimulation. David particularly appreciated hearing eminent historian G.M. Trevelyan twice, and also the head of Pathfinders, Australian Air Vice Marshal Bennett, and Earl Templeton, known as 'the father of the House of Commons'.

Every week the men were taken for a ramble in the countryside, where the loveliness of spring unfolding was a delight and played an important part in David's healing, bringing new hope. As the milder weather thawed his winter-chilled body, spring's promise warmed his grief-numbed heart. He revelled in each new sign – fruit trees bursting into blossom, hedgerows and hawthorns beginning to tinge with green, the first daffodils, the joyous song of birds. And in mid-March he was able to write, *It is so good to be alive and about these days! Particularly as a more optimistic view can now be taken of the European war.* In December the Allies had taken Ravenna in Italy; in January the Russians had captured Warsaw and Krakow and reached the Oder; while in February British troops reached the Rhine on a ten-mile front and by mid-March the Allies controlled its west bank.

He reported proudly to his parents, *I have now cut down the number of letters I owe from over 100 to 27.* For three months people from all over Australia and Britain had been writing to congratulate him on his DFC and wish him a speedy recovery. And in his meticulous way he was determined to answer every letter. He particularly appreciated one from Drew's wife, Thel, who wrote, *Thank you again for what you did. The thought of what might have happened still gives me the creeps. I know the boys are proud of you.*

His first headmaster wrote, *If your ears have been burning, it will be because you have been the subject of much talk among the young things here.*

His Uncle Arthur wrote, *Good for you doing your best to defend democracy and thereby helping to make the bad old world better and happier. An example of duty to country and conscience. You are young and have had the great advantage of visiting other countries, the experiences which will or should be of inestimable value to you in after life. Would that I had had them when young, my mental horizon would have been much expanded.*

Back home, his parents had also been receiving telegrams and letters from every Australian state as people read in the papers of David's feat, his devotion to duty, his award, and wrote offering congratulations and best wishes for his recovery. They ranged from an aunt who remembered nursing David as *a fat and lovely baby*, to those, including teachers, who had watched him grow up. All shared memories and sentiments to comfort and uphold his parents. A former neighbour wrote, *My mind goes back to the first time I saw him in the garden at 'Fairlawn', with his red jumper, a very bonny boy. How little we realised just what the future had in store for him so young. But he has proved what sort of a man he is.*

His last headmaster gave wise encouragement. *He is having great experience now, and will return with a knowledge and breadth of vision that will make him a man a generation ahead in development compared with when he went away.*

Peter Lord's mother wrote, *Do you know David sent me a cable from hospital. Wasn't it marvellous of him? I do hope you will be having him home soon. Peter wrote to me about a friend of his that did not return – 'If your number is up there is no more to it.' We are unlucky. When David comes home I would very much like to see him.*

Perhaps the most touching of all was from Frank's mother, who wrote to David's, *No one knows but a mother, what the anxiety about our boys is to us. Frank's brother hoped in his last letter that Frank would be home for Christmas. He only knows that he is missing. I want him to keep hoping with me that our Frank is returning. I can't think any other way.*

David also received a number of letters from parents of airmen who had been killed or gone missing, desperate for more information about their son's fate than official communications provided. These were the most difficult letters to answer and he spent much time in correspondence with Air Force headquarters, and networking among friends and acquaintances trying to glean any available details. Usually there were none, or none that would bring any comfort to bereaved and grieving parents. But he did his best and was moved by the pathetically grateful replies he received.

The mother of Allen Morgan, one of the boys with whom he had spent time in New York, wrote, *Many thanks for your letter. Yes, it was a terrible shock losing Allen. We never gave up hope until quite recently. Although I realise now he is gone, in my heart he still lives.* David had sent her a snapshot taken in New York, for which she was grateful. *Not a very good one of him, as you said, but the most recent.* For that reason he was

L-R: Fred Clarke, Allen Morgan, David in New York. They travelled together to Britain, but after spending their first weeks at Brighton, were posted to different units and did not meet again. As a gunner, Allen was sent on ops much earlier than pilots, who needed more training.
He was killed, aged 20, over Berlin on 29 January 1944.
He is buried in the Berlin 1939-1945 War Cemetery.

glad he had continued the expensive practice of having studio portraits taken to send home. They could be all that was left for his parents. Mrs Morgan went on to ask for help in tracking down two of her son's crew who had been taken prisoner, in hopes that they might be able to tell her something. So did Ron Leonard's mother. David and Ron had trained together at Point Cook and Ron had helped celebrate David's 21st birthday in Wellington. Now he was in enemy hands.

No wonder a friend of his mother had written, *Many hearts must feel like breaking these days*. Everyone was looking forward to the time 'when the boys come home'. Not least the boys themselves.

APRIL   4th Month   1945

15 Sun—2nd after Easter

Appleton	All O.K.	—
Bowell	7 killed	7
Edwards	1 killed	1
Finlay	4 killed 2 P.O.W.	6
Friend	6 P.O.W.	6

16 Mon

Gilbert	1 wounded	1
Gooding	All O.K.	—
Huxtable	1 killed	1
Leonard	7 P.O.W.	7
Lord	1 killed 6 P.O.W.	7

17 Tues

Mattingley	2 wounded	2
McLelland	All O.K.	—
Mifler	6 killed 1 P.O.W.	7
Ordell	6 killed 1 P.O.W.	7
Richins	6 killed	6

18 Wed

Roze	All O.K.	—
Staples	7 killed	7
Jocchini	1 killed	1
Walker	6 killed	6

19 Victory At Last!

On 21 April David wrote in his diary, *Today is the great day – at last I am free from hospitals and similar institutions. Five months have been quite sufficient, and the doctors have done a good job, although my right hand is still much weaker than my left.* His hand had been declared fit for flying a heavy bomber again. But in another irony of war, he was told that because of the damage to the tendons he would not be able to play the piano.

Never again would he feel the cool smooth ivories rippling beneath his fingers. Never again would he hear melodies produced by his hands. Never again would the organ respond to his touch. He thought of the piano waiting in the sitting room at home, the small organ in the corner of the dining room, the organ in the little church at Bridport where he sometimes played hymns for the Christmas and Easter services. He remembered the walks, the bike rides, winter and summer, to music lessons. His

Page from David's pocket diary, later copied into his regular diary

painstaking teacher who on frosty nights always put an eiderdown over the grand piano, which was his pride and joy. David was one of the few pupils allowed to play it. The hours and hours of practice, concerts, exams, theory with which he wrestled. The pile of music books. The thrill of mastering a new piece. Etudes, mazurkas, waltzes, sonatinas flooded back through his mind as he stood swaying in the train to London, going on nine days' leave.

His first stop of course was the Boomerang Club, where his confidence was rather shaken when fellows with whom he had trained commented on how his hospital stay had aged him.

Cambridge was David's next destination for three therapeutic days with Dr and Mrs Noble. Physically relaxed and mentally rejuvenated, he then went to Nottingham for his next commitment – as best man to Des Hadden at his wedding to a local girl. *Sheila was one of the prettiest brides I have seen, and Des was extra happy*, he wrote.

Festivities over, he caught a train to Lincoln to meet Drew, Pop and Boz and spend a cheerful evening reminiscing.

'So when are you going to get married?' Drew asked Pop and David. 'Who's going to be first?'

They looked sheepish. Pop shrugged his shoulders. David replied, 'No plans.'

'It would have been more interesting if you'd said "No comment",' Drew teased.

'You don't know what you're missing,' Boz told them. 'You ought to start looking and get yourselves an English bride too before we go home,' he urged.

*Flying Officer
David Mattingley
in 1945*

*Wedding of Des
Hadden and Sheila
Houghton, David
as best man, Brian
(R in cap) in guard
of honour*

Drew would not give up. 'Surely there were a couple of pretty bridesmaids at the wedding?' he persisted.

'No comment,' David grinned.

Going home. It was on everyone's mind and something that everyone talked about now. Surely the war in Europe could not last much longer. But it was far from over on the Japanese front. They could be sent to India. Or Burma. Or the Pacific. They all knew that for Australians there was still more action. But at least they would be closer to home.

With the decreasing need for air offensive, wartime airfields which had sprung up all over Lincolnshire and Yorkshire were being closed. David found many changes at Kelstern.

It took two days to track down, collect and repack all his kit for the move to his next posting with the squadron. He wrote, *I do not like breaking the ties with Kelstern*. But the last op from Kelstern had been flown on 4 April, and next day, 4 May, he also was off to rejoin the squadron now based at Scampton. There the Personnel Officer wanted to send him back to a Heavy Conversion Unit.

David, however, had other views. He phoned the Wingco, *he was most pleased to have me back*, and the Wingco arranged that he should take over the crew of the B Flight Commander, who had finished his tour – an all-British crew except for one lively Irishman. *It is remarkable how few folk I know on 625 now – there are only two crews who were on the squadron when I left. The others have 'had it' or have been screened. Today the Wingco left. He was very good to me and I am sorry to see him go*, he wrote.

On 25 April 625 Squadron had flown its last mission. The target had been Berchtesgaden, Hitler's retreat in the Bavarian Alps. It proved to be the last daylight bombing operation of the war.

With 23 missions to his credit, David's days and nights as a bomber pilot were over.

Now with growing excitement he and everyone on the station anticipated the collapse or capitulation of Germany, and listened eagerly to every fresh news bulletin.

On 7 May he wrote, *I was in the Mess most of the day listening to the news bulletins. Each one has been better than the previous one and the climax came with the great news of unconditional surrender.* Immediately he went over to Hemswell to be with Drew, Pop and Boz, *with whom we did our little bit towards victory.* They were sorry that Murga had gone back to Australia and that Cyril and Birdy were on screening leave. *But*, he wrote, *it was great for the four of us to be together.*

Tuesday 8 May, the official VE Day, dawned fine at Scampton, where all personnel attended a thanksgiving church parade in No. 1 Hangar. David wrote to his parents, *It is as if a cloud has been lifted from the face of Britain.*

In his diary he wrote more soberly: *It is wonderful to think that the victory for which we have striven for over five and a half years is at last here. What losses there have been in this struggle which has come to such a happy conclusion! Bomber Command in the course of dropping almost 1 000 000 tons of bombs has lost nearly 10 000 aircraft by enemy action alone. Others were brought down by ice, some crashed in England, and others were too badly damaged to be of further use.*

Over 50 000 men were killed, while others were POW or wounded, out of 110 000 men who passed through the Command. This is the price that one branch of one service has paid.

In fact nearly 26 000 of those who died flew from Lincolnshire, and the anniversary of Frank's death, on a mission from Scampton, was only days away. David spent the afternoon quietly; reflecting, remembering. Frank, Peter, Tas, Allen, Ollie, Arthur, Jimmy, the Brock brothers Jim and Joe...and so many others he had known.

He listened to Churchill's historic speech and went with friends into Lincoln, where they found a gala atmosphere, streets and buildings bedecked with flags of many nations. At 9 pm they gathered in the celebrated White Hart Hotel to hear the King's speech. After darkness fell, the cathedral was illuminated by searchlights, a magnificent sight which David would never forget. From its towers rang out peal upon peal of victory joybells. People thronged the narrow streets and began dancing. Joy and thankfulness embraced everyone as strangers hugged and laughed and sang in the elation of victory. Back at Scampton, although all pyrotechnics had been locked up, David and a mate had managed to secure a substantial supply, and he wrote *We made good use of them and eventually got to bed as dawn was breaking.*

David, *being now in the position on the squadron that I can do almost anything I wish*, decided to go flying with a scratch crew. *There seem to be a number of chaps, including some erks, who want to fly with me, so we shall take them whenever possible. All 625 staff seem pleased to see me back again, but I am the one who is most glad.* It was exhilarating to be in the air again. David hoped to go on mercy missions, dropping food to the starving Dutch, bringing back POWs, and also taking ground crew on 'Cooks Tours' to view some of the op sites.

But on 25 May all Australians were grounded and withdrawn from crews.

David had made his last flight as a Lancaster pilot.

The consolation was that they would get some leave. He headed for London where victory celebrations continued. A gala atmosphere still reigned, with flags and bunting brightening the drab, war-weary streets whose buildings had not had a coat of paint throughout the war. It was thronged with service men and women, and after the years of stress and tension an air of relief prevailed.

Eager to catch up with friends and acquaintances and to find out all he could about others, he spent two days at the Boomerang Club. Most POWs he met were fitter than he expected. But he wrote, *Some have had very gruelling experiences in German hands. Many had to do forced marches in the depths of winter, with very little food. Those who were liberated by the Russians did not enjoy the treatment by them.* He was glad to meet Ron Leonard, who with his whole crew had been POWs. Another POW was the only survivor when the 'Oh! My profile!' pilot's plane was shot down.

He spent time at Kodak House, too, on the grim business of making enquiries about casualties, and he wrote, *The toll of war is not light and there are many faces that one misses in the Air Force, which has had such heavy casualties. Looking back on the happy times we all had at Church Broughton I thought of those we shall never see again. Out of 19 crews only 3 survived their ops intact.* He listed them in his diary. *Seventy two men out of 133 became casualties. Three men were wounded, 23 became prisoners of war, and 46 were killed.*

But they were not just numbers. Not just statistics. They were men. Each had a name. And every one of them had a family. And friends. So the pain and suffering spread far beyond each man who had gone through the horrors of hell and the valley of the shadow of a hideous death. Into distant homes where they would live on as a photo on a mantelpiece, a snapshot in an album, a bundle of letters in a drawer, a story of courage and gallantry remembered and recounted at Christmas. Into faraway communities where, when snow lay in drifts over Lincolnshire, Yorkshire and Derbyshire, heat would be rising from parched grass or dust would be blowing in willy-willies. Where names newly chiselled into monuments topped by a statue of a World War I digger would glint more brightly than the heroes of Anzac. For a time. Until they too were faded, lichened. Names. Not men driving tractors across wide paddocks. Or standing in front of classes of upturned faces. Out on a cricket pitch on a Saturday afternoon. Taking their sons fishing. Or their daughters to ballet lessons. Sitting on the verandah with their wives, watching the sunset, talking about the future.

David still had many places on his must-see, must-do list, so after days listening to POW stories, it was a relief to take time out to visit Windsor Castle with Pop, and Runnymede, where Magna Carta was signed. 'Another seminal site in the history of England that I've now seen!' he exclaimed.

When he met his cousin Eric, back from almost two years in the Middle East, they made the trip into Hampshire together to visit Mattingley. They were thrilled to discover a picture-book village with charming thatched cottages clustered around the green and a 13th century church. Well pleased with their excursion into family history, they quaffed a pint in the Leather Bottle Inn.

In Nottingham catching up with Des, David fulfilled another long-held wish. Wandering among the great oak trees in Sherwood Forest, he said to Des, 'I've always wanted to come here. Do you remember we did *Robin Hood* as a play in primary school?'

'How could I forget?' Des replied. 'You were Robin Hood!'

'And now you're a Merry Man indeed, with your Maid Marian,' David teased his old friend about his local lass, Sheila. But as he scuffled through last year's leaves and rolled silken-smooth acorns in the palm of his war-damaged hand, he wondered, not for the first time, if he would ever find his own Maid Marian.

Reg Watson and David enjoying leave in Wales

A concert at London's Albert Hall was a highlight, and David was able to write home that he was standing only a few feet from the Queen and the Princesses. But he told his parents nothing of his private grief as he had listened to the celebrated pianist Dame Myra Hess, knowing that he would never again be able to play.

One memorable day, after collecting eleven parcels at the Base Post Office at Kodak House he calculated that his mother alone had sent him more than seventy parcels, over one third of a ton of food! 'But I must write and tell everyone not to send any more,' he reminded himself. 'They mightn't arrive before I sail for home.'

Sailing for home. It was in all their thoughts. In all their conversations. But David hoped his embarkation call would not come just yet. He had signed up for a week's British Council course in Stratford-upon-Avon, a week at Cambridge University, and a month at Oxford University. And he was keen to do them.

Back at Scampton, it was time to pack up yet again. As David surveyed all that he had accumulated since his last move, he consoled himself that he did not have a frying pan to pack, as did his Irish crew member!

But the letters… Oh, the letters. Although he had always discarded most after answering them, there were still too many to keep and he would have to discard more. Sitting on his bed, he began re-reading them, smiling, chuckling, blinking away tears. He would have to destroy those from his parents. But he wanted to keep the many messages of congratulation and well wishes for his recovery. From Drew and the rest of the crew. And the Wingco and the padre. And the last letters. He bit his lips as he picked up envelopes with the familiar handwriting of Frank, Peter, Tas and others. This was not the time to read them. Later. Much later. Perhaps when his heart was stronger again.

On the last night everyone joined in a farewell party in the Mess and eventually they made their way to bed at 4 am. 'What a night! It's a party we'll all remember.'

More farewells were yet to be said before leaving next day for Gamston, the base where all Australians in Bomber Command had to hand in their surplus gear and be processed for repatriation. Twelve hundred men had already been through since VE Day, and had gone on to Brighton to await embarkation. The air was tense with expectation and excitement, loud with laughter, greetings and cries of 'Australia, here we come!' 'And I'm drooling at the thought of lemon meringue pies again!' Birdy crowed.

David met up with Drew, Pop and Boz and others. Drew was counting the days till he might see his Thel, but Boz was trying to get his time in Britain extended, to be as long as possible with his English Ann.

David was pleased that he and Pop had managed to get their departure deferred. But sad indeed to wave goodbye to Drew, who shouted 'Bomb doors closed!' and gave his usual cheeky thumbs-up sign as the bus pulled away through the station gates and passed out of sight. No longer would it be 'Enemy coast ahead' for him, but 'Australia ahoy!'

noise from railway engines, answered
by factory sirens. Peace had been
declared!' Having dressed again, I
walked up to Carfax, where an ever-
growing bonfire was lighting up the
centre of the road. Fuel seemed to
appear from nowhere, as did the crowd.
The announcement at midnight had
found many of them in bed. Soon
there were numerous figures running
round the fire, having a hilarious
and riotous time. We eventually
went to bed shortly before 5 a.m.

Wednesday 15
    The great day is here, and
there is peace on earth again, after
6 years of war. What a rejoicing
there is; and yet the full significance
has not struck us all. For many
it is a day of bitter-sweet feelings, as
so many friends have given their
lives for those who remain. This
afternoon I went for a quiet walk

Brooklyn, not
famous bridge
is uninspiring
Barber times De
very corrupt
ship we can
Britain, U.S
Sweden, and
a surprise
ships on i

Sunday
evening, a
cleared d
authoriti
on the g
all New
true it
thirty
They a
varies
Irish

American
ews and
supplements!
paper

U.S.A. at 5.45
car to the
Borough Hall),
der the river by
Station at
ness centre
ductors or ticket
and subways, as
heir place!
icket in the slot
nywhere on
sit system. Thus
very long ride for
in tea with Fred
Union Jack Club
we set out to explore
d seems really
parks and reserves
has most of the

*Entry in David's diary for 15 August 1945, describing
Victory celebrations in Oxford. Entry in open diary below describes
his first impressions of New York on 15 August 1943.*

20 'In hospital again. Nothing serious. Don't worry.'

After spending his twenty-third birthday at Stratford-upon-Avon with Pop and his friend w/op Mark Beresford, David set out on a series of farewell visits, first to Cyril's family where Mrs Bailey provided a splendid dinner.

'But you should not have used up all your meat coupons,' David remonstrated.

'Only the best is good enough for you boys,' Mrs Bailey declared. 'Without you lads where would we all have been?'

'I was lucky to have such a good flight engineer. Thanks to you both,' David said to Cyril's parents as he left. No looking back, he reminded himself, wondering if he would ever see this generous family again.

Then it was off to Scotland to say goodbye to the McNeills, before a trip to Ireland with Pop and Mark. In Dublin he bought a Donegal tweed sports coat and, as it was the first time he had worn civvies for years, it felt quite strange. They indulged in the rich, unrationed Irish fare like kids in a lolly shop. Now it really was beginning to feel like peacetime!

The week in Cambridge was one of the best in David's stay in Britain. The lectures about history and world events by knowledgeable, witty dons were manna for a mind which had so long grappled with the mechanics of engines and airframes and the mathematics of navigation, gunnery and bomb aiming. The opportunities to visit colleges with their proud traditions of scholarship and learning, and to be shown their treasures was manna for the spirit whose focus had perforce been so long on destruction. The last lecture entitled *Why read poetry* was, for David, a perfect finale.

At Oxford for the four-week course on education, David again enjoyed the opportunities for debate and discussion, as well as afternoons exploring some of the colleges.

Within days of atom bombs being dropped on Hiroshima and Nagasaki, Japan finally surrendered. On 14 August David had just gone to bed when blasts from factory sirens, tooting railway engines and the first revellers banging tin cans alerted him that the war was over. At last! Dressing hastily, he hurried to the heart of the city, where people were bringing anything they could to add to the bonfire, the centre of hilarious and riotous celebrations which continued until 5 am. Next day, victory peals rang out from all Oxford's church bells and David attended a thanksgiving service, before listening to the King's speech and joining in the dancing in the streets again.

In his diary he wrote, *The great day is here, and there is peace on earth again, after 6 years of war. What a rejoicing*

'In hospital again. Nothing serious. Don't worry.'

there is; and yet the full significance has not struck us all. For many it is a day of bitter-sweet feelings, as so many friends have given their lives for those who remain. In the afternoon he went for a quiet walk, remembering Rupert Brooke's lines about the dead who 'poured out the red Sweet wine of youth; gave up the years to be Of work and joy...'

Wandering Oxford's streets he was pleasantly surprised to come across various acquaintances. Best of all was meeting Sam Salter, Peter's instructor from Southrop, and spending two evenings together. On the first they talked about old times and people they both knew. But on the second they talked of the future. Sam had decided his vocation was in the church. 'Have you considered that?' he asked.

David nodded. 'But I don't believe it is my calling. I'm thinking of teaching. I've had a taste of that and I liked it. And it's a way of putting something back. Rebuilding. If young people learn something about history, surely the next generation will not repeat the mistakes of the past,' he said hopefully. 'History really is important.'

Later, as they sipped port by the fire, Sam said, 'Marriage?'

David was silent, looking into the friendly flames, so different from those others.

Sam sat quietly, and then went on, 'It's a path I want to go down. But I'll have to wait a while until I've finished my training.'

'I don't think I'm ready for it yet,' David said. Slowly he added, 'Getting close to someone makes you very vulnerable, doesn't it? I don't know whether I can risk it again.'

Sam nodded. The wounds of war went very deep. Healing would be slow. But pray God it would come in time.

David had not been feeling well for some while, and on a trip to Cornwall he became ill. On 3 September he wrote, *It is now 2 years since I arrived in this country, during which time I have seen a good deal of it and the way it has suffered from 6 years of war.* So many had paid the full price with their lives in that war. He was fortunate that he had only paid an instalment with a part of his.

But another instalment was due.

Back at base he reported sick and was sent off to the Royal Doncaster Infirmary. With a high temperature and rapid pulse, he was diagnosed with acute pleurisy, accounting for the excruciating pain in his chest. He was not told the results of X-rays and a blood test, but simply informed he would be hospitalised for some time. So he sent another cable to his parents. IN HOSPITAL AGAIN. NOTHING SERIOUS. DON'T WORRY.

Although he had a small room to himself, it was connected to the children's ward, with the constant sound of children vomiting and crying.

Five ounces of fluid were removed from his left lung in a painful procedure. But he had no energy. Too weak to shave, even reading tired him. Six days later he wrote, *I spend most of the time just lying and thinking, an art I acquired when in Rauceby Hospital.* Pop brought pyjamas and other comforts. But then he also left for Brighton on his way home. And David wrote, *I wonder how long it will be now before I leave?*

Fortunately, Brian was transferred to a nearby station, so David was not bereft of visitors. When Brian, who had been awarded a DFC after completing his tour of duty, was posted to Gamston at the beginning of October, David wrote, *I may not see him again until we reach home. Almost everyone I know is now on the high seas or back in Australia.*

After three long lonely weeks he was pleased to be able to shave himself and after four began to write letters home again. But he was becoming restive. So after a dense fog on 1 October, a sure sign of approaching winter, he *had a chat with the doctor and pointed out that the sooner I am on my way home and in a warm climate the better.*

A sympathetic nurse brought him a tomato from her parent's greenhouse – luxury indeed – and the kindly medico invited him to his house whenever he wished for time out. But after learning that he had lost 10 pounds, which brought his weight loss to two-and-a-half stone since arriving in England, David determined to find out more about his condition. He waited until the nurses' station was unattended to go and 'borrow' his records. He wedged the chair against the door of his room and sat on his bed to read them.

It was not good reading. His pleurisy was tuberculous.

David's spirits lifted with news that the important part Cyril had played in bringing Dog back from Dortmund had been recognised with a Distinguished Flying Medal. Birdy also had been gazetted for a DFM after completion of his tour.

At last, on a sunny day David was allowed outside for a fifteen-minute walk, and wrote, *I can now imagine how a bird feels on being released from a cage.*

But two days later he received another devastating blow. When he opened the carefully recycled wartime envelope addressed in Mrs McNeill's firm square hand there was nothing to prepare him for the news she shared. *We have lost our Darling David. As you know we were looking every day for him coming home. But he died suddenly last Sunday evening in hospital in Gloucester.* Bonnie David, such a fine lad, so true and warm-hearted and brave. Another part of Dights' heart crumpled and died with him. In a daze of pain he read on. It was the infection he had contracted in the Middle East which affected his heart. Yet when he was home only three weeks earlier he had seemed so happy and full of life, talking of getting back to university, carrying on where he left off.

What a waste, David breathed. What a cruel waste. The words of the 'Lament for the Battle of Flodden' were running through his mind. 'The flowers of the forest are a' wede away.' And he could hear the dirge of bagpipes, as they had heard them when David lad proudly had taken him to Edinburgh Castle eighteen months ago. The fierce crushing pain which gripped him was like a pleurisy of the heart, flooding it, drowning it in the bitter tears he could not shed.

Scottish David's last words to his mother in the hospital were, 'Goodnight, Mummy. Dinna worry about me. I'll be all right.' And she wrote to David, *I'm just trying to remember those words every minute of the day. He has just gone on a wee while before me. We hope to meet him some day in a better world than this.*

She wrote again twelve days later to thank David for his letter of sympathy. This time the envelope was black edged, as was the paper. *Had David been properly treated when he returned or been discharged this would never have happened. All my life I shall never be able to forgive the RAF for their carelessness. David, we are all heart broken. He was so very happy about being demobbed. He had all his plans made for the next three years. It's just as well one doesn't know what's before one.*

Just as well indeed.

After yet more X-rays and blood tests, David was told the results were good. The pleurisy had eased considerably and if he continued to improve he should be ready for repatriation early in the new year.

The bad news was that in the meantime he was to be transferred back to Rauceby.

On 29 November he wrote *It is a year ago today that I did my last op and came into this hospital.* And he had spent eight of those twelve months in hospitals. After three more dreary weeks at Rauceby he was sent on to another convalescent unit. This was a great improvement on the former asylum. It was Harewood House, the beautiful 18th century Yorkshire home of the Earl of Harewood and Princess Mary, the King's sister, who had graciously made one of the wings available for servicemen.

The house was set in hundreds of acres of parklands and, free to spend the time as he wished, on fine days David went for long walks, letting the peace seep through his whole being.

When the weather was wild or wet, there was plenty indoors to engage his attention. The elaborate Rococo ceilings and many fine paintings revealed so much about the past, the occupants of the house and their activities, as well as the landscape.

On Christmas Eve they cut greenery to decorate the house, festooning the rooms with holly, and David grinned to himself, thinking what Drew and Boz would say if they could see him hanging mistletoe in strategic places.

On Christmas morning, after the service in the old stone church in the grounds and a substantial breakfast with real eggs, David met Princess Mary and the Earl, enjoying a long informal chat with them. All the meals at Harewood were good, in contrast to the poor hospital fare, and Christmas dinner was no exception. Afterwards, the Princess gave each officer a copy of a book about the Royal Family, personally inscribed, and they listened to the King's speech, his first peacetime one in six years.

Social activities were an important part of life at Harewood and a vital part of healing, with VADs, a cheerful group of young women, providing the nursing assistance any men might require, but even more importantly giving them company as they adjusted towards everyday life again. Meals were usually segregated, but not this night. Everyone joined in a merry evening of party games. David was chuffed that he and his VAD partner, the dark-haired Barbara, distinguished themselves by winning dancing and musical chairs competitions. If only Drew and Boz had been there to see that!

Festivities continued on Boxing Day, when the patients put on VADs' uniforms and waited on them at lunch. Afterwards, David and the Princess talked again as they washed up together. On the second evening of dancing David found himself really enjoying female company once more, commenting on what a pleasure it was to see girls in evening dress again. Barbara was good fun. They took walks together, and often made up a foursome to go off to the cinema or for meals. One day David and a British major with whom he had become friendly swapped uniforms and thoroughly enjoyed the prank.

He hated having to leave Harewood to return to cheerless Rauceby early in the New Year. Further X-rays and a blood test were satisfactory and he was told that he would leave England on a hospital ship in two to three weeks. But when bad weather postponed sailing, David was glad to be given leave from Rauceby. Although the McNeills had extended a warm invitation to return at any time, he could not face going back. It seemed so unfair, now that David was gone. Why one David but not the other? It was unfathomable and he did not want to inflict any more sorrow on the grieving family.

So he went back to Harewood. Climbing the hill with Barbara in the sunlight for a last look across the park to the beautiful home where he had been so happy, both felt they were in another world. *Remote from this one with all its strife.*

On 31 January 1946 a small group of Australian airmen with David in charge left Rauceby by ambulance for London. On 1 February they boarded the white hospital ship *Maunganui*, with its distinctive green line and green crosses on its funnel. An old New Zealand vessel of 7500 tons, it had been fitted out to carry war brides as well as patients, both Australian and Kiwi, from the three services. Air Vice Marshal Wrigley, Air Officer Commanding RAAF Overseas, who had visited David in Rauceby, came to the docks to see them off. Nearing midnight, the ship moved out into the Thames.

David looked up the river towards Westminster, the cradle of democracy, where so many of the war's hard decisions had been made. After almost two and a half years in Britain he was leaving with very mixed feelings. England, Scotland, Wales. London, Edinburgh, York, Lincoln, Canterbury, Cambridge, Oxford. Dozens of other smaller and special places. Good times, bad times. Making friends, losing friends. Loving. Losing. And learning. Always learning. Immeasurably enlarged. Sadder. Wiser. Wondering. Would he ever come back again?

Hospital ship Maunganui. Note distinguishing crosses and band.

21 Going Home

A severe storm forced *Maunganui* to anchor where the roadstead was crowded with vessels flying flags of many countries, all waiting for the weather to improve. Later, as the ship proceeded down the Channel, David had his final glimpse of the white cliffs of Dover. Rising forbidding from an angry sea with ominous clouds above, they seemed to epitomise the rugged British defiance, its people stalwart against the turmoil of war. England, bastion of freedom, unconquered since 1066. And he had played a part in her history.

In violent conditions in the Bay of Biscay, David, one of the few still on his feet, spent the solitary hours reliving his memories as he painstakingly made a model Lancaster.

Maunganui steamed through the Mediterranean, scene of so many recent naval battles, and Italy's defeated navy beached at Taranto; onwards into Suez, that other amazing canal, and its bustling Port Said; through fierce

Model Lancaster made by David on voyage, with RAAF cap badge

desert sandstorms into the Red Sea's searing heat; into the cooler Indian Ocean.

In colourful tropical Colombo, their third port of call, David bought a handmade lace tablecloth for his mother. Then, standing by the ship's rail watching the silhouette of Ceylon's mountains receding, David envisaged the welcome being prepared for him. His mother baking, his aunt polishing, while by the front steps his father placed pots which he had planted weeks before with red and white petunias and blue lobelias, and his uncle contrived some little treat, the way he had always loved to do when the boys were small. Would they come to the ferry to meet him? Or would he surprise them? Arriving unannounced. Running up the slope to the house where an Australian flag and a Union Jack had been draped by the front door, and where a big sign in his aunt's careful printing proclaimed, WELCOME HOME DAVID!

He looked up into the sky. Not long now before he would see the Southern Cross again...

Since he had left home in May 1943 he had circumnavigated the world. Not as fast as Jules Verne's Phileas Fogg, but with a great deal more at stake. In thirty-three months he had experienced something of life and culture in New Zealand, Panama, USA, England, Scotland, Wales, Eire, Italy, Egypt and Ceylon. And he had fought against Nazism and all its evils, helping win the victory. He had not made a Jules Verne journey to the centre of the earth. But he had been to hell. And back, thank God. And to heaven, too, in the exhilaration and ecstasy of flying: Tiger Moths, Oxfords, Ansons, Wellingtons, Halifaxes and Lancasters. He had felt the joy of taking off into the unknown, soaring above the clouds, discovering distant horizons. He had seen the earth from 20 000 feet and more. On wings heaven-high. And he had made a journey to the centre of his being. A long deep journey.

By the last light of northern stars he watched the ship's wake foaming and glittering and took a deep breath of the warm salty air. One more day and they would reach the Equator.

Everyone counted the days, the hours, until their longed-for Australian landfall. Each advance of the clock was a bonus and when seagulls began to follow the ship there was great excitement. One gull landed on the deck and was treated like a VIP. Binoculars were pulled from kitbags as everyone began contending to be the first to see the coastline. Who would be first to smell the welcoming scent of eucalyptus?

When they woke on Sunday 10 March 1946, the low

coastline of Western Australia was in sight. By 9 am the ship had berthed in Fremantle and there was a rush to get ashore. To set foot on Australian soil. Again. At last.

Squinting in the bright sunlight, surprised at how low the buildings all looked, David made his way to the city and found the GPO. Carefully he counted out the coins in his pocket, so different from the English ones he had become used to. No farthings here. Anyway, it would cost more than farthings for a trunk call to Tasmania. But it would be worth every penny, every shilling, every florin with its kangaroo and emu coat of arms. He booked the call and waited.

Lucky that WA time was behind Tasmanian, David thought. His parents should be back from church by now. He could almost smell the Sunday roast. He could hear the phone ringing. Echoing down the long hall. He could see his mother coming from the kitchen, wiping her hands on her apron as she hurried. His father was hastening in from the garden. Who would get there first?

His mother answered.

'I'm home!' David shouted. The line echoed. Home, Home, Home.

He could hear the tears of joy in his mother's voice as she said, 'Welcome back, Viddy! Everything's ready here for your coming!'

Then he set off to see his uncle and aunt, the parents of Frank, who would never come home.

Epilogue

Death's no respecter in this unjust spring,
No chooser under the callous rain: but, brothers,
All is won when men who find a cause to die for, live.

John Pudney, 'Spring', *1942*

Back in Tasmania, David visited more families he
knew whose sons did not return. Then, after some very
welcome home leave, he had to go to Heidelberg Military
Hospital in Melbourne for further tests prior to discharge.
He was finally demobilised in January 1947, four and a
half years after enlistment. Twenty months after VE Day,
17 months after VJ Day, David's war was over. Officially.
But its marks have remained for over sixty years.

During these years, David has paid three more
instalments of the cost of his years as a pilot. While he
was still at university in Tasmania he had to return to the
Repatriation Hospital in Hobart for six months, delaying
the completion of his Arts degree by a year. Then his

fledgling career in Commonwealth Archives was brought to a close by another period of war-related illness.

David and I met at the University of Tasmania in March 1948. He was a few months off 26, a Commonwealth Reconstruction Training Scheme Student in his second year. I was a fresher, just over 16 years old.

He was one of the few students on campus who had a car. But it was the man, not the car, to whom I was instantly attracted. Tall, good-looking, in his grey Savile Row suit, and grey and green tie from Burlington Arcade, he stood out.

First appearances did not lead to disappointment. He proved to be quietly spoken, courteous and chivalrous, thoughtful, with a wisdom even beyond his more mature years. And his sense of humour was most endearing. We began to meet regularly in the morning when our timetables allowed, to walk downtown for coffee. One day David told me that he would not be able to meet me next morning. I knew it was not because of lectures, but he gave no explanation. For two days and nights I wondered if it was the end of our friendship.

Then at breakfast on the third day, my mother, reading the *Mercury*, exclaimed, 'David Mattingley was invested with the Distinguished Flying Cross at Government House yesterday morning!'

Our friendship deepened and five years later we were married.

My parents liked and respected David immensely but were concerned about his health record and its possible future effects. So they insisted that I should acquire professional qualifications beyond my degree before we married. Our marriage took place in December 1953 and we went off to David's beloved England, thinking we might settle and make our life there. But with 'only a colonial degree', an appointment to the sort of school where David wanted to teach was not easy to obtain, and the pay was minimal, less than half of what he could earn in Australia. After some short-term contracts including a year at Marlborough College, we regretfully decided that it was better for us to return to Australia to raise a family.

But we had had almost two years to see some of Britain. We renewed some of David's wartime friendships. In London David bought books on British, German, French and Russian history at Bumpus' Bookshop in Oxford Street. We visited the RAF Memorial at Runnymede, where airmen with no known grave, including Hugh Brodie, are commemorated. We went to Lincoln and even drove along the deserted runways at Kelstern, now reverted to farmland. We made a pilgrimage to the ancient cathedral of St David's in Wales, where the jackdaws chuckled and swooped round the squat grey building, laboriously built stone by stone so long ago to the glory of God. We explored quite a lot of Europe, where the effects of war were still painfully evident in many places. The great cemeteries of World War I spread over the fertile fields of northern France were especially moving. And shocking.

In 1960, before the birth of our second child, David paid the final instalment of the cost of being a pilot and was out of action for most of my pregnancy. In all, his war participation has cost him almost three years in hospitals. But throughout bad times and good his faith has upheld him. We have worshipped in our parish church, St David's,

Burnside, for 49 years. In 1989 he attended a 625 Squadron reunion at Scampton and at the Squadron memorial at Kelstern, and in London was delighted to see St Clement Dane's beautifully restored as the Royal Air Force church. We also visited Harewood House and Lincoln Cathedral, where we spent some time in the Airmen's Chapel. Later, realising the ongoing need for support for the cathedral's restoration, and how much it meant to David, I made him a life member of the Friends of Lincoln Cathedral.

David gave devoted service for 32 years, teaching English and Modern European history and coaching rowing at Prince Alfred College, Adelaide. He also wrote a small book on two of his heroes, both Lincolnshire men, Matthew Flinders and George Bass. (*Matthew Flinders and George Bass*, Melbourne, Oxford University Press, 1961, reprinted 1971).

On his long-service leave in 1974 we took our three children to Europe so that they might learn something of their English heritage and other cultures too, experiencing what it was like to be a foreigner, and hopefully becoming world citizens. Subsequently they have all returned to Europe. Two worked for many years in other countries and married partners from South Africa and Sweden. We have visited Germany a number of times, lived there for several months in the 1970s and have many good German friends.

Since 1958, David has been active in the Australian Institute of International Affairs and the University of Adelaide has named a prize in his honour. He has maintained his involvement with Community Aid Abroad (now Oxfam), since we started the South Australian arm of the organisation in 1964.

Sadly, he lost touch with the McNeill family after a letter in 1968 was returned 'No longer at this address', and also with the Bailey family after taking our children to visit in 1974. Mrs Bailey was in ill-health, but 'held on so that she could see David again'. She died soon afterwards. Since beginning work on this project we have managed to re-establish links to both families by writing letters to the local newspapers in Kent and East Lothian, and this has been a great joy.

At the baptism of each of our three children, David's mother wore the suit made from the Scottish tweed he had bought for her. At his 80th birthday party in 2002 we used the handmade lace tablecloth he had bought for her in Ceylon on his way back to Australia in 1946.

On the eve of our 50th wedding anniversary in December 2003 we were present at the unveiling of G for George, the newly restored Lancaster at the Australian War Memorial in Canberra, where the sound and light re-creation of an operation over Germany reduced veterans to tears. We placed scarlet poppies by seven names on the Wall of Honour and in the late afternoon sun we stood in the Court of Remembrance as it echoed with the sound of the Last Post. We remembered. And gave thanks.

On the day I was finishing the last chapter, the Sunday psalm proclaimed:

Though I walk in the midst of danger yet will you preserve my life: you will stretch out your hand against the fury of my enemies and your right hand shall save me. The Lord will complete his purpose for me. Psalm 138: 7–8a.

David and Christobel while working on this story

About the Others

Frank Mattingley, Gunner, was killed on his first operation, over Duisburg, Germany. According to a report from the Missing, Research and Enquiry Unit forwarded to his mother on 30 July 1947, Frank's aircraft crashed on 22 May 1944 in a field between Horst and Handerath, approximately 19 miles north of Aachen, Germany. His body and those of five of the crew were recovered from the wreckage by local residents and buried in a communal grave in the Handerath cemetery. The seventh crew members body was discovered a mile from the crash and buried in the village cemetery at Horst. The bodies were later exhumed, identified and re-interred in individual graves in the British Military Cemetery at Rheinberg, cared for by the Commonwealth War Graves Commission.

Replying to David's letter of condolence, Frank's mother wrote on 12 June 1945, *I have felt the blow more and more as the time has lingered on and I had not given up all hopes of him returning. Yes we do feel sad and lonely seeing other boys returning, then get a pang and think of our Frank's fate.*

We have recently made contact with Frank's nephews.

When he came home, David went to Devonport to visit the parents of **Peter Lord**, also killed on his first op, and buried in Düsseldorf, Germany. A few months later David was a

293

pall bearer at the funeral of Peter's father. Recently, we have managed to make contact with Peter's two married sisters.

David tried to keep in touch with all his crew at least once a year, at Christmas.

Cyril Bailey DFM, Flight Engineer, is now the only other surviving member. After the crew was disbanded, he married Dot before being sent to India with the RAF in 1945. On demobilisation he went back into engineering, finally becoming a senior quality assurance test engineer on Ministry of Defence missile fuse heads. Now retired, he and Dot live in a bungalow with a garden he enjoys tending, in the London suburb of Surbiton. They adopted two children and take great pleasure in their grandchildren. We lost touch after his parents' death and were unable to trace them in the massive London telephone directories. Since being told of David's letter in the *Isle of Thanet Gazette* seeking news of him, he has written a number of times, sent copies of old photos and documents, and dredged up memories to help answer my queries. He also shared the graphic detail that some of the pages in his flight notebook are still stuck together with David's blood.

Drew Fisher, Bomb Aimer, went back to teaching and was principal in several country primary schools in Queensland. With his beautiful script and lively manner his classes were never dull. David visited him several times before he died in 1976, aged 63. His widow, Thel, is now in a nursing home. Drew's logbook and the personal diary he had made at David's suggestion contained accounts of all the operations they had flown together.

Reg Murr (Murga), Navigator, repatriated early in 1945 and discharged because of ill health, returned to his wife, Mary, and her family, the McGoldricks, who ran the Empire Hotel in Toowoomba, Queensland. He and Mary and their baby daughter Rosemary lived with his mother in his old family home, for which he made beautiful furniture. He went back to his job with the Toowoomba Railway Office, and also began studying to become a draftsman, hoping for a career in architecture. But he was hospitalised several times. Soon after the birth of a son, named David after his skipper, in August 1947, Reg was again in hospital when David went to see him. He died a month later, aged 37. David lost contact with his widow, and after many unsuccessful enquiries we have recently succeeded in re-establishing it. Mary, now 94, lives in Brisbane with her daughter Rosemary. David is a Senior Counsel in Sydney. As they did not know their father, Reg's children have deeply appreciated learning something of him, seeing photos and letters he wrote to David. We learned from them that Reg's father had emigrated from Germany to Australia in the early 1900s, from the *Gemeinde Murr*, a region close to Stuttgart. Reg never mentioned this and we wondered what his thoughts must have been while flying ops over Germany, especially to Stuttgart.

Reg Watson (Pop), Wireless Operator, went back to his position in a Sydney accountant's office, and eventually set up his own business. He never married but was very fond of Mark Beresford's children, and kept in close touch with Mark's family. David went to see him in Sydney several times. He died in 1999.

Noel Ferguson (Boz), Mid Upper Gunner, had put his age up to marry Ann, who had seen a whole gun crew blown up on her nineteenth birthday. He returned to his job in spare parts for the automotive industry in Newcastle, NSW, where he and his English bride made their home. Later he set up a successful business of his own. They lost two of their six children as babies, but now have eleven grandchildren and seven great-grandchildren from their surviving four. Ann, who thought 'the sun, moon and stars shone out of Noel,' said, 'Daddy was everything to the children.' She always took them to see him in the Anzac Day march and never wore her own medals until after he died. When David's crew was disbanded in December 1944 Noel had some bad experiences in the new one to which he was assigned. This resulted in bouts of depression which became more frequent and severe in later years. David made the trip to Newcastle to see him prior to his death in 2003.

Allan Avery DFM (Birdy), Rear Gunner, rejoined the RAAF as a permanent serving member and with his streak of daring, trained to become a fighter pilot, flying Meteors. In his last letter to David in May 1951 he was expecting to go to Korea. On service there he was mentioned in despatches (MiD) and was killed in a flying accident in a storm over the Sea of Japan on 1 September 1952, aged 27. He is buried on the island of Okinawa. One of his old school friends named his son Allan after him, and he is remembered with great affection by childhood playmates. He did not marry but loved his motorbike. When David visited Newcastle to see him, Allan took him for a burn, literally. There was no pillion, and seated on the luggage rack with his foot against the exhaust, David found the heel of his shoe had melted!

Jackson was not the real name of the Pilot Officer put into David's care for one night at Kelstern. His fate is not known.

Charles Gardiner DFC, Navigator, who took Reg Murr's place, was posted to another station soon after David was hospitalised. They lost touch and we have been unable to find any more details.

David has stayed in touch with his English pilot friends on 625 Squadron at Kelstern, **Jack Ball, Clem Koder** and **Sandy Lane** and caught up with them on our visits to England. Jack worked and travelled for Shell, and Clem worked for ICI. We stayed with Sandy and his wife Sybil in Wales and they stayed with us on a visit to Australia before Sandy's death some years ago. Clem designed the Lancaster rose badge for the 625 Squadron Association, the memorial erected at Kelstern where a service is held each May. He died in 2006.

'Ted' Bear, Wireless Operator on 625 Squadron, injured in the same raid as David and in the same ward at Rauceby Hospital, returned to his farm in Western Australia. He came to meet us when our ship berthed in Fremantle on our way to the UK in 1954. He kept in touch until his death some years ago.

Des Hadden, Pilot, and David's school friend, returned to university in Melbourne and later ran an electrical business. He and Sheila retired to Hobart, where we stayed with them several times. When he visited us after her death, we took him to Victor Harbor to see the mansion 'Mount Breckan', which was converted in wartime to an Initial Training School, where he did his training.

Ian Vickers was posted to an OTU in Palestine, then to an HCU in Egypt to fly Liberators. He joined 614 Pathfinder Squadron, flying on Biscuit Bomber trips supplying food to advanced ground forces in Northern Italy, and operations over Austria. He returned to Tasmania, studied engineering and rejoined the Hydro-Electric Commission. Serendipitously, his daughter Christine, who met me at a children's literature conference in 1985, asked me to be her daughter Lyndal's godmother. Only later did we discover the connection between her father and David.

Gordon Lawson, Pilot, who also trained in the Middle East, was posted to a different squadron and flew bomber operations from Italy. He returned to his prewar job with the ANZ Bank in Launceston and later joined the staff of the Apple and Pear Board. He married and his children live in Launceston. He sponsored his Flight Engineer as a migrant to Tasmania.

Alan Scott, Navigator, and his wife Chloe made us welcome when we first came to live in Adelaide in 1955, but we lost touch when they moved away. After discharge he qualified in mechanical engineering, and worked in many parts of South Australia and interstate, finally with Santos on the Moomba gas fields. We were glad to make contact again a few years ago after he returned to Adelaide, not long before he died in 1999.

Sam Salter, Peter Lord's instructor, became an Anglican priest. He served as a chaplain at Cheltenham College, a part-time RAF chaplain and a parish priest in Sussex and Lincolnshire. He obtained some photos for David's book on the Lincolnshire explorers Flinders and Bass. We have stayed with him and his wife Margaret in Chichester, Cheltenham and Grantham, and always looked forward each Christmas to his quirky letter, until his death in 2005.

Mark Beresford, Wireless Operator like his close friend Reg Watson, returned to his sheep and horses on his property in northern New South Wales, where he made David welcome. We later visited him and his wife Gwen, before they retired to Coonabarabran, and also stayed with one of his daughters in Armidale. We still keep in touch.

Phil O'Halloran, Pilot, David's cousin, joined Qantas and later IATA. He died in 1996, aged 75. He married Shirley, a WRAN in WW2. She had been widowed at 18, three months after her marriage to Keith, aged 20, who was an RAAF Rear Gunner killed on operations.

Max Mattingley, Lieutenant, served in the Royal Australian Navy for four years before returning to teaching in Tasmania, Western Australia and Queensland. He joined the Brotherhood of St Barnabas, and as a Bush Brother was Headmaster of All Souls' School, Charters Towers, Queensland, where he died at a chapel service, aged 58 in 1971.

Brian Mattingley DFC, Navigator, and David had their DFCs conferred in a unique private ceremony at Government House in Hobart in 1948. He returned to The Armidale School, NSW, where he was a housemaster, organist and at various times acting headmaster. He taught English, Classics and lifesaving and coached successful swimming and rifle teams until his retirement in 1979. He never married but devoted himself through Legacy to assisting war widows and their children. In 1980 he became a non-stipendiary Anglican priest in Tasmania, serving several country parishes. He died at the age of 90 in December 2004.

During David's time with 625 Squadron he served under three Commanding Officers, all permanent RAF officers. The first was **Wing Commander Douglas Haig, DSO, DFC and Bar**, at Kelstern for six months. He had unusually rapid promotions at a very young age and was very popular. After the war he worked in Norway, and on returning to England became a guard on British Rail, to supplement his pension.

Wing Commander I.G. Mackay spent only six weeks on the Squadron. He was then promoted to Group Captain and posted elsewhere as Station Commander.

Wing Commander John L. Barker, who then took over, was very helpful to David. Barker eventually became an Air Vice Marshal and head of the Royal Ceylon Air Force.

The dark-haired **Barbara** married the British Army major with whom David had swapped uniforms at Harewood House.

Writing *Battle Order 204:*
a Love Story,
NOT a Grocery List

For many years, David spoke little of his wartime experiences, but he did allow me to read his diaries, which I found very moving, realising that while I was just a schoolgirl during World War II, he and many young men like him had been living so dangerously and with such valour.

During his years as a history teacher, David sometimes drew on his experiences to educate the young men about the folly of war, and occasionally allowed people to read his diaries. As I was by that time a published author, they invariably said to me, 'When are you going to write David's story?' My glib reply was always, 'Never. That's his story. He can write it if he wants to.'

But in 1979, when I was researching for a film script on women artists, I discovered the work of Stella Bowen, one of three Australian women war artists in World War Two, at the Australian War Memorial. I shall never forget standing in front of her portrait of an RAAF bomber crew in 1944, now a well-known image, but then almost unknown. Looking at the baby-faced boys and older men whose tight-closed lips would never tell of the horrors their anguished eyes had seen, the tears streamed down my face. It could have been David and his crew under the wings of the great black Lancaster. This crew did not come back, but their image stayed always in my mind.

In December 2002, 49 years after our marriage, I was recovering from major surgery for cancer and wondering why I was still here. I had written 43 books. What was there still that I had not done?

Six months later, still wondering, I was sitting in Melbourne with a publisher who was suggesting that I write my autobiography. Suddenly, like a Damscus road flash, I knew the story I still had to write. And it was not mine. It was right beside me and had been for 55 years.

Fortunately, the archivist/historian streak in David had ensured that he preserved not only his wartime diaries, but also his photos, carefully annotated with names, dates and places; his logbook; operational diaries; service records; lecture notes; airgraphs and letters to his family; and a significant collection of books and pamphlets about the RAF and Bomber Command. All were ordered and organised.

So with the new war in Iraq horrifying the world, David, just turned 81, and I, 71, embarked on a new project together, to help the young and not-so-young people to understand how war affects the lives of ordinary men and women, the cruel waste it causes, the pain and grief it inflicts.

David, going through the letters I sent him while he was in hospital during his university years, smiled and showed me one I had written after I had just completed several big essay assignments. *I am sick of writing,* I declared with eighteen-year-old passion, *and in future I never want to write anything but grocery lists!*

I hope that *Battle Order 204* is more than a grocery list. It has been a labour of love.

Christobel Mattingley
Stonyfell, South Australia.

Acknowledgements

My grateful thanks are due to John Coleman for his most timely contribution. In 2003, three days after I had commenced work, still with some misgivings, on this project, I received a phone call from someone in Queensland I did not know. John Coleman was going through the family papers of his late wife Judith, daughter of Drew and Thel Fisher. Having heard Drew speak so often of David, his old skipper, whom he had held in such regard, John was offering to make a copy of his late father-in-law's logbook and the personal diary Drew had made at David's suggestion. Coming so unexpectedly, it seemed to me a confirmation that I was indeed meant to write this story. John Coleman's care in copying and sharing the voluminous material is deeply appreciated. Drew's accounts, supplemented with photos of his targets and newspaper accounts of the raids, have been invaluable, his forthright breezy style complementing David's carefully worded records. His heartfelt letters to David were also very revealing. Between them, John Coleman and Drew Fisher have added an important dimension to the story.

I thank Cyril Bailey for his memories and help in verifying certain details, and for copies of several documents in his possession.

I am grateful that before I had envisaged this account, Mark Beresford sent David a copy of Reg Watson's official logbook entries for the sorties they flew together. Reg's frequently reiterated comment, 'Poor bloody civilians', was important. We thank Noel Ferguson's widow Ann for sharing her memories with us and lending us her photos, including the precious tattered one of Noel which she pinned up over her bunk in the various huts where she was stationed on anti-aircraft duty. We also appreciate Pat McKenzie and Jo Goulder responding to our letter in the *Newcastle Herald*, with memories of their childhood playmate and friend Allan Avery, and Allan's sisters, Pat Inglis who lent photos and a copy of Allan's logbook, and Elizabeth Babington who also lent photos. Des Hadden's long friendship, memories and the loan of his copy of *Tasmanians at War* are much appreciated. Eric Thale's gift in 1990 of one of only three copies of *No. 625 Squadron Diary*, which he researched and produced, has proved a most useful source of dates and information about operations and names of personnel. We thank the McGoldrick family of Toowoomba, who provided the contact which ended our long search for Reg Murr's widow and children.

We thank Major-General Steve Gower AO, Director of the Australian War Memorial, for inviting us to the official opening of the Lancaster G for George in December 2003 and to the commemorative ceremony for 460 Squadron. I am particularly grateful he gave his permission for me to view the interior of the aircraft. We also thank him and John White, Senior Curator of Aircraft, for reading the manuscript, and John for the notes and information he supplied.

I thank Max Fatchen who also read the manuscript and offered a most useful suggestion. He has been stalwart in his encouragement and support. Mike Garbett, world authority on the Lancaster and its crews, wrote to David for the first time after we had commenced this project. This unexpected contact from Britain was another confirmation of the importance of telling this story, and we thank him for his interest and comments.

We thank the *Isle of Thanet Gazette* and the *East Lothian Courier* for their help, by publishing David's letters seeking information about the Bailey and McNeill families, which led to the renewal of contact after so many years; and also the *Newcastle Herald* for publishing David's letter seeking information about Allan Avery, which brought several welcome responses. Ted Field, Senior Librarian at the Devonport Library, was most helpful in finding details of Peter Lord's family, enabling us to make contact with Peter's sisters, Katharine Robertson and Valerie Lloyd-Green. Katharine kindly lent us photos.

We thank members of the Association of the Friends of Lincoln Cathedral for their interest: Len Curtis for his boyhood memories of a Lancaster crash near his home; Keith Jones for placing David's name on the prayer list in the Airmen's Chapel; Jean Pritchard for her letters and for suggesting to her sister Marion and husband Joe Benson that they should look us up on their trip to Australia, and the Bensons for their visit and gift of a print of Lincoln Cathedral and some ancient handmade nails retrieved during restoration. We were grateful that they made a pilgrimage on our behalf to Scopwick Church cemetery to place on John Magee's grave the red poppy we had sent. David Cordingley's visit was also an unexpected pleasure, as was the recent visit of Katherine and Brian Maddison.

Barbara Ives of the University of South Australia helped with information about the works of John Pudney, as did my former literary agent Michael Horniman. Rainer

Scharenberg advised on a German phrase. Our son Stephen and our daughter Rosemary searched for information on various obscure details and read the manuscript, as did our son Christopher. Margaret Smith listened to my reading of the manuscript with acute attention and perspicacity. Jan Wetherall's cheerful help with the vagaries of my computer and her skill in locating lost chapters was timely, and Monte Goulding's computer advice has also been helpful. Robert Andrew, a former student of David, has prepared perceptive teacher notes. I thank Fiona Inglis, my agent, for understanding how much this book means to me.

I thank publisher Erica Wagner for her long time faith in me and her belief in this story; and Susannah Chambers for her thoughtful editing.

Finally I thank my husband David, without whom I could not have written this book. I am grateful for his unfailing patience and support as I grappled with the complexities and difficulties of the story, for answering endless questions day and night, explaining technicalities and procedures, recounting anecdotes, directing me to references and research sources. Most of all I have been moved by his willingness to recall painful memories as together we have relived that wartime experience, so that others may know something of the ongoing cost of war. I regret I never had the privilege of meeting any of his crew, except Cyril, but now Drew, Murga, Pop, Boz and Birdy have become very real to me and I am deeply grateful to them all for their loyalty and devotion to their Skip.

About the Poems

The three poems quoted in their entirety, *Wings, High Flight* and *An Airman's Prayer* I found in David's diaries. *Wings* and *High Flight* were carbon copy typescript on small slips of paper, typical of wartime economy. Obviously they expressed sentiments which resonated, were shared, circulated and cherished. There was no attribution for *Wings*, and *High Flight* was simply entitled *Sonnet* with the author's name misspelt. *An Airman's Prayer* was on a small yellowed newspaper cutting, with the poignant details about its author.

Research has revealed that *Wings* was written by the well-loved English author Cecil Roberts and has appeared under several other titles, *Wings of the Wind, An Air Force Pilot's Prayer* and *Prayer for a Pilot*.

Sonnet's title is *High Flight* and its author is John Gillespie Magee, born in Shanghai in 1922 of missionary parents, American father John Gillespie Magee, and British mother Faith Backhouse Magee. John Jr was educated in Nanking and at Rugby School in England, where he won the Poetry Prize for 1939 with his poem *Brave New World*. He went to the USA in 1939 where he had won a scholarship to Yale University. But instead he enlisted in the Royal Canadian Air Force, gained his Wings in June 1941 and served with RAF Fighter Command in 412 Squadron as a Spitfire pilot. One of the first US war casualties, killed at the age of 19 in a midair collision on 11 December 1941 over Britain, he is buried in the war graves section of the Holy Cross Church, Scopwick, Lincolnshire. *High Flight*, written in September 1941, was first published in his father's Washington parish magazine. It was included in a Library of Congress exhibition of poetry entitled 'Faith and Freedom' and widely re-published by American and British newspapers. Lines were quoted by US President Ronald Reagan in a tribute to the American astronauts in 1986 after the Challenger 7 space shuttle disaster. Two are also quoted on the Royal Australian Air Force Memorial, Anzac Way, Canberra. Several Friends of Lincoln Cathedral recently visited Scopwick at my request and laid a poppy from the Australian War Memorial on his grave.

An Airman's Prayer was written by Melbourne-born Flight Sergeant Hugh Rowell Brodie, who had been both student and teacher at Melbourne High School and who enlisted in September 1940. A member of 460 Squadron, he was officially presumed killed over Germany on 3 June 1942 at the age of 30, with no known burial place. He is commemorated at the Runnymede Royal Air Force Memorial in Britain, and on Memorial Panel 107 at the Australian War Memorial, Canberra. The poem was found among his possessions with a letter to the boys of his old school.

Quotations from other poems are as follows:

Chapter 4: *green and pleasant land* from William Blake's *From 'Milton'*; *blunt, bow-headed, whalebacked Downs* from Rudyard Kipling's *Sussex*; *the lark at heaven's gate* from William Shakespeare's *Cymbeline*.

Chapter 5: *Each in his narrow cell forever laid, The rude forefathers of the hamlet sleep* and *leaving the world to darkness and to me* from Thomas Gray's 'Elegy Written in a Country Churchyard'.

Chapter 8: *These, wishing life, must range the falling sky, Whom an heroic moment calls to die* and *You shall have your revenge who flew and died, Spending your daylight hours before the day began* from John Pudney's 'The Dead', and *Enough of death! It looms too large in words...Enjoy the sky, Possess the field of air, Cloud be your step, The west wind be your stair* from Pudney's 'Men Alive'.

Chapter 14: *If I should die, think only this of me: That there's some corner of a foreign field That is forever England ... A dust whom England bore, shaped, made aware* from Rupert Brooke's 'The Soldier'.

Chapter 15: chapter title *Bold, cautious, true and my loving comrade* from Walt Whitman's 'As Toilsome I wander'd Virginia's Woods'; *They shall not grow old, as we that are left grow old; Age shall not weary them, nor the years condemn. At the going down of the sun and in the morning We will remember them* and *They went with songs to the battle, they were young, Straight of limb, true of eye, steady and aglow, They were staunch to the end against odds uncounted* from Laurence Binyon's 'For the Fallen'; *I shall never love the snow again Since Maurice died: With corniced drift it blocked the lane, And sheeted in a desolate plain The countryside* from Robert Bridges' 'Since Maurice died'.

Chapter 18: *When day is gone, and night is come, And a' folk bound to sleep, I think on him that's far awa' The lee-lang night and weep* from Robert Burns' 'The Farewell'; *It's yet for a' that That man to man the world o'er Shall brothers be for a' that* from Burns' 'For a' that, and a' that'; *Should auld acquaintance be forgot And never brought to min'? Should auld acquaintance be forgot And days of auld lang syne?* And *a cup of kindness* from Burns' 'Auld lang syne'.

Chapter 20: *poured out the red Sweet wine of youth; gave up the years to be Of work and joy* from Rupert Brooke's 'The Dead'; *The flowers of the forest are a' wede away* from 'Lament for the Battle of Flodden' by Jane Elliot.

Epilogue: *Death's no respecter in this unjust spring, No chooser under the callous rain: but brothers, All is won when men who find a cause to die for, live.* From John Pudney's 'Spring, 1942'.

All John Pudney poems quoted are from *Dispersal Point and other Air Poems*. London, John Lane the Bodley Head, 1942.

Glossary

Aldis lamp	A portable lamp used for signalling
Beam	a radar approach aid
Bod	a person
Boob	a foolish mistake, a blunder
Bought it	euphemism for killed
Bumps	landings, touchdowns
Clamp	close in (weather)
Commission	the position or rank of an officer
Coned	caught (in the crossbeams of searchlights)
Cookie	a huge 4000-pound bomb
Corkscrew	violent evasive action
Crate	slang for aircraft
Demobilised	discharged from the armed services
Dispersal	areas where aircraft are parked
Duff	slang for poor, no good
Erk	ground crew
Flak	anti-aircraft fire and the accompanying shrapnel
Flights	office accommodation near dispersals
Gee	a radar navigation aid
Gen	slang for genuine information, good
Get the chop	euphemism for killed
Go for a burton	euphemism for killed
Gone in	euphemism for killed
Groupie	Group Captain
Jetties	slang for jet aircraft

Jink	a sudden evasive movement
Kite	slang for aircraft
Luftwaffe	German Air Force
Mae West	slang for an inflatable life jacket, named after a film star of the 1930s
Magneto	electric spark generator for starting and running engines
Mustering	grouping according to skill
Ops	operations. Air Force term for bombing raids
Penny section	maximum tram ride for a penny
Pukka	correct, genuine, good
Ropey	inferior, risky, dangerous
Second dickey	pilot assigned to another, more senior, to gain experience
Snag book	book in which aircrew record malfunctions or damage
Stooge	fly about, move around
Tannoy	Trade name for public address system
ten/tenths	full cloud cover
U-boat	German submarine
Very light	a small coloured flare used for illumination or signalling
Wingco	Wing Commander
Y	radar navigation aid
AA	Anti-aircraft fire
AC2	Aircraftman Class 2
AFU	Advanced Flying Unit
ATS	Auxiliary Territorial Service
B/A	Bomb Aimer
BAT	Beam Approach Training
CO	Commanding Officer
CRTS	Commonwealth Reconstruction Training Scheme
DFC	Distinguished Flying Cross
DFM	Distinguished Flying Medal
DI	Daily inspection
DSO	Distinguished Service Order

ED	Embarkation Depot
EFTS	Elementary Flying Training School
F/O	Flying Officer
HCU	Heavy Conversion Unit
HE	High Explosive
ITS	Initial Training School
LAC	Leading Aircraftman
MO	Medical Officer
NCO	Noncommissioned Officer
OTU	Operational Training Unit
PDRC	Personnel Despatch and Reception Centre
P/O	Pilot Officer
POW	Prisoner of War
SFTS	Service Flying Training School
TI	Target Indicator, pyrotechnics dropped by Pathfinders to indicate the bombing target
u/s	unserviceable
VAD	(member of) Voluntary Aid Detachment
WAAF	(member of) Women's Auxiliary Air Force
W/Op	Wireless operator

A note about imperial measurements

Throughout *Battle Order 204*, weights and volumes have been quoted in the imperial measurements that were used at the time. Converting specific imperial measurements to metric often produces awkward numbers. For instance, a 500-pound bomb would be a 226.8 kilogram bomb.

Here are some basic conversions:

1 foot = 30.48 centimetres

20 000 feet = 6096 metres

1 mile = 1.61 kilometres

1 pound = 0.45 kilograms

1 stone = 6.35 kilograms

1 gallon = 4.55 litres

Following convention, the 24-hour clock has been used for times in operational sequences.

Sources

Primary sources

David Mattingley's papers including:
    official flying logbook October 1942 to May 1945
    personal operational diaries, 3 volumes, September 1944 to
       November 1944
    personal diaries, 3 volumes, from embarkation 5 June 1943
       to return 10 March 1946
    RAAF records
    address book and other personal papers
    photograph albums 1943–45
    letters and airgraphs to family 1943–45
    correspondence to David and to his parents 1942–46
Drew Fisher's official flying logbook and operational diary
    September 1944 to November 1944. Photocopy
Reg Watson's official flying logbook entries October 1944 to
    November 1944. Photocopy
No. 625 Squadron diary October 1943 to September 1945: a
    compilation of information extracted from Squadron records
    by Eric Thale. Only 3 copies were made.

Secondary sources

*Aircraft identification: Part 1 British monoplanes; Part 2
German monoplanes; Part 1 revised British and German
fighters and bombers; Part 3 Italian fighters, bombers and*

seaplanes; Part 4 American types for the RAF. London, The Aeroplane, 1940–42

Air crew entry under the Empire Air Scheme: notes for the information of candidates. Melbourne, R.A.A.F. Publications No. 78 (May 1940)

Taylor, Leonard (ed) Allied aircraft illustrated: a selection of pictures from the Air Training Corps Gazette. London, Air League of the British Empire, [n.d. ca 1946]

Brooke, Rupert. The complete poems. Sydney, Hicks, Smith & Wright, 1944

Burns, Robert. Poetical works. London, Oxford University Press 1942

Cassell's Anthology of English poetry. Selected and edited by Margaret and Desmond Flower. London, Cassell, 1942

Fletcher, Hanslip. Bombed London: a collection of thirty eight drawings of historic buildings damaged during the bombing of London in the Second World War 1939–1945, with an introduction by Professor A.E. Richardson, R.A., F.R.I.B.A. London, Cassell, 1947

Garbett, Mike and Goulding, Brian. The Lancaster at war. Part 1 (1971) and Part 2 (1979). Leicester, Reed Editions Australia, 1992

Harris, Sir Arthur. Bomber offensive. London, Collins, 1947

Hastings, Max. Bomber Command. London, Pan Books, 1981

Jimmy 'This is London!'. London, Alliance Press, [n.d. ca 1942]

Johnson, Sue and Winspear, Brian. Tasmanians at war in the air 1939–45. Hobart, Brian Winspear, 2002

Johnson, Syd. H. It's never dark above the clouds: the experiences of an Australian navigator-bomb aimer with Bomber Command. Perth. Privately published. [n.d.]

Kings of the Clouds. Sydney, Frank Johnson, 1943

McCarthy, John. A last call of Empire: Australian aircrew, Britain and the Empire Air Training Scheme. Canberra, Australian War Memorial, 1988

Nelmes, Michael V. & Jenkins, Ian. G-for-George: a memorial to RAAF Bomber Crews 1939–45. Maryborough, Banner Books, 2002

Otter, Patrick. *Maximum effort: the story of the North Lincolnshire bombers*. Grimsby, *Grimsby Evening Telegraph*, 1990

Pilot's and flight engineer's notes: Lancaster Mark I, III and X. Air Publication 2062A, London, Air Ministry, 1944

Pudney, John & Treece, Henry. *Air force poetry*. London, Bodley Head 1944

Pudney, John. *Dispersal point and other air poems*. London, Bodley Head, 1942

Pudney, John. *Collected poems*. New York, Putnam, 1957

Rapier, Brian J. and Bowyer, Chaz. *Halifax and Wellington at War*. Leicester, Promotional Reprint Co, 1994

The R.A.F in action. London, Adam & Charles Black, 1941

R.A.F. in action: photographic exhibition. Canberra, Australian War Memorial, [n.d. ca 1946]

Robertson, Bruce. *Lancaster – the story of a famous bomber*. Letchworth. Privately published. 1964

Rothenstein, Sir William. Men *of the RAF: Forty portraits with some account of life in the RAF*. London, OUP, 1942

Williams, Neville. *Chronology of the Modern World 1763–1965*. London, Penguin, 1975

Wilkins, Lola. *Stella Bowen: Art, love & war*. Canberra, Australian War Memorial, 2002

Video

Air war 1939 to 1945. Time Life video Century of Warfare series. [n.d.]

G for George sound and image presentation. Canberra, Australian War Memorial, 2003